MW00462713

Wild Gales
and
Tattered Sails

De Profundis, Veritas

Wild Gales and Tattered Sails

by

Paul John Creviere, Jr.

The Shipwrecks of Northwest Lake Michigan from Two Creeks, Wisconsin to Dutch Johns Point, Michigan and all of the Bay of Green Bay

Copyright © 1997
Paul J. Creviere, Jr.

Wild Gales and Tattered Sails
First Edition, 1997

Copyright © 1997 Paul John Creviere, Jr.
All rights reserved.

ISBN 0-9660328-1-0

Library of Congress Card Catalog Number: 97-92528

Table of Contents

Foreword

Probably like a lot of Door County divers, my first guide to the area's many shipwrecks was the venerable *Fredrickson's Chart of Ships Wrecked in the Vicinity of Door County, Wisconsin*. With its accompanying two paperback volumes, *Ships and Shipwrecks of Door County, Wisconsin*, the 1959 *Fredrickson's Chart* was the major published source on Door County shipwrecks until Walter and Mary Hirthe's excellent *Schooner Days in Door County* appeared in 1986. I can well remember the first time I laid hands upon a copy of *Fredrickson's Chart*, at about the age of nine. Encountering it under a pile of tomes in the back of a second-hand bookstore, the yellowed, dusty document with its cryptic notations seemed like a pirate map of old, and the offshore world of the Door, sunken mysteries beckoned to me as it did to so many.

A number of other publications on Door County shipwrecks have appeared since 1959, including articles and a book on the "Mystery Ship" *Alvin Clark*, several diver's guides, and a series of underwater archaeological surveys of individual wrecks. However, none of these publications have done what *Fredrickson's Chart* attempted to do: create an inventory of all known wrecks in Door County waters.

That is, until now. Paul J. Creviere's *Wild Gales and Tattered Sails* is the most comprehensive inventory of northeastern Wisconsin shipwrecks ever published. Over a decade of careful research, gleaned from local archives and newspapers, have produced a remarkable volume of new information about the many wrecks, salvages, and legends of this historic expanse of freshwater. Creviere's research does not stop at the Door, but extends into the upper and lower reaches of Green Bay, into the Fox River, and down the Lake Michigan coastline to Two Creeks.

With historical summaries and references for each shipwreck, supplemented by historical photographs and essays on associated maritime topics, *Wild Gales and Tattered Sails* is an invaluable resource for historians, divers, maritime museums, underwater archaeologists, and local history buffs alike. Anyone who has conducted research on shipwrecks knows and will appreciate the years of painstaking effort that this study entailed.

Wild Gales and Tattered Sails will no doubt become a basic reference for all future shipwreck research in northeastern Wisconsin, furthering the study and preservation of the area's maritime historical and underwater archaeological treasures.

David J. Cooper
State Underwater Archaeologist
State Historical Society of Wisconsin

Introduction

This region of the Great Lakes has always had a proud maritime legacy and, I think, always will. The marine trade that built and sailed ships here, and once endeavored to deliver groceries, later reached out to the national market and, indeed, made world history. The first ship to engage German shore batteries on the Normandy coast on D-Day, June 6, 1944, (and later the first to be sunk by those batteries), was a U.S. Navy sub-chaser built in Sturgeon Bay, Wisconsin.

This legacy grew from an area that has always had much to offer. Beside cargoes of grain and fruit and vegetables, we have shipped lumber, iron ore and fish and yes, ships, to the rest of the world. From the mightiest lumber baron to the humblest potato farmer, merchants hustled to ship their products to a waiting market. In a day and age before the railroads had arrived, before roads could be considered reliable, commerce took to the Lakes.

As trade developed, the trade routes stretched out to accommodate it. Particularly after the Civil War, shipbuilding exploded, in an effort to meet the demand. All over the Great Lakes, shipyards blossomed like spring clover. Hardly a day went by without the announcement of another ship launching. The port of Chicago became the busiest in the United States and in one 48 hour period in the 1870s, over 230 ships arrived there. Piers sprang up near every shoreside community and even some that were not shoreside. Casco, Wisconsin, is three miles from Lake Michigan...but there was a Casco Pier.

As trade and technology changed through the decades, transportation changed with it. The piers that had been built to accommodate it were, one by one, abandoned. The Door Peninsula boasted dozens of piers in the 1870s. By 1895 there were only eight still in use. Ships became larger in size though smaller in number. Sails were replaced by steam and still later by diesel power. More and more the schooners and early steamers that once did proud service on Lake Michigan were found in its estuaries and mud flats where they were left to rot and decay.

This book is about those ships...and where possible, the people who sailed them. The people are gone. But occasionally, oaken ribs will wash ashore, a tree-head bolt will push through the sand, or an obscure blip on a sonar screen will suddenly rip the down riggers off a fishing charter. All as if to say, "I once sailed these waters. Hear my tale."

A resident recalling the story of the Griffon (see ship-wreck No. 1), commented that there were thousands of ships wrecked on these shores. While there is some truth to that, there were also thousands that were recovered, restored and returned to business. I have sorted out the stories of some 400 vessels that did not. Included also are the stories of almost two dozen other ships whose remains are thought to be in this area but were in fact salvaged. These particular vessels (and one car) have given their names to shoals, have been the subject of a diver's fruitless search or in some other way have become intertwined with the shipwreck tales for this part of the Lake. To leave them out is to leave unfinished the story of the maritime trade here.

On behalf of the beachcomber who finds a ship's knee, the fisherman who pulls aboard a cabin lamp with his nets, or the history buff who simply enjoys a good sea story I have tried to piece together as full and accurate an account of these vessels as resources would allow.

This is the culmination of 14 years of research. In spite of my exhaustive effort to make it as complete as possible, anyone knowledgeable in the lore of this area may recognize some deficiencies. The "missing bomber" is a large airplane interchangeably located near Washington Island or St. Martin Island and has been described as a DC-3, a B-29, and a B-17. While I have talked to people who were aware of it, no one has ever been able to give consistent details and a location. Also there are stories of a freight train lost off Fayette, Michigan. Once again, I have never been able to find a source.

"Thank You"s should be extended to all who made this book possible. Lou Hamms of the Delta County Historical Society was the person who said, "This isn't a research project, it's a book...you HAVE to publish this." Dennis Frederick and Ann Marie Laes assisted with proof reading and style changes. Dave Cooper provided invaluable advice on research. Katherine VerHaagh graciously typed my notes. Rick Nell provided advice on copyright requirements. All of the librarians at the Brown County Library have been of great service, and it was they who suggested that I index everything, to the extent that I have, and use as many names as possible. Special thanks goes to Joan Kloster, of the Wisconsin Maritime Museum of Manitowoc, who gave tremendous assistance. I appreciate the help and patience of Kevin Smet, Jim Baye, and Roger Carson who helped with indexing, researching and, in some cases, searching for wrecks never found. Keith Orde is remembered for his impatience. Keith hounded me for years to continue my work on this book and see it through to fruition. And of course, to Mom and Dad just for being there.

Paul John Creviere, Jr.
July, 1997

Area of Lake Michigan encompassed by this book.

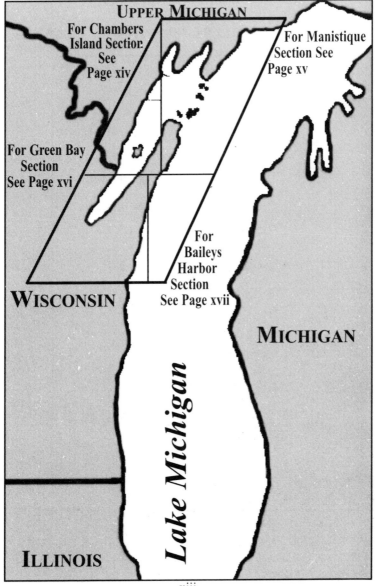

UPPER MICHIGAN

For Chambers
Island Section
See
Page xiv

For Manistique
Section See
Page xv

For Green Bay
Section
See Page xvi

For
Baileys
Harbor
Section
See Page xvii

WISCONSIN

MICHIGAN

Lake Michigan

ILLINOIS

Shipwreck locations are marked with a number corresponding with that ship's chronological listing.

All locations are approximate.

These maps were drawn by the author specifically for this book.

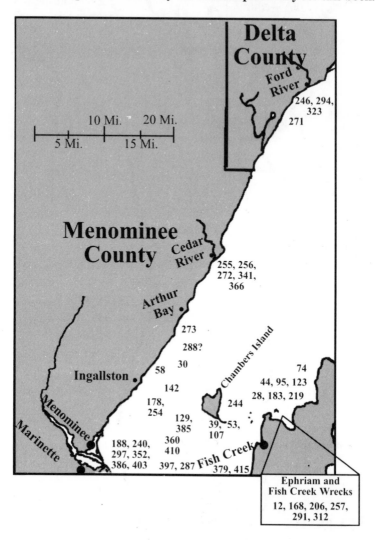

Delta County

Ford River

246, 294, 323
271

10 Mi.   20 Mi.
5 Mi.   15 Mi.

Menominee County

Cedar River

255, 256, 272, 341, 366

Arthur Bay

273

288?

Chambers Island

58   30

74

Ingallston

142

44, 95, 123
28, 183, 219

178, 254

244

129, 385

39, 53, 107

Menominee

188, 240, 297, 352, 386, 403

360
410

Marinette

397, 287   Fish Creek

379, 415

Ephriam and Fish Creek Wrecks

12, 168, 206, 257, 291, 312

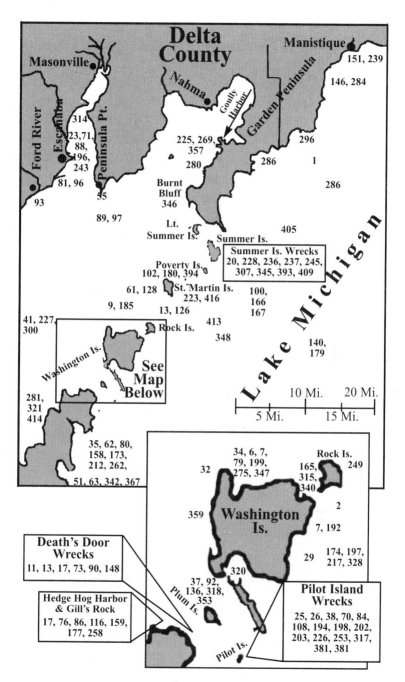

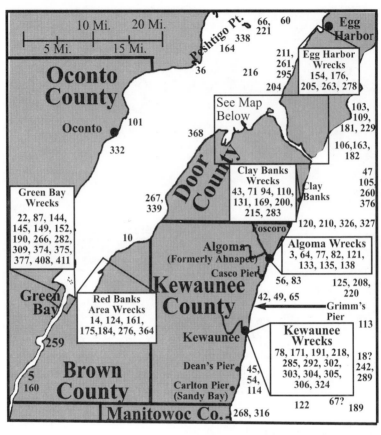

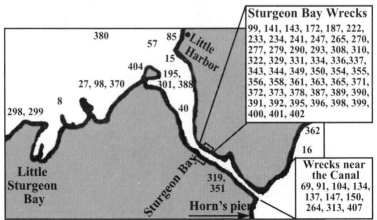

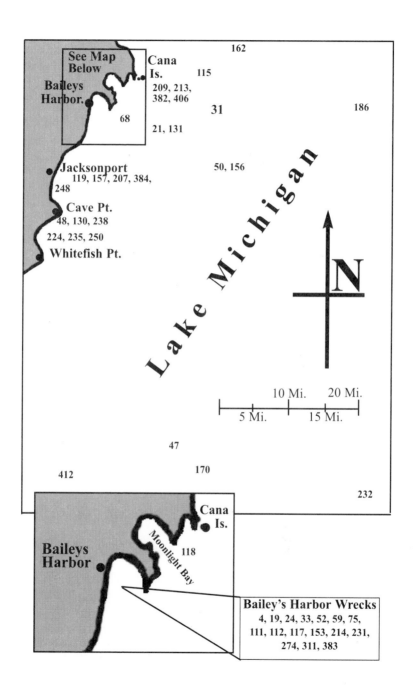

162

See Map Below

Cana Is.

115

Baileys Harbor

209, 213, 382, 406

68

31

186

21, 131

Jacksonport

50, 156

119, 157, 207, 384, 248

Cave Pt.

48, 130, 238

224, 235, 250

Whitefish Pt.

L a k e   M i c h i g a n

N

10 Mi.   20 Mi.

5 Mi.   15 Mi.

47

412

170

232

Cana Is.

Moonlight Bay

118

Baileys Harbor

Bailey's Harbor Wrecks
4, 19, 24, 33, 52, 59, 75,
111, 112, 117, 153, 214, 231,
274, 311, 383

Ships, yachts and other losses on the Bay of Green Bay and the northwest shore of Lake Michigan

Part 1:
Vessels lost before 1874

1) *Griffon*, Bark, Foundered Sometime after September 18, 1679.

The *Griffon* had come to anchor off Washington Island to make contact with a group of men the vessel's master, Robert Rene Cavalier, Sieur de la Salle, had sent to gather furs. According to Father Louis Hennepin, chaplain and chronicler for the expedition, LaSalle decided to send the *Griffon* back to Niagara with the furs to settle his debts. Hennepin wrote,

"Our pilot and five men with him were therefore sent back, and ordered to return with all imaginable speed, to join us toward the southern parts of the lake where we should stay for them among the Illinois. They sailed on the 18th of September with a westerly wind, and fired a gun to take their leave. Though the wind was favourable, it was never known what course they steered nor how they perished; for after all the enquiries we have been able to make, we could never learn anything else but the following particulars. The ship came to an anchor to the north of the lake of the Illinois[1], where she was seen by some savages who told us that they advised our men to sail along the coast and not towards the middle of the lake, because of the sands that make the navigation dangerous when there is any high wind. Our pilot, Luke, as I said before was dissatisfied, and would steer as he pleased, without hearkning to the advice of the savages, who, generally speaking, have more sense than Europeans think at first. But the ship was hardly a league[2] from the coast when it was tossed up by a violent storm in such a manner that our men were never heard of since; and it is supposed that the ship struck upon a sand and was there buried."

La Salle and the rest of his men continued along the lakeshore to the mouth of the St. Joseph River to await the arrival of the *Griffon* and twenty men that had been left behind at the Straits of Mackinac.

By mid-November, La Salle was growing apprehensive about the loss of his vessel. The part of his crew that had been left at Mackinac Straits reached La Salle from there on November 20. According to Hennepin, "They told us that our ship had not put into the Bay of Mackinac as they were ordered and that they had heard nothing of her since we sailed, notwithstanding they had enquired as much as they could from the savages inhabiting the coast of the lake."

The Griffon as drawn by artist Karl Kuttruff.
Photo courtesy of the Great Lakes Marine Collection
of the Milwaukee Public Library/ Wisconsin Marine Historical Society

The *Griffon* was named for the Griffins in the coat of arms for Count Frontenac, the French Governor of Canada. She was built on the shore of the Niagara River near the mouth of the Cayuga Creek, with work beginning on January 22, 1679. The vessel was rigged and ready to sail by the end of July. Originally, Hennepin said the bark was 60 tons but in his "A Description of Louisiana" states that she was 45 tons. He wrote in his earlier work that, "She carried five small guns, two were of brass, and three 'harquebuze a-crock'[3]. The beak head was adorned with a flying griffon and an eagle above it; and the rest of the ship had the same ornaments as men of war use to have."

In the three centuries since her disappearance, the *Griffon* was reported found in various points in Lake Michigan and Lake Huron. Guy McCracken of Door County reported in the 1930s, that as a youngster in the 1880s, he knew of a wreck off Lily Bay that was thought, by local fishermen, to be the *Griffon*. This wreck was approximately 70 feet long and was built with trunnels or wooden dowels. Peter Johnson, a local fisherman who was familiar with the wreck, said that local residents removed a bell and a small cannon in the late 1870s. John Mitchell of Escanaba claimed to have found the bark near Pointe aux Barques in the late 1940s. Richard Brownes of Detroit claimed to have found her east of Drummond Island in 1969. Harry G. Tucker of Owen Sound, Ontario reported in 1929 that he found the *Griffon* near Grand Manitoulin Island. Other Canadians reported, in 1930, the bark was west of Manitoulin Island. Orrie Vail of Tobermory, Ontario claimed in 1969 that he found the craft near Grenough Point. Eugene McDonald, onetime president of the Zenith Corporation, dived on what he stated was the *Griffon's* remains near Cockburn Island. No one has ever proven the location of the missing bark and its whereabouts remain a mystery to this day. [1]Lake Michigan as it was then known. [2]About three and a quarter statute miles. [3]A harquebuze was a heavy cannon used in the 15th and 16th centuries. "A-crock" means they were without a carriage or cradle. Father Louis Hennepin, A New Discovery of a Vast Country in America, by 1681, reprinted from the second London issue of 1698 by Reuben Gold Thwaites, A.C. McClurg & Co., Chicago, 1903, p. 82 - 144. Father Louis Hennepin, A Description of Louisiana, trans. from the edition of 1683 by John Gilmary Shea, New York, 1880. DOOR COUNTY ADVOCATE, August 23, 29, September 5, October 3, 1930. DOOR COUNTY ADVOCATE, April 21, 1960. GREEN BAY PRESS-GAZETTE, December 14, 1969.

2) *Eclipse*, Schooner, Stranded late November of 1843.

The *Eclipse* was bound from Mackinac Island to the Village of Green Bay when she struck a reef near Louse Island (either Rock or Washington Island) and became a total wreck. The vessel was bound there with a cargo of iron for the foundry and merchandise for Messrs. Francis Gilbert, Nathan Goodell, and D. Butler of Green Bay. Part of the cargo was thrown overboard for the purpose of lightening her to float her off, but the effort was futile. Most of the cargo was saved. Gilbert's loss was the greatest because his order of salt and sugar dissolved in the water. The GREEN BAY REPUBLICAN reported, *"Mr. Hagedon and a companion were all that were on board at the time of the disaster [and] reached here last week, nearly worn down with hunger, cold and fatigue; having traveled 80 miles on foot in a trackless wilderness through mud, ice and water, with no covering at night, and little to eat."* The vessel was owned by Luther Hagedon of Green Bay. In April of 1844, the sloop *Rudolph* arrived from Louse Island with *Eclipse's* cargo. GREEN BAY REPUBLICAN, December 5, 1843. GREEN BAY REPUBLICAN, April 23, 1844.

3) *Toledo*, Brig, Stranded Autumn, 1848.

This vessel was blown ashore at Ahnapee (now Algoma) and was stretched across the Wolf River. Her crew abandoned her. She was visited by Bradford R. White in a fish boat. He was, at the time, the only white settler in the area. DOOR COUNTY ADVOCATE, May 26, 1893

4) *Janette*, Schooner, Stranded May 1, 1851.

The *Janette* ran ashore at Baileys Harbor in a late snow storm. The *Janette* had cleared Manitowoc loaded with a full supply of stores and fishing tackle. She was bound for "the fishing grounds"* and was beating her way north along the Door County shoreline when she was struck by the snowsquall. In the squall she mistook Baileys Harbor for Mud Bay and struck the north reef of Baileys Harbor. The vessel soon became a total wreck. The *Janette* was owned by Messr. Smith who had their families along, totaling ten to fifteen people. The owners had on board two Mackinac boats and passengers and crew were able to leave the wreck in safety. It was understood that none of the stores were saved and the ship went to pieces shortly thereafter. *A story in the GREEN BAY ADVOCATE, June 26, 1851, defined the principal fishing points as Grand Traverse, Fish Creek, Washington Harbor, Rock Island, Fox and Beaver Islands, St. Martin's Island, Big Summer Island, and what was then Fisherman's Island, (now Fisherman's Shoal.) GREEN BAY ADVOCATE, May 8, 1851 (reprinted from the MANITOWOC HERALD of May 3, 1851).

5) *Indianna*, Side-wheel Steamer, Sank September 11, 1851.

The *Indianna* sank in the Fox River near the mouth of Apple Creek below Wrightstown. Her machinery was removed and placed in the steamer *Morgan L. Martin* which had been built to replace her. The *Indianna* had been in the command of Capt. George Battershell at the time. She had been brought to Green Bay in the summer of 1850 by Grand Rapids parties who placed her on a daily Green Bay to Wrightstown route. When the Rapide de Croche lock was completed, her route was extended to include Kaukauna. In the spring of 1851, Nathan Goodell purchased the vessel, and created a daily route up and down the river opposite the steamer Pioneer which had been built at Fort Howard by Dr. U.H. Peak and managed by his son, Hillman. The *Indianna* had been brought around Lake Michigan to Green Bay by Capt. Wm. O. Lyon with Capt. Battershell as second officer. The *Indianna* had struck a rock near Bridgeport (now Wrightstown) and was damaged so badly that there was no hope of raising her. Mr. Goodell removed the engine, furniture and other valuable material for the construction of a new boat. "Early Navigation on the Fox," DOOR COUNTY ADVOCATE, July 22, 1899. GREEN BAY ADVOCATE, September 18, 1851

6) *Scott*, Brig, Stranded November 11, 1852.

The *Scott* was reported driven ashore and completely wrecked at Washington Harbor, in a heavy gale. The *Scott* was thought to be owned at Chicago. The *General Scott* was later reported to be wrecked on the eastern side of the lake. GREEN BAY ADVOCATE, November 25, December 2, 1852.

7) Unnamed Vessels, Stranded November 11, 1852.

Three unnamed vessels were blown ashore at Washington Harbor. One was a small craft owned at Washington Harbor by William Magee. Another vessel was owned by Mr. Sensibee of Washington Harbor. All were in the fishing trade. The owner of the third boat was unidentified. GREEN BAY ADVOCATE, November 25, 1852.

8) *Red Rover*, Scow, Stranded June 10, 1852.

The GREEN BAY ADVOCATE reported, "SCOW WRECKED— The Spectator says that the *Red Rover* was cast away near Gibraltor (Green Bay) a fortnight since and has gone to pieces. She had a cargo of fish for Messrs. Albright and Crosby,* a portion of which was saved." *Albright and Crosby were Green Bay merchants. GREEN BAY ADVOCATE, June 24, 1852.

9) *George C. Smalley*, Schooner Capsized September 5, 1853.

The GREEN BAY ADVOCATE of September 15, 1853 reported:

"Loss of the Schr. Geo. C. Smalley-Three Lives Lost.-Through the kindness of Capt. Winegar, of the steamer Franklin Moore, *we are enabled to present our readers with the principal particulars of the loss of the* Geo. C. Smalley, *with three of her passengers. She left St. Martin's for Washington Harbor on the 5th inst., with eight persons on board; when about two hours out, she filled with water and capsized, placing the persons on board in an awful situation; soon after, a little girl, unable to cling longer to the boat, was drowned; from 3 o'clock P.M. on Monday until 5 A.M. on Tuesday, the boat drifted about in the bay, during which, time two more persons, Mr. N. Curtis and his wife, parents of the little girl previously lost, were drowned; the wreck then struck on the northern beach of Washington Island, where the almost exhausted survivors were extricated from their awful situation."*

10) *Little Sarah,* Schooner, Capsized November 17, 1854.

In the November 23, 1854 issue of the GREEN BAY ADVOCATE, appeared this article.

"Boat Capsized.-On Friday last, the schooner Little Sarah, *bound from Big Suamico to Oconto, with a full load of freight and 15 passengers capsized a little below the mouth of Little Suamico. At the time the wind was blowing fresh from the west, and the schooner had every stitch of her canvass spread. The passengers were all in the cabin when she capsized. The cabin nearly filled with water, and those in it were barely able to keep their heads out of water by clinging to the ceiling. Mr. Danforth Perrigo, who with his wife and two or three children were on board, was enabled to make his way out of the cabin, and with the crew got upon the side of the schooner, in which they floated about three hours, when they attracted the attention of an Indian on the beach, about 1¹/₂ miles distant, who immediately gave notice of their perilous situation to Mr. Gross, a fisherman in that vicinity, who came promptly to their rescue. By cutting a hole in the side of the vessel, the women and children were all enabled to escape, with the exception of a little daughter of Mr. Perrigo. It is supposed that she became chilled through, and lost her hold. She was lifeless when taken out. The wind blew so hard that it was impossible to tow the schooner to the shore, or to save any of her freight. Mr. Perrigo, who was moving to Oconto, lost a chest of carpenters' tools, his household furniture, and every article of wearing apparel he and his family possessed, save what they had upon their backs. The schooner has not been seen since. The rescued ones unite in giving great praise to Mr. Gross for his noble exertions in their behalf. They say that they could not have survived but a very short-his timely arrival and noble efforts saved them from a watery grave."*

Three weeks later, the GREEN BAY ADVOCATE published this letter from Milo Montgomery, who identified himself as the *Little Sarah*'s Captain.

"Mr. Editor:-Seeing a statement in your paper of the capsizing of

7

the schooner Little Sarah, *I would respectfully observe that the greater part of it is a mistake. With regard to her carrying canvass, she was carrying close reefed canvass at the time she went over. The wind was north-west, and very squally and baffling. A moment before she went over, the wind struck her in the head and stopped her headway, and before she gathered again, another puff struck her right abeam and threw her upon beams end. The passengers, (fifteen in number, men, women and children,) being somewhat alarmed, jumped down to leeward, the vessel thus carrying over a ton in weight with her, so that she could not right again; the water at the same time rushed into the cabin, driving the passengers all back in a mass. I was the only one outside when she went over, and it was probably five minutes before any of them succeeded in getting out, by diving down through the companion way, and when they came up they were nearly gone-so much so, that it was all that I could do to get them up onto her side, until the whole nine men were all safe, leaving two women, three children, and my brother-in-law, (a boy,) inside of the vessel.- They succeeded in getting to the upperside of the cabin, in the wing of the berths, so that they would just get their heads out of the water and hang on to the clamps with their fingers. My brother-in-law caught a little boy, belonging to Mr. Perrigo, by the collar of the coat, and held him up for three hours. As soon as I got the passengers on to her side, I got a pole, which I had previously saved as it was drifting away, and caught an apron which floated out of the cabin, belonging to one of the ladies below, and rigged a signal, but with little hopes of being discovered, being a mile and a half from land and having continual snow squalls. After swaying my signal to and fro for an hour and a half, to our great joy we saw a boat coming, belonging to Mr. Grosse, a fisherman near Suamico, who had been warned by an old Indian who saw us and had to travel nearly two miles, to send a boat to our rescue, and it was a good two hours before they got along side. It was freezing very hard, so that we could not have stood more than five hours without perishing; our clothes were frozen perfectly stiff in less than a quarter of an hour. When the* *boat arrived, we had no means of making a hole into the vessel to get the remainder of the sufferers, nor could we have carried them had we got means to do so. The men who were outside piled in immediately, so that it loaded the boat down, I took off my jacket and pulled an oar for life against a gale for two miles, and had to go half a mile to get an axe, and back, before we could relieve the sufferers inside of the vessel. While we were gone, a little daughter belonging to Mr. Perrigo got so benumbed, that she let go her hold and was drowned. Mrs. Rice had a boy, about two years old, which she dropped when the vessel first filled, and she went down and brought up her child and saved him. It was just three hours after the vessel went over before we got the sufferers out of the vessel. They were so thoroughly chilled, that they could not help themselves at all. We capsized at half past two o'clock, and it was dark when we left the vessel. I see there is another statement that Mr. Perrigo lost every thing he had, including a chest of tools; but this is a mistake. Mr. P. had no chest of tools on board, and the rest of his stuff was mostly saved. A trunk, belonging to his wife, was found opened and robbed of its contents below Red Banks. My vessel drifted on to Point au Sable bar where the 'Arabs' went aboard and stripped her, cutting her rigging up in a horrible manner. As far as capsizing the vessel is concerned, I do not consider myself at all to blame. I have the praise of being as careful as the next man, and I do not mean that my reputation shall suffer injury through the slanderous tongue of a man whom, with his family, I used the greatest exertions to save. Had I been drowned, there was not a man there who had presence of mind enough to do anything to save himself or the helpless beings inside the vessel. They all gave up in despair, and on their hands and knees called upon the Almighty to save them, but they would not help themselves. Yours truly, MILO MONTGOMERY."* *Mr. Gross (or Grosse) maybe Charles Gross, who was involved in subsequent rescues.

11) Leland, Schooner, Stranded 1855.

The GREEN BAY ADVOCATE, August 9, 1855 reported, "The

schooner *Leland,* which went ashore some time ago near Death's Door will not be got off. The lumber has been taken off." No other information on the schooner, her destination or situation were available.

12) *Roelofsen,* Bark, Stranded September of 1855.

The *Roelofsen* reportedly went ashore on a reef six miles from Eagle Harbor. She was bound for Chicago with a cargo of 300,000 board feet of lumber. The crew was "left destitute on the island." It was thought that the steamer *Huron,* which was bound for the area, would rescue them. The vessel was chartered by and loaded for Col. D. Jones at Oconto. The lumber was thought to be saved, but the vessel was a complete wreck. The vessel was owned by Nichols, Whitcomb & Co. and hailed from Detroit. Reprinted from the MILWAUKEE SENTINEL, September 22, 1855, by the GREEN BAY ADVOCATE, September 27, 1855.

13) *Windham,* Schooner, Stranded December of 1855.

The *Windham* went ashore on Death's Door Reef* while on her way to Chicago with a load of lumber. Last accounts reported the sea breaking over her. She hailed from Grand Rapids and was owned by her captain and Mrs. Munroe and others. *Entrance to Green Bay. GREEN BAY ADVOCATE, December 13, 1855. GREEN BAY ADVOCATE, December 20, 1855.

14) *Arkansas,* Schooner, Stranded December of 1855.

The *Arkansas* was reported ashore and breaking up near Green Bay according to the GREEN BAY ADVOCATE, December 13, 1855. No other information is available.

15) *Etta,* Sloop, Foundered August 1, 1856.

The *Etta* sank in a heavy gale off Sturgeon Bay Bluff and settled in 60 feet of water. She was bound for Green Bay at the time and was loaded with a cargo of stone for C. Kitchen. The crew was saved. The *Etta* hailed from De Pere. —GREEN BAY ADVOCATE, August 7, 1856.

16) *Homes*, Schooner, Sunk by collision September 15, 1856.

The *Homes* was run down by the schooner *William Fisk* in a dense fog, fifteen miles southeast of Mud Bay (now Moonlight Bay). The *Fisk* took on board the crew members of the *Homes* and towed the stricken vessel into Mud Bay, where they ran her into the mud. A northeast gale blew over the area for three days and the *Homes* was later found in Lily Bay, totally wrecked by wind and waves. She was stripped of her cargo of shingles, bolts and her nautical equipment and then abandoned. The *Homes* was bound from Leland, Michigan for Racine.—Retold by William Jackson who piloted the *Homes* into Mud Bay, published in the DOOR COUNTY ADVOCATE, March 14, 1896.

17) *Columbia*, Brig, Stranded June 4,1859.

The *Columbia* was wrecked on a small bay between Door Bluff and Hedgehog Harbor. The brig, in the command of Jacob Hansen, was bound from Chicago to Sturgeon Bay with a cargo of general merchandise for the upper mill company. The vessel sailed into a northerly blow and took shelter in the lee of Plum Island. In time the wind changed to the northeast and with the drop in temperature, rain turned to snow. The *Columbia's* position had become dangerous so sail was made for a better anchorage. She stood off on a port tack but on coming about, she missed stays. In danger of drifting ashore, the big anchor was dropped but the cable broke. The small anchor was likewise lost and "only a few moments elapsed before the brig went ashore in a small bight between Door Bluff and Hedgehog Harbor. The shore was very bold at this place and the vessel was about two fathoms from dry land when she struck." The yard arm became caught in the trees at the top of the bluff and the crew was able to escape by climbing the masts and crossing the yards to the bluff. Over the next day, or so much of the cargo was brought to shore and saved. The *Columbia* was owned by Joseph Harris and Jesse Birmingham. Birmingham happened to be along on the voyage and went for the assistance of a tugboat. None could be found, except in Green Bay, and when he returned four or five days later, the brig had been finished off by a

The brig Columbia as she may have appeared in 1855.

(Photo courtesy of Ohio Historical Society)

second storm. The *Columbia* measured 177 tons burden, with a length of 91 feet and a beam of 29 feet and was not insured. The year before she was lost, she earned her place in Great Lakes history, under a different owner, Captain Judson Wells, by becoming the first vessel to carry iron ore out of the Lake Superior Region. She is also remembered for having delivered in 1857, the locomotive, "Sevastopol" to Marquette, Michigan, the first locomotive in upper Michigan.

In September of 1875, Mr. A.J. Sibley left Sturgeon Bay for the Gulf Coast by way of the Fox, Wisconsin, and Mississippi Rivers. He, his wife and five children were all sailing to the destination in the yawl, *Columbia.* This yawl had, originally belonged to the brig *Columbia*, until she had been wrecked near Death's Door. The yawl was about 25 years old and had long been considered unsafe. The venture was viewed as most foolish, especially in September.

GREEN BAY ADVOCATE, September 30, 1875. DOOR COUNTY ADVOCATE, April 20, 1889.

Herman G. Runge Collection of the Milwaukee Public Library/Wisconsin Marine Historical Society.

18) *St. Mary*, Schooner, Foundered September 7, 1860.

The *St. Mary* sank mysteriously with all hands while on her way from Kewaunee to Cedar River, Michigan. It was thought to have gone down in the same gale that prevailed when the *Lady Elgin* was sunk. The *St. Mary* was headed north to pick up a cargo of lumber for her owner, John Caffery of Kewaunee. She was loaded with a cargo of pig iron to ballast her and it was supposed, at the time, that this sent her straight to the bottom. Fears were entertained of her loss but nothing was confirmed until one of her small boats drifted ashore near Lill's Brewery.* Shortly thereafter a body recovered from the lake was identified as that of William Jameson, one of the nine crewmen aboard. Two passengers also perished with the vessel. The *St. Mary* was kept by Mr. Caffery for the sole purpose of carrying lumber from Cedar River. She was valued at $6,000 and was uninsured. A later article quotes, "LOSS OF THE SCHR. ST. MARY CONFIRMED-Chicago, Sept. 28 It is now positively certain that the Schr. *St. Mary* foundered on the night of the *Lady Elgin* disaster. One of her small boats drifted ashore Sunday, a short distance north of this city. One body, supposed to have been lost off the *Lady Elgin*, has been identified as one of the schooner's crew. There were eleven persons, including crew, on board. The vessel was valued at $6,000-no insurance." *The Lill's Brewery, mentioned in the story, has never been identified. It is not known if the small boat was found north of Green Bay or north of Chicago.
GREEN BAY ADVOCATE,October 4, 1860. KEWAUNEE ENTERPRISE, October 10, 1860.

19) *Forrest Queen*, Type unknown, Stranded Late November, 1860.

This vessel ran aground and sank in a storm at Baileys Harbor. Circumstances were not confirmed but it was thought that she was trying to make the port for shelter and either struck the reef and sank on the spot or was run aground to prevent her sinking in deep water. She was bound from Milwaukee with 14,000 bushels of wheat for Buffalo. The cargo was insured. She was owned by Richmond of Chicago and was considered an old boat and of little value.—Reprinted from the MILWAUKEE SENTINEL by the GREEN BAY ADVOCATE, December 6, 1860.

20) *Minnesota*, Steam Propeller, Stranded September 26, 1861.

The *Minnesota* was bound north from Chicago when she "broke her arches" and sprang a leak off Baileys Harbor. The ship's cargo of corn had to be jettisoned. Later, when the leak increased, she was run ashore on Summer Island in the early morning of the 26th to prevent her from sinking. She soon parted and went to pieces in a heavy gale blowing from the south at the time. The rigging and furniture saved from the propeller were loaded on board the propeller *Union*.

The *Minnesota* had a number of bouts with calamity. She suffered $2,000 worth of damage in a Lake Erie gale in 1853. The following autumn, she ran on a rock in the Detroit River and spent the winter sitting on the bottom near Belle Isle, Michigan. The vessel was later repaired and returned to service. In 1855, she collided with the propeller, *Jersey City* and 400 barrels of whiskey and flour had to be thrown overboard to keep her afloat.

The *Minnesota* was built in 1851 at Maumee, Ohio for the Holt, Palmer & Co. of Buffalo and registered 749 tons. GREEN BAY ADVOCATE, October 3, 31, 1861. CHICAGO TRIBUNE, August 18, 1869

21) *Agnes Willie*, Type unknown, Capsized November 4, 1862.

The *Agnes Willie* was bound from Green Bay to an unknown destination with a cargo of apples when she capsized seven miles off Baileys Harbor. Her two owners, Alexander Doak and Robert Dickinson, were the only ones aboard and were rescued by fishermen from Mud Bay (now Moonlight Bay). She drifted ashore and became a total loss. Vessel and cargo were valued at $500 for which there was no insurance. She hailed from De Pere. DOOR COUNTY ADVOCATE, November 8, 1862.

22) *Unknown Scow*, Foundered August 21, 1863.

This unnamed vessel sank on her way from Grass Point to Green Bay with a load of sand. Her story is best told by this newspaper article:

"THE STORM-Loss of Life-The storm on Friday afternoon was the most sudden and severe that we had this season. In the afternoon, while the weather was clear and pleasant, three men, Martin Counard, Peter Vandenbrook, and Theodore Johnson, started with a scow load of sand from Grass Point for the city, and when about half way to the mouth of the river the storm struck them and carried away their sail, when the scow commenced to fill with water. The men seeing that the scow must soon sink, tore loose the small cabin on her which they got on to where two of them remained for about five hours, until taken off, one at a time by Charles Gross. Young Johnson could not swim and was several times brought back to the floating cabin by his more fortunate comrades, when washed off, but he finally sank exhausted, out of their reach. Mr. Gross deserves much praise for his exertions in saving VANDEN BROOK and COUNARD. When they reached the house of Mr. Atkinson, at Bay Settlement late in the evening they were nearly exhausted, but kind care from Mr. and Mrs. A. so far restored them as to enable them to reach their home in this city the next morning."

The story was followed by an account of a small boating accident in the same storm and this post script: "P.S.-The body of young Johnson was found floating near the mouth of the river on Tuesday, forenoon, by some boys, and brought to this city by them and buried the same afternoon by friends."— GREEN BAY ADVOCATE, August 27, 1863.

23) *Lady Cornelia*, Sailboat, Capsized November 3, 1865.

The *Lady Cornelia* capsized early in the morning off Sand Point near Escanaba. Only one of the five occupants, a Mr. Steward, reached shore on the wreckage after drifting for six or seven hours. Lost from the craft, were Burt Sensibee of Fort Howard; William

Moulton, sheriff of Delta county; Andy Morehead, and Joseph Herdmanc, a fifteen year-old boy who had run away from his home in New York City. Sheriff Moulton hung on to the wreck until it washed ashore but did not have the strength to make his way through the surf. Stewart crawled two miles on his hands and knees until he reached the nearest house. The *Lady Cornelia* sank two years before, October 3, 1863, in a blow off Point Sauble, eight miles north of Green Bay. In that incident, Captain Alex Laurie and David Sawyer, both drowned, after they left that morning for Green Bay to pick up winter supplies. The vessel was found by an Indian.—Recounted in the DOOR COUNTY ADVOCATE, January 21, 1909. GREEN BAY ADVOCATE, November 9, 1865. KEWAUNEE ENTERPRISE, November 15, 1865.

24) *H. Mitchell*, Schooner, Stranded May, 1863.

The *Mitchell* went ashore at Baileys Harbor. The *Mitchell* was a vessel of 194 tons and bound from Chicago to Green Bay. The ship was valued at $5,000 and was insured for $3,600. She was owned by J.T. Kelly of Milan, Ohio. The crew escaped to shore.— MARINE CASUALTIES ON THE GREAT LAKES, 1863.

25) *Henry (Harry) Norton*, Schooner, Stranded October, 1863.

This ship blew ashore at Pilot Island while on her way from Green Bay to Chicago. The *Norton* registered 153 tons and was owned by the Judd Co. of Milwaukee. The crew made their way to shore safely. The vessel was valued at $9,000 and was insured for $2,000. The cargo was valued at $2,000 and was not insured. A story reprinted from the MENOMINEE HERALD, related that the *Henry Norton*, a top sail schooner, was blown ashore on Pilot Island in a storm. The *Norton* had sailed for Menominee with a cargo of lumber from an unnamed port. The cargo, which belonged to the Kirby-Carpenter Co. and to Joseph Wise, was a total loss as was the vessel. The crew, however, was saved. MARINE CASUALTIES ON THE GREAT LAKES, 1863. GREEN BAY ADVOCATE, October 1, 1863.

26) *Daniel Slauson*, Schooner, Stranded October, 1863.

The *Slauson* was wrecked near Death's Door while on her way to
Buffalo with a load of wheat. The captain and crew were able to
save themselves and arrived at Racine, Wisconsin, on October
24th. The vessel was insured with Home Insurance Co. and her
cargo was insured with Mercantile Mutual. According to the
MARINE CASUALTIES ON THE GREAT LAKES, 1863, the *"D. Slauson"*
was bound from Chicago to Buffalo when she stranded at Pilot
Island. She was rated at 273 tons and hailed from Racine where she
was owned by Slauson & Co. Loss on the ship was placed at
$17,500, of which insurance covered $10,000. Loss on the cargo
was valued at $35,000, with $15,000 coverage. Reprinted from the DAILY
WISCONSIN of October 26, 1863 by the KEWAUNEE ENTERPRISE, October 28, 1863.

27) Unnamed Schooner, Stranded November, 1863.

A small news item described a three masted schooner driven
ashore on "Pond Island" at the mouth of Little Sturgeon Bay. The
vessel was blown ashore in a storm. (Author's note: Pond Island
has also been known as Basin Island and Snake Island.) DOOR COUNTY
ADVOCATE, November 19, 1863.

28) *Menominee Belle*, Stranded November, 1863.

The *Menominee Belle* was blown ashore at Little Sister Bay, in a
storm and was severely damaged. The crewmembers were able to
save themselves by swimming to shore. DOOR COUNTY ADVOCATE,
November 19, 1863.

29) Ramsey Crooks, Brig, Foundered Autumn of 1863.

The *Crooks* sank off the east shore of Washington Island. Captain
Henry Knudson was taking her to the island with a cargo of general
freight which included, among other things, a barrel of whiskey.
Before the crew started unloading cargo, they opened the barrel and
"indulging pretty freely in the fiery stuff, they became unmanageable." A storm blew up while the crew was under the influence and

The brig, Ramsey Crooks
Photo courtesy of the Great Lakes Marine Collection
of the Milwaukee Public Library/Wisconsin Marine Historical Society

the *Crooks* dragged her anchors, struck bottom and went to pieces. The government steamer *Search* went to the scene the next day to save what was left, but the brig was so old and rotten that nothing could be saved.

The Ramsey Crooks was built in Detroit in 1836 for the American Fur Company. She measure 100 feet in length, 28 feet across the beam, 9 feet in depth and registered 247 net tons. DOOR COUNTY ADVOCATE, November 24, 1888. Beasly, Norman. "Freighters of Fortune, The Story of the Great Lakes." Harper & Brothers. New York. 1930. p.23.

30) *Alvin Clark*, Schooner, Capsized June 29, 1864.

The *Clark* was capsized in a gale about 5 p.m. off Chambers Island. She was light and bound for Oconto to pick up a cargo of lumber at the time. Her captain, mate, and one crewman were drowned. The surviving crewmen were picked up by a passing schooner. The vessel was owned by a Mr. Higgie of Racine. Captains of vessels who passed the wreck stated that she was lay-ing off Chambers Island in 9 fathoms of water with her stern float-ing out of the water. The day the *Clark* capsized, the weather was warm with a strong wind out of the south-southwest, until 5 p.m. when it suddenly shifted to the northeast and blew a squall that tore up trees, "picking up the water before it and carrying it for hun-dreds of feet ahead." Plans were made to raise the *Alvin Clark* and it was thought that she could be brought up with slight damage. The tug *Sarah E. Bryant* was sent from Buffalo with a steam pump and anything else she needed to raise the craft. MARINE CASUALTIES ON THE GREAT LAKES, 1864 confirms most of this information and adds only that she was valued at $2,500 for which there was $1,500 coverage.

The *Clark* was found again on February 19, 1898 by Menominee fisherman, James Shaw, who was fishing through the ice with nets near Chambers Island. Shaw caught and ripped his nets on some-thing and remnants of the nets came up with rust and pieces of wood. Older marine men believed it to be the *Alvin Clark*, a large two masted schooner which capsized and sank in the 1860's.

On November 1, 1967 the *Clark* was found again, this time by Menominee fisherman Dick Garbowski, who caught his nets on it. Frank Hoffman, a diver from Egg Harbor was called in to free the nets and discovered they were entangled on the vessel's mast. Hoffman began an 18 month struggle to raise the *Clark* from 19 fathoms and succeeded in bringing her to the surface on July 23, 1969. The craft, by this time dubbed the "Mystery Ship," was taken to Menominee harbor were Hoffman turned her into a museum. He lacked the funds to give her the care and preservation she required, and the *Clark* suffered terribly from dry rot. Hoffman sold

The Alvin Clark after she was raised.

Photo courtesy of the Great Lakes Marine Collection
of the Milwaukee Public Library/Wisconsin Marine Historical Society

the marina where she was on display and her new owner ultimately had her bulldozed into the ground.

The *Alvin Clark* was built in Detroit in 1846 and was named for Alvin S. Clark, youngest son of John Pearson Clark, one of the pioneers who brought the fishing industry to Lake Michigan. John P. Clark later established a successful shipyard and drydock in

Detroit. July 7, 1864. Reprinted from the MENOMINEE HERALD by the GREEN BAY ADVOCATE, July 14, 1864. GREEN BAY ADVOCATE, August 4, 1864. DOOR COUNTY ADVOCATE, February 26, 1898. History of the Great Lakes, Illustrated. Chicago: J.H. Beers & Co. 1899. Vol. 2, 66 - 67. Thomas Avery, The Mystery Ship from 19 Fathoms Au Train, Michigan, Avery Color Studios, 1974, p. 35 - 42.

31) *J.C. Fremont*, Schooner, Foundered June 26, 1865.

The *Fremont* sank after a collision in the fog with the barque, *American Union*, off Baileys Harbor. The vessel sank five minutes after the barque broke loose, but the crew was rescued by the *American Union*. The *Fremont* was owned by A.E. Curtis of Chicago. A government report agrees with the newspaper account and adds that the *Fremont* was bound from Buffalo for Chicago with no cargo at the time. The report further states that she was 288 tons, hailing from *Fremont* and was valued at $8,000 with insurance of $6,000. However, the *Fremont* is listed as having been sunk in June of 1864, and under the ownership of Fleist & White. DOOR COUNTY ADVOCATE, June 29, 1865. MARINE CASUALTIES ON THE GREAT LAKES, 1864.

32) Unnamed Fishing Boat, Capsized July 5, 1865.

This unidentified boat capsized off Boyer's Bluff on her way to the island. Three men on board, James Lowe, Frank Woolf, and Edward Warren were all lost. Lowe's body was the only one recovered. All three were from Washington Harbor. The boat was loaded with nets, tackle, etc. GREEN BAY ADVOCATE, July 13, 1865.

33) *Lewis Cass*, Schooner, Stranded Mid-September, 1865.

The *Cass* went ashore at Baileys Harbor on the reef opposite the lighthouse. A tug sent up from Milwaukee was unable to pull her off. She was later described as having been abandoned to the underwriters. CHICAGO TRIBUNE, September 22,1865. DOOR COUNTY ADVOCATE, November 9, 1865.

34) *Flash*, Sloop, Stranded Mid-November, 1866.

According to a one line item in the DOOR COUNTY ADVOCATE,

November 15, 1866, the *Flash* went ashore in Washington Harbor.

35) *T. Baker*, Schooner, Stranded November 11, 1866.

The *Baker* ran aground on "Hogs Back Reef" between North Bay and Rowley Bay. She was bound from Cleveland to Escanaba with a load of hay at the time. DOOR COUNTY ADVOCATE, November 15, 1866.

36) *Josephine*, Schooner, Stranded December, 1866.

The *Josephine* was the subject of different and conflicting news items. The DOOR COUNTY ADVOCATE, December 13, 1866, reported her ashore and going to pieces on Peshtigo reef. The freight, rigging and sails were saved. Her owner, Captain Robert Graham, sold the hull for $150, however, efforts to release her were unsuccessful. In a story reprinted from the ADVOCATE, the KEWAUNEE ENTERPRISE reported January 16, 1867 that Robert Graham had started building another vessel to replace the *Josephine* lost in the fall of '66. The DOOR COUNTY ADVOCATE, May 2, 1867, refers to the *Josephine* as being afloat as of April 29 of that year. This late reference may be of a second vessel by that name.

37) *Grapeshot*, #10265, Schooner, Stranded November 1, 1867.

The *Grapeshot* went ashore on the north end of Plum Island. She was described in one news article as being "upon a bed of solid rock, with her bow out about four feet, while at the stern she is decks to in the water." The tug, *Leviathan*, and a steam pump were sent from Chicago. The steamer *George Dunbar* later arrived to take over the job. The schooner was thought to be little damaged and easily saved once her cargo was removed and her hold pumped out. She'd been loaded with lumber at the time. A story in the DOOR COUNTY ADVOCATE, July 23, 1868 confirmed that the *Grapeshot* had been stripped and abandoned. She was known to have had two masts. The List of Merchant Vessels of the United States, 1867, describes the vessel as a scow-schooner, measuring 267.78 tons. She had a length of 131 ft., a beam of 28 ft. and a 10 ft. depth of hold. She was built in Buffalo in 1855 and hailed from

Chicago. She was dropped from the registration list the following year. CHICAGO TRIBUNE, November 8, December 20, 1867. DOOR COUNTY ADVOCATE, November 14, 1867. DOOR COUNTY ADVOCATE, July 23, 1868.

38) *Maple Leaf,* #16422, Scow-Schooner, Stranded November 1, 1867.

The *Maple Leaf* went ashore on Pilot Island early in November of 1867.* The schooner's bottom was so badly stove in, that salvage was hopeless and she was partially stripped and abandoned. She carried no cargo at the time. A later DOOR COUNTY ADVOCATE article, confirmed this. Two years later, Captain Thomas Parker sold the ship's outfit. The new owner had to travel from Green Bay across the ice to Pilot Island to retrieve his property. An August 25, 1870 news item in this same newspaper referred to her as being ashore "near the Door." The *Maple Leaf* was built in Buffalo, New York in 1854 and rebuilt nine years later. The List of Merchant Vessels of the U.S. of 1867 describes her as 222.99 ton vessel that hailed from Chicago. She was dropped from registration the following year. *One news article stated she was on Detroit Island.

CHICAGO TRIBUNE, November 8, 1867. DOOR COUNTY ADVOCATE, November 14, 1867. DOOR COUNTY ADVOCATE, July 23, 1868. CHICAGO TRIBUNE, April 15, August 23, 1869. List of Merchant Vessels of the U.S., 1867, p. 124.

39) *Hanover,* #11142, Schooner, Stranded November 7, 1867.

The *Hanover* was reported ashore on Strawberry Reef near Fish Creek. She was a total loss. The very next day she started to break up and Captain John McElligott ordered her stripped. The vessel was bound for Oconto for a cargo of lumber but was light (empty) at the time. The location of her loss may be farther south, near Chambers Island, on what is now called Hanover Shoal. The *Hanover* was built in 1832 at Irving, New York and received an extensive rebuild in 1865 which restored her status as a staunch vessel. She was valued at $7,000 "gold value." According to the the List of Merchant Vessels of the U.S., 1867, she measured 188.31 tons and hailed from Buffalo. CHICAGO TRIBUNE, November 13,

1867. DOOR COUNTY ADVOCATE, November 14, 1867. List of Merchant Vessels of the U.S., 1867, p. 83.

40) *H.B. Steele*, #11302, Schooner, Stranded November 9, 1867.

The *Steele* was blown ashore at Sturgeon Bay near Brandt's pier where she had taken on a load of poles. There was no loss of life. The vessel was formerly owned at St. Clair by the Bashlow Co. but had just recently been purchased by Milwaukee parties for $6,000 in cash. She was insured for $3,000. She measured 118 tons and was built in St. Clair, Michigan in 1858. (One news account of the wreck of the schooner, *Medora* in 1868, gives brief mention of the *H.B. Steele* as afloat. It may be an error or, in spite of all of the statements of her demise, the *Steele* might have been rescued after all.)

DOOR COUNTY ADVOCATE, November 14, 1867. CHICAGO TRIBUNE, November 23, December 20, 1867. CHICAGO TRIBUNE, November 3, 1868. List of Merchant Vessels of the U.S., 1867, p. 81. MARINE CASUALTIES ON THE GREAT LAKES, 1867.

41) *Sam Hale*, #22345, Brig, Stranded September 22, 1868.

The *Sam Hale* went ashore on the "Whales' Back" just north of Chamber's Island. The crew went to Cedar River for help, leaving two men behind. While the "rescue party" was gone, the vessel went to pieces. Both seamen were able to escape the sinking vessel in relative safety and grab a piece of floating wreckage. One crewman floated around the northern Bay of Green Bay for twelve hours before he was picked up near Death's Door by the steamer *Washington*. The other sailor had clung to a part of the cargo of lumber for 24 hours before being rescued by the steamer *Saginaw*. The *Hale* was loaded with lumber for Chicago by Spalding & Porter. She lost part of her deckload when she went on the reef. The captain came in at Cedarville (Cedar River) and telegraphed at Menominee for a tug and three scows but none had come to his assistance. It was later reported that she had gone to pieces. The vessel and her cargo of lumber were a total loss.

Years later, the CHICAGO TRIBUNE reported, "While setting buoys in Green Bay, Capt. Hart fished up considerable iron. Among other things he found the rudder post of the old schr Sam Hale."

According to the List of Merchant Vessels of the U.S., 1867, she measured 225.96 tons and hailed from Chicago. DOOR COUNTY ADVOCATE, October 8, 1868. Reprinted from the MENOMINEE HERALD by the GREEN BAY ADVOCATE, October 1, 1868. CHICAGO TRIBUNE, December 14, 1868. STURGEON BAY ADVOCATE, December 31, 1868 quoting the MILWAUKEE SENTINEL. CHICAGO TRIBUNE, May 29, 1875. List of Merchant Vessels of the U.S., 1867, p. 170.

42) *Medora*, #16451, Schooner, Stranded November 1, 1868.

The *Medora* was taking on a load of bark at Grimm's pier when a storm sprang up. She was next to the *H.B. Steele* at the time and the Steele was blown around the end of the pier, into the *Medora*. The scow was severely damaged and sank in seven feet of water. She was reported to have gone to pieces. She had been loaded with a cargo of wood for John Dorner of Milwaukee. This was also lost.

The *Medora* was valued at $2,000 and was insured. She was built at Clayton, Michigan in 1861 and measured 64 tons. She was owned by Edward Readey of Detroit. CHICAGO TRIBUNE, November 3, 1868. List of Merchant Vessels of the U.S., 1867, page 134.

43) *S.L. Noble*, #23103, Schooner, Foundered November 16, 1868.

The *Noble* sank in a storm at T.F. Gillilland's pier at Clay Banks. She had just taken on a load of cordwood when a southeast gale came up. The on-shore wind prevented her from seeking the safety of deeper water. Trapped in the shallows in heavy seas, she pounded on the bottom until her hull gave out. The DOOR COUNTY ADVOCATE, December 31, 1868 by way of a MILWAUKEE SENTINEL article confirmed that she was ashore at Clay Banks and had become a total loss. The CHICAGO TRIBUNE of November 17, 1868, stated the the *Noble* was ashore at Clay Banks, Michigan—on Lake Erie. The List of Merchant Vessels of the U.S., of 1867 listed her as a scow-schooner of 88.40 tons, hailing from Port Huron, Michigan. List of Merchant Vessels of the U.S., 1867, p. 168.

44) *W.M. Arbuckle*, #26167, Schooner, Stranded November 25, 1868.

The *Arbuckle* had sprung a leak and was run ashore at Sister Bay to prevent her from foundering in deep water. A steam pump was sent up from Milwaukee and efforts were made to pump her out. When that failed she was abandoned as a total loss. Late reports stated she was sitting in an exposed position and would go to pieces soon for her bottom seemed to be already demolished.

The *W.M. Arbuckle* was valued at $4,500 and insured for $2,500. She was built in Erie, Pennsylvania in 1854, registered 174 tons and was owned by Brearley, Pritchard and Williams of Racine.

CHICAGO TRIBUNE, November 28, December 4, 1868. Reprinted from the MILWAUKEE SENTINEL by the DOOR COUNTY ADVOCATE, December 31, 1868. List of Merchant Vessels of the U.S., 1867, p. 196.

45) *Mount Vernon*, #16405, Schooner, Stranded April 9, 1869.

The *Mount Vernon* went ashore at Dean's Mill, six miles south of Kewaunee. She had landed at the mill dock that morning and had taken on 2,800 ties for Taylor & Bach. More ties were to be loaded the next morning and the vessel was left moored. That evening a strong northeast wind developed and the captain pulled in his lines intending to get away from the pier. The vessel would not answer the helm and drifted upon a shoal "200 feet north of the pier and 150 feet inside" where she pounded on the bottom until she sprang a leak and sank. The water was even with her deck. It was thought that the vessel could be recovered if good weather prevailed and the captain went to Manitowoc the next day and telegraphed Chicago for a tug boat. A steam pump was also sent from Chicago. The tug, *Union*, came to the aid of the craft but was unable to do anything. The *Mount Vernon* had, by this time, settled three feet in to the sand and her deck was underwater. The crew from the *Union* placed a pump aboard the wreck and a trench, nine feet deep, was dredged away from the wreck, but as soon as she was pulled into deeper water, she settled on the bottom as firm as ever. The stress of rough weather caused her to leak faster than the pump could handle and she was abandoned. Within three weeks of her stranding she started breaking up. Her final resting place was the same distance from shore and fifty feet closer to the pier from where she first struck. She was owned and sailed by Captain F.O. Beryson. He had purchased the *Mount Vernon* the previous year and, at great expense, had repaired the vessel. This was his first trip. His loss of the vessel, tug expenses, and other costs totaled $3,000 to $4,000. The ties were expected to be recovered. The *Mount Vernon* was an old vessel and was valued at $7,000 to $8,000. She was insured for $5,000. The *Mount Vernon* measured 171.95 tons and hailed from Chicago according to the List of Merchant Vessels of the U.S., 1867. KEWAUNEE ENTERPRISE, April 14, 21, 28, 1869. CHICAGO TRIBUNE, April 20, 21, 24, 1869. List of Merchant Vessels of the U.S., 1867, p. 139.

46) Unnamed vessel, Capsized May of 1866.

In the May 29, 1869 issue, the GREEN BAY ADVOCATE published a small item about a man, Frank Welch, who had found a bottle floating in the bay near Grass Point. The bottle had been tightly corked and looked as though it had been in the water for some time. Inside was a Dousman & Elmore dray delivery ticket. On one side was written in pencil, "Upset off Washington Island, May, 1866, James P. (unintelligeable), Frank Hogg, John Nickle." On the other side of the card was written "My poor wife. What will she do. Life insured." The card was thought to be an old one based on the style of cardboard and was known to have been originally printed in the ADVOCATE office. The location, and size of the crew suggests that it was probably a fishing boat. The article is interesting in that it illustrates that vessels and men could disappear in that day and age, leaving no official record of their loss.

47) *J.G. McCullough*, #12974, Schooner, Foundered July 3, 1869.

The *McCullough* sank after a collision with the bark, *Pensaukee*, in the fog twenty miles off Clay Banks. The *Pensaukee* struck the *McCullough* just aft of the main mast, "making a fearful breach." The force of the blow broke the *McCullough's* mast into 3 pieces sending the main and foremast crashing into the cabin demolishing it and the ship's lifeboat. The watch had just been changed and all of the schooner's crew members were on deck at the time. The captain, mate and one crewman scrambled aboard the *Pensaukee*. Two other crewmen were able to climb aboard the *Pensaukee's* lifeboat. All lost their personal belongings and only the ship's papers were saved. Ten minutes after she was struck, the *McCullough* sank in 200 feet of water. The *McCullough* hailed from Kenosha and was bound for that port with a cargo of pig iron from Escanaba. She was in command of her owner, Captain A. Miller. The vessel was valued at $6,000 and was insured for $4,000. She measured 86 tons burthen. The vessel was officially registered as the *J.G. McCulloch* and hailed from Kenosha, Wisconsin, according to the List of Merchant Vessels of the U.S., 1867. CHICAGO TRIBUNE, July 7, 1869. Reprinted from the MILWAUKEE SENTINEL by the KEWAUNEE ENTERPRISE, July 14, 1869. List of Merchant Vessels of the U.S., 1867, p. 96.

48) *Gray Eagle*, #10341, Schooner, Stranded July 17, 1869.

The *Gray Eagle* went ashore in a gale on the north point of Whitefish Bay. Her captain thought she'd be a total loss. A large bark and a topsail schooner, the *E.R. Blake* went ashore on the south point of Whitefish Bay in the same storm, however, they were later recovered. The *Blake* lost her large anchor and fifteen fathoms of chain. The *Gray Eagle* on the other hand became a total wreck with the big seas that pounded her making short work of her old and poor hull. Her "outfit" was taken off by the crew of the *Yankee Trader* and returned to its owner in Milwaukee. Everything else was lost. The remains of the scow were ultimately burned, it was thought, by fishermen in hopes of retrieving the ship's spikes and other iron.

The *Gray Eagle* measured 287.07 tons, hailed from Milwaukee and was owned by Ferdinand Vogel, Captain Johnson and Thomas Carroll of that city. She was built at Buffalo in 1857 and was insured for $10,000. DOOR COUNTY ADVOCATE, July 15, 22, 1869. CHICAGO TRIBUNE, July 15, 16, 17, 20, August 5, September 11, 18, 1869. DOOR COUNTY

49) *Rival*, #21693, Schooner, Stranded September 10, 1869.

The *Rival* struck a rock and sank while trying to leave Grimm's Pier, five miles north of Kewaunee. She had loaded 50 cords of wood for Jacob Grimm during the day. That night she tried to set sail. There was little wind at the time, but a heavy swell was rolling in. When about 300 feet northeast of the end of the pier, she struck hard on a sunken rock and stove in her bottom planking. She sank immediately, settling on the rocky bottom. Her captain, called the tug, *G.W. Tift*, to come from Milwaukee for assistance. When the *Tift* arrived the she found the *Rival* blown over the reef and in the shallows with her bottom pounded out. The tug was unable to help and returned to port that same day with the craft's small boat, running gear and canvas. The scow's standing rigging, spars, anchors, and chain were to be removed when the weather subsided. The *Rival* was uninsured and was valued at $2,000. Up to that time the vessel was still deemed salvageable, but a week later, September 22, the KEWAUNEE ENTERPRISE announced, "the scow, *Rival* now lies on the beach near Grimm's Pier, a total wreck, having been stripped and abandoned by her owner." She was owned by Henry Kasten, Henry Lippert, Henry Herter and Adam Kuntz of Milwaukee. She was built at Port Huron, Michigan in 1861 and registered 47.71 tons. KEWAUNEE ENTERPRISE, September 15, 1869. CHICAGO TRIBUNE, September 16, 1869. List of Merchant Vessels of the U.S., 1867, p. 164.

50) *Ocean Wave*, #18912, Schooner, Foundered September 23, 1869.

The *Ocean Wave* struck a piece of timber or floating wreckage and sank "fifteen or twenty miles southeast Baileys Harbor" and twelve miles off shore. She had left Mud Bay with a load of 53 cords of building stone intended for harbor improvements at White Lake and had been experiencing foul weather all the way. The captain, Fletcher Hackett and his crew had only time enough to launch the ship's lifeboat before she sank in 300 feet of water. They lost everything except the clothes on their backs. The captain also lost $160 in "greenbacks" which had been in his state room. The crew rowed for shore and found land near Whitefish Bay.

Three years earlier, the *Ocean Wave* capsized and sank off of Chambers Island. Over three months of effort were required to bring her back to the surface. The *Ocean Wave* was built at Cleveland in 1853 and measured 213.61 tons. She was valued at $5,000 and had been insured for $3,000 only three weeks before. The vessel was originally rigged as a barkentine but at the time of her loss was rigged as a three masted schooner with no yards. She hailed from Chicago. CHICAGO TRIBUNE, July 8, October 26, 1866. CHICAGO TRIBUNE, September 25, October 16, 1869. DOOR COUNTY ADVOCATE, September 30, 1869. DOOR COUNTY ADVOCATE, March 4, 1909. List of Merchant Vessels of the U.S., 1867, p. 147

51) *Sunshine*, #23057, Schooner, Stranded September 29, 1869.

The *Sunshine* was bound from White Lake, Michigan for Chicago with a cargo of lumber when she was overcome by a violent southwest gale. She was headed for shore and reached North Bay waterlogged and unmanageable. The scow was filled with water and sitting low so the captain ordered her deckload of lumber thrown overboard allowing her to float higher on to the shore. The vessel was ultimately beached on the north point of North Bay. When her crew left her she was still in one piece but sitting on a rock ledge and pounding. By December she was still beached, still loaded with lumber, but her sides had separated from the bottom. The *Sunshine* measured 115.56 tons and and was owned by Captains Hauser and Durbin of Chicago. She was built Mt. Clemens, Michigan in 1856, was valued at $6,000 and insured for $4,000. CHICAGO TRIBUNE, October 6, 11, December 9, 1869. DOOR COUNTY ADVOCATE, August 25, 1870. List of Merchant Vessels of the U.S., 1867, p. 181.

52) *Fairfield*, #9195, Schooner, Stranded September 30, 1869.

The *Fairfield* ran on the reef off the north point of Baileys Harbor while on her way to pick up a cargo of wood. She carried no cargo at the time and was scuttled to prevent her from pounding on the bottom. She was later joined by the schooners *Magic* and *Blue Belle*, both of which were rescued. The DOOR COUNTY ADVOCATE reported "There now lies three schooners within 70 rods of each other entirely north of the channel where vessels never have any business to go and close to the lighthouse."

The tug *O.B. Green* was brought up to salvage her and had a "fair prospect" of succeeding. The schooner had been blown broadside on to the rock ledge and the *Green* had towed her two ship's lengths with the schooner plowing the rocks away as she went. Her rescuers thought she could be rescued if fair weather held. If southern gales showed their fury, the *Fairfield* would have only a slim chance of recovery. The next week when south southeast seas rolled into Baileys Harbor, the *Fairfield* was summarily abandoned to the elements. She was later stripped and abandoned and by the third week in October, her masts washed away indicating that the hull was going to pieces. By early spring of 1870, much of the vessel had washed ashore. The *Fairfield* hailed from Chicago and was bound from that port for Green Bay at the time she ran aground. Loss to the vessel was estimated at $5,000 of which $3,000 was covered by insurance. Years later, parts of the *Fairfield* began to wash ashore again, creating fears that some unknown ship had gone to pieces with all hands somewhere out in the lake. The *Fairfield* measured 223 tons and was built in Niagara, New York in 1846. DOOR COUNTY ADVOCATE, October 7, 21, 1869. CHICAGO TRIBUNE, October 6, 8, 12, 22, 1869. DOOR COUNTY ADVOCATE, June 4, 1870. MARINE CASUALTIES ON THE GREAT LAKES, 1869. List of Merchant Vessels of the U.S., 1867, p. 63.

53) *D.O. Dickinson*, #6133, Schooner, Stranded October 8, 1869.

The *Dickinson* ran up on "Strawberry Shoal" while she was on her way from Oconto to Chicago with a cargo of lumber. The vessel was declared a total loss, estimated at $12,000. Insurance covered $10,000 of that.

When the crew of the *Dickinson* reached Chicago, the CHICAGO

TRIBUNE ran a story of their adventure. The account prompted a letter to the editor from Captain William Cardwell who was not completely satisfied with its accuracy. This letter gives many details of the disaster and does so with vivid color. It is therefore reprinted here, full and complete.

To the Editor of the Chicago Tribune;

In your issue of the 21st inst. appears an account of the loss to the schooner Daniel O. Dickinson, *which is somewhat incorrect. The crew did not return to Chicago on the* Franklin; *they came on the propeller* Truesdell, *and, instead of being one day from Oconto when the schooner got ashore, we were only four and one half hours. We left Oconto at 11 p.m. on the 7th and got aground at 3:50 a.m. on the 8th. The facts simply are, that, the night being very dark and hazy, we did not see the light on Green Island, and to the best of my opinion, in which the majority of the crew concur, the light was not there at the time. In consequence, we ran ashore upon the southeast end of Chambers Island, generally known as Strawberry Reef; so that your informant must have been half-seas-over, or else very little acquainted with Green Bay and its many shoals and islands, to get his account of the wreck so much mixed up as he has done. As to the crew losing control of the vessel, and part of them going to Menominee, such was not the case. My officers and crew acted nobly, and cheerfully obeyed every order, doing their duty fully, to a man. There was a heavy sea, and a strong wind sprung up after our getting on the beach, so that we could not get our anchors out to heave her off; so I took four of the crew with myself in the yawl, went to Menominee and procured the tug* Reindeer, *and returned to the schooner at 5 p.m. The wind had now changed to the southwest, and was blowing very hard. The tug could not get near the schooner, so myself and crew boarded her in the yawl, and the tug returned to Menominee. Next day, the 9th, the tug returned, with a scow and ten hands as far as Green Island, but could not approach near enough to render us any aid. During that night we all remained on board, it being very dark and the wind blowing very hard from the southwest. At 3 a.m. on the 9th, the sea was breaking all over her, and the water was up and over the cabin floor. I could have got on shore with my crew but unfortunately I had my sister and her little boy, Willie Lane, five years old, on board; also young Robert Emmet, son of A.L. Morrison of this city. Although they were but children, they acted like heroes, and never even murmured. We all left the vessel at daylight on the 9th, in the yawl, and safely landed on Chambers Island, one mile and a half from the wreck, the seas running fearfully high. We remained encamped in the woods until the following Tuesday, the 12th inst. Fortunately for my sister and the two children, we met a good Samaritan, in a poor fisherman, the only inhabitant on that end of the island, who generously gave up possession of his little hut, about 10 by 4, and camped out in the woods with us himself. On that evening, on board the little schooner* Cecilia, *we embarked with all the sails and running gear which we had been able to rescue. In beating to Menominee, we were towed by the wrecking tug* Leviathan, *which had been sent to our assistance by the Republic Insurance Company. The schooner got broken amidships during the gale from the southwest on the 9th and 10th; and with the exception of a lull on the 11th, and 12th, it continued to blow until the 15th, in the afternoon. At 11 a.m. on the 16th, the wind having risen again at midnight, both masts went by the board; her decks burst open, and floated away, She then finally, washed over the reef, and disappeared from view. I was sitting at the time on the top of Fish Creek Hill, four miles distant, and watched the wreck through my glass until the last stick of the well-known schooner* D.O. Dickinson *disappeared from view beneath the waters of Green Bay. We lost all our personal property, but saved the "green flag."* Respectfully, Wm. P. Cardwell, Last Master of the ill-fated schooner* D.O. Dickinson. *Chicago, Oct. 23, 1869.*

The *Dickenson* hailed from Chicago where she was owned by Captain Cardwell. She measured 241.82 tons. *Captain Cardwell may be referring to a "gin pennant" and may be implying that they drank a toast to the schooner. CHICAGO TRIBUNE, October 15, 19, 21, 22, 24, 1869. DOOR COUNTY ADVOCATE, October 28, 1869. MARINE CASUALTIES ON THE GREAT

54) *Iowa*, Barge, Stranded November 14, 1869

The *Iowa* blew ashore a mile and a half north of Taylor & Bash's pier. She had been in tow of the tug, *Admiral D.D. Porter* at the time. The tug, like her consort, also ran aground but was able to free herself. The *Porter* with the assistance of the tug, *Kitty Smoke*, tried unsuccessfully to free the stranded barge. She was laying on rocks, badly damaged, and it was decided that she was to be stripped of her outfit and abandoned. KEWAUNEE ENTERPRISE correspondent, J.M. Read, of Carlton, made this observation: "A good new vessel would, perhaps, have been off before this, but this one is the hull of an old steamer, and being large, and heavy, and decayed, she could not stand it. The weather has been very still ever since she went on." The *Iowa* was owned by the Peshtigo Lumber Co. and was north bound at the time she went on, (presumably on her way to Peshtigo, by way of Death's Door.-Author) The KEEWAUNEE ENTERPRISE later reported, "Last Wednesday some person, who had nothing better to do, set fire to the wreck of the barge, *Iowa*, which went on the rocks four miles and a half south of the place in the town of Carlton, about a month ago. It took the old hulk two days to burn down to the water, and then what was left of her floated ashore Thursday night." The *Iowa* was not listed in the <u>List of Merchant Vessels</u> and as it is likely that she was cut down to an unpowered barge before official numbers were assigned, it's possible that no documentation number was assigned.

The *Iowa* was built as a paddlewheel steamer and later converted to a propeller. In the spring of 1867 she was taken to a Peshtigo shipyard where she was cut down and converted to a lumber barge. The $15,000 conversion left her with a single mast for a large sail and a major dependence on her intended escort, the tug *Admiral D.D. Porter*. Her sole purpose was carrying lumber from Peshtigo to Chicago for which her capacity was estimated at one million board feet of lumber. CHICAGO TRIBUNE, September 17, October 9, November 17,

22, 1867. Kewaunee Enterprise, November 17, December 15, 1869. Door County Advocate, November 25, 1869.

55) *W.H. Craig*, #26216, Schooner, Stranded November 26, 1869.

The *Craig* was bound from Escanaba to Cleveland when she ran aground on Peninsula Point. She was loaded with 468 tons of iron ore from the New York Mine. She was thought to be safe if the bay froze over before southern winds broke her up. She was last seen breaking up and was lost for want of a steam pump. She measured 275.74 tons and hailed from Chicago. Escanaba Tribune, December 9, 16, 1869. List of Merchant Vessels of the U.S., page 195.

56) *Ottawa*, Propeller, Stranded in Autumn of 1869.

Remains of the *Ottawa* were found on the beach, two miles south of Ahnapee where she'd been destroyed by fire in the fall of 1869. She had belonged to the Goodrich Steamboat Line before being sold to the Chicago and Green Bay Line and was replaced by the *G.J. Truesdell*. Three different vessels by this name were listed in the List of Merchant Vessels of the U.S., for 1867: #18914-Milwaukee, Wis., 578.14 tons, #18922-Detroit, Michigan, 220.11 tons, #19107-Sandusky, Ohio, 57.66 tons. No reference was made to the burning of the *Ottawa*, in either the Kewaunee Enterprise, or the Door County Advocate anytime prior to this. Door County Advocate, June 20, 1896. List of Merchant Vessels of the U.S., 1867, p. 150.

57) *Free Trader*, Schooner, Foundered December of 1869.

The *Free Trader* was found in distress by the steamer *St. Joseph*. The small schooner was leaking badly, so her cargo of fish was loaded onto the steamer and the schooner taken in tow. She was brought to Sturgeon Bay where she was shoved onto the "middle ground" by Dunlap Reef where she filled with water. Several days later, she floated free and was last seen drifting into the Bay of Green Bay. She was presumed to have foundered. Door County Advocate, December 9, 1869.

58) *Ostrich*, #18967, Schooner, Stranded September 6, 1870.

The *Ostrich* blew ashore just north of Point Rocherean, fifteen miles north of Menominee. She went on in a heavy fog, with a gale blowing from the southeast at the time. Her foresails and headgear were carried away. The vessel was a foot out of water, but her skipper, Captain Ferguson thought she could be gotten off. According to the Carus Marine Notes of the Wisconsin Maritime Museum, the *Ostrich* sank in December of that year. The List of Merchant Vessels of the U.S., 1867, lists the *Ostrich* as a 284.43 ton vessel, hailing from Milwaukee. Reprinted from the MENOMINEE HERALD by the DOOR COUNTY ADVOCATE, September 8, 1870. Edward Carus Marine Notes, Wisconsin Maritime Museum, Manitowoc, Wisconsin. List of Merchant Vessels of the U.S., 1867, p. 150.

59) *Joseph Cochrane*, #12755, Schooner, Stranded October 23, 1870.

The *Cochrane* had taken on a cargo of lumber at Cheboygan, Michigan and was bound for Chicago when she started taking on water. The following morning she was able to reach Baileys Harbor but missed the channel and stranded upon the north reef of the harbor. The seas were running so high that no attempt could be made to rescue Captain Anderson and his crew. They were stranded on the doomed vessel until the next day when a boat from the brig *H.E. Mussey* succeeded in taking them off. Her stern broke off and her situation was deemed hopeless. Within two days of her stranding, the *Cochrane* started to break up, spilling her cargo of lumber, which later washed ashore. Of the 236,000 board feet of lumber, 100,000 was later salvaged by the schooner *Market Drayton*. The rigging was also salvaged.

A CHICAGO TIMES article described her as a three masted schooner of 326 tons burthen, built at Charlotte in 1856 and valued at $10,000. The List of Merchant Vessels of the U.S. for 1867 lists her as a schooner of 245.33 tons. CHICAGO TIMES, October 28, November 2, 15, 1870. DOOR COUNTY ADVOCATE, November 3, 1870. List of Merchant Vessels of the U.S., 1867, p. 107.

60) *Carrington*, #4342, Schooner, Stranded October 30, 1870.

The *Carrington* ran aground on Hat Island Reef on her way from Green Bay to Chicago. She was loaded with 190 tons of pig iron from the Green Bay Iron Furnace Co. and 1,500,000 shingles from the Earle & Case Co. The cargo was valued at $10,000 and was insured for $9,600 by Western Fire & Marine Insurance Co. of Buffalo through the Green Bay agency of Fuss & Heineman. The *Carrington* was in command of Captain Connell, who with his brother, owned the schooner. Captain Connell told the GREEN BAY ADVOCATE that the ship hit the rocks about 2:30 in the morning. She filled with water in twenty minutes and they knew she would prove a total loss. About 9 a.m. the captain and crew left the vessel in the ship's yawl and rowed fourteen miles to Menominee. That night, while they were still away, the *Carrington* slid off the reef. She was valued at $12,500 and was insured for $5,080 by Albany City Insurance Co. and for $5,000 by National Insurance of Boston.

The job of salvaging the cargo of iron, began in early February with deep sea divers working through the ice. By March, they had raised 125 tons of iron. Thomas Wilson, owner of the rigging from the *Carrington*, was one of a party of salvors working on the wreck and provided some information for the GREEN BAY ADVOCATE. He stated that the vessel was a rotten old hulk and broke in two amidships when she struck the reef. Part of the hull was laying in eight feet of water, part in fifty feet of water. The Earle & Case Co. engaged George Martin and George Jackson as divers, and Wilson and six other men to work on the wreck. They worked on the wreck for about twenty days and raised 154 tons of pig iron, chains, the compass, hourglass and many other articles. The pig iron was taken to Thorpe's dock in Egg Harbor. Wilson said they intended to return at the end of May and retrieve the small quantity of iron that remained as well as the standing rigging and anchors. The cabin of the wreck drifted ashore as did the clock which found a use in Egg Harbor. Years later, a party was formed to study the possibilities of salvaging still more iron from the wreck.

The <u>List of Merchant Vessels for 1867</u> listed the *Carrington* as measuring 215.70 tons and hailing from Chicago. She was built in Cleveland in 1853. DOOR COUNTY ADVOCATE, February 9, 1871. DOOR COUNTY ADVOCATE, November 3, 1870. GREEN BAY ADVOCATE, November 3, 1870. CHICAGO TIMES, November 3, 5, 1870. GREEN BAY ADVOCATE, November 10, 1870. GREEN BAY ADVOCATE, March 2, 1871. DOOR COUNTY ADVOCATE, March 30, 1871. DOOR COUNTY ADVOCATE, February 16, 1911. <u>List of Merchant Vessels of the U.S.</u>, 1867, p. 30.

61) *Dauntless*, #6128, Schooner, Stranded in December of 1870.

The *Dauntless* went ashore on St. Martin's Island, between Washington Island and the Michigan shore, and went to pieces. (The vessel was probably coming from Escanaba. - Author.) Her "outfit" of sails, rigging, etc. was salvaged. She was loaded with 525 tons of iron ore at the time. The craft was valued at $15,000 and insured for $10,000. The *Dauntless* measured 299.39 tons, and hailed from Chicago, according to the 1867 <u>List of Merchant Vessels</u>. According to accounts in the CHICAGO TIMES, she measured 433 tons and was built in Buffalo in 1857 where she was owned by a Mr. Doyle. CHICAGO TIMES, November 2, 30, 1870. DOOR COUNTY ADVOCATE, December 8, 1870. <u>List of Merchant Vessels of the U.S.</u>, 1867, p. 45.

62) *General W. Scott*, #10225, Schooner, Capsized August 24, 1871.

The *Scott* was bound for Chicago with a load of lumber from Menominee when she capsized off Spider Island. The schooner had sailed through the "Door" only to meet a southeast gale. When outside of Spider Island, the ship labored so much that her captain, Henry Faith, ordered the head sails taken in. The watch no more than finished this chore when it was discovered she was "making" water. The main sail was double-reefed but the ship lurched suddenly and went over on her beam. The crew hung on to the railing for over twelve hours before they were rescued at noon the next day by the schooner, *Ethan Allan*. The *Scott* was three miles from land when the accident occurred and Captain Faith, (who was also part owner) believed she had gone up on the rocks of Spider Island.

The *Scott* filled so quickly that her pumps were unable to keep up with the deluge. She rolled over about 10 p.m. when her deckload shifted. Captain Faith went back to Menominee for necessary paperwork before returning to the scene in hopes of towing the vessel to some port for repairs. The GREEN BAY ADVOCATE reported September 14, 1871, "The schooner *Winfield Scott* whose capsizing off Spider Island we announced last week, went ashore on Hog Island, east of Washington Island. She was found there, careened over, with all sails set and is now a total wreck. Her cargo was taken out of her by the fishermen in the area." The *Scott* was built at Cleveland by William Jones and was valued at $10,000 with insurance coverage of $8,000. Her cargo was not insured. While the *Scott* was often referred to as the "*Winfield Scott*," she was officially registered as the "*General W. Scott*." She measured 213.46 tons and hailed from Chicago. - List of Merchant Vessels of the U.S.,1867. The Wisconsin Maritime Museum's Carus Marine Notes confirm the date and locations. DOOR COUNTY ADVOCATE, August 31, 1870. MENOMINEE HERALD, August 31, 1870. Edward Carus Marine Notes, Wisconsin Maritime Museum, Manitowoc, Wisconsin. List of Merchant Vessels of the U.S., 1867, p. 74.

63) *Dan Tindall*, #6137, Schooner, Stranded September 18, 1871.

According to the DOOR COUNTY ADVOCATE, (September 28, 1871), the *Tindall* went ashore on the north point of North Bay and became a total loss. She was bound from Oconto to Chicago and was loaded with 270,000 board feet of lumber at the time. The vessel had just been rebuilt the previous year and was insured for $12,000. The CARUS MARINE NOTES report the *Tindall* wrecked at Manitowoc at this same time. However, the ESCANABA TRIBUNE story of September 23, 1871, agrees that the *Tindall* was ashore at North Bay, adding, "She was loaded with lumber and our informant states that she was badly broken up." The *Tindall* registered 299.24 gross tons. Edward Carus Marine Notes, Wisconsin Maritime Museum, Manitowoc, Wisconsin. List of Merchant Vessels of the U.S., 1867, p. 44.

64) *Howes*, Scow-Schooner, Stranded September 22, 1871.

The *Howes* dragged her anchor and went ashore north of the north pier at Ahnapee. She'd been lying off shore when the heavy southeast wind hit her. The *Howes* was loaded with $3,000 worth of supplies for Hitt & Davidson of Clay Banks. She was owned by Racine interests and was valued at $1,500. The vessel was declared a total loss. The *Howes* was not listed in the List of Merchant Vessels for 1867, or 1871. KEWAUNEE ENTERPRISE, September 27, 1871.

65) *Swallow*, #22558, Sloop, Stranded October 12, 1871.

The *Swallow* was blown on the rocks just north of Grimm's Pier, four miles north of Kewaunee. She had taken on a cargo of 1,000 ties at the pier but was compelled to leave the shallow mooring and seek deeper water when rough weather came up. On October 12th, she was attempting to return to the pier. As she was approaching, she struck a rock, filled and sank. The ties were the property of Mr. Grimm. The *Swallow* was owned jointly by A. Carlson and the vessel's captain, Ole Johnson. She hailed from Milwaukee and was a small vessel at 10.77 gross tons. The *Swallow* was valued at $3,000 and was not insured. KEWAUNEE ENTERPRISE, October 18, 1871. List of Merchant Vessels of the U.S., 1867, p. 183.

66) *George L. Newman*, #10339, Schooner, Stranded Mid-October of 1871.

The *George L. Newman* was reported ashore on the southeast point of Green Island. The *Newman* hailed from Racine and was laden with lumber from Little Suamico. Captain Trowell of the Saginaw told the GREEN BAY ADVOCATE that she was full of water, her cabin washed out, and she was abandoned as a wreck. The *Newman* measured 249.47 tons. GREEN BAY ADVOCATE, October 19, 1871. List of Merchant Vessels of the U.S., 1871, p. 104.

67) *Almira*, #1577, Scow-Schooner, Foundered December 2, 1871.

The *Almira* was thought to have been lost in a gale. She had gone north to Clay Banks for a cargo of wood. She left there December

1, 1871 bound for Racine and was never seen again. A gale had blown across Lake Michigan on December 2nd and it was presumed that she fell victim to it. On board were Captain Connor, his son, Lawrence Connor who was mate, and crewmen Arthur McFay, Edward Stewart, and Patrick Rogan. It was feared that she was caught in the ice, cut through and sunk with all on board. The *Almira* was a small vessel at 54.87 gross tons. GREEN BAY ADVOCATE, January 18, 1872. List of Merchant Vessels of the U.S., 1871, p. 14.

68) Unnamed Sailboat, Foundered In Early September of 1872.

Captain William Jackson, his son, and a third man were bound for Cana Island when the craft capsized a mile and a half off the old lighthouse in Baileys Harbor. Jackson and the others were forced to abandon the boat and swim for shore. The vessel drifted out into the lake where she presumably sank. Jackson was keeper of the Cana Island light. DOOR COUNTY ADVOCATE, September 15, 1872.

69) Unknown Vessel, Stranded September 24, 1872.

The craft went ashore during a gale at Tuft's Pier near the portage and went to pieces quickly. She had taken on cargo when the gale hit and tried to get underway. DOOR COUNTY ADVOCATE, September 26, 1872.

70) *Lydia Case*, #14800, Schooner, Stranded September, 1872.

The ESCANABA TRIBUNE of October 5, 1872, stated only that the "*Alida Case*" of Racine was ashore on Pilot Island. The GREEN BAY ADVOCATE was a little more informative. A news item of October 3, 1872 stated that Captain S. Gunderson of the schooner *Mary Nau* reported to that newspaper that the "*Alida Case*" of Racine was blown ashore on Pilot Island in a northeaster that blew through Lake Michigan for most of the last week in September. The ADVOCATE announced on Nov. 6, 1873, "The schooner *Lydia Case*, which was wrecked last season at Death's Door, it will be remembered had on board a cargo of coal. Messrs. Van Nostrand & Son have bought the coal from the insurance company and the steamer *Union* is now engaged in bringing the same to this city."

The AHNAPEE RECORD reported that Captain Johnny Doak had gone to Pilot Island with a crew to take the coal out of the sunken schooner. The *Case* measure 246.61 tons. GREEN BAY ADVOCATE, July 9, 1874. List of Merchant Vessels of the U.S., 1867, p. 121.

71) *Glenham*, Scow, Stranded September 28, 1872.

The *Glenham* snapped her mooring lines and drifted out to sea while she was being loaded with bark at the Hitt & Davidson pier at Clay Banks. Several crewmen were stranded on board at the time. The vessel later drifted ashore a mile north of Clay Banks. The sailors aboard were rescued by the efforts of George Roberts and some of his friends, but not before the crewmen received a "thorough wetting and freezing." She was considered old and rotten and was expected to be a total loss. The cargo was saved. The *Glenham* was not listed in the List of Merchant Vessels of the U.S., for 1867. DOOR COUNTY ADVOCATE, October 3, 17, 1872.

72) Unnamed Barge, Foundered May 11, 1873.

She broke in two and sank while loading ore at the west end, south side of the Escanaba ore dock. She was the consort of the Green Bay Iron Company's propeller, *Neptune*, and had taken on 260 gross tons of ore at the time. Later it was reported that efforts were underway to raise the barge but were, so far, unsuccessful. She was described as "badly broken up and will probably be nearly worthless after the ore is taken out." ESCANABA TRIBUNE, May 31, June 7, 1873.

73) *Hampton*, #11305, Brig, Capsized September 20, 1873.

The *Hampton* capsized and sank in Lake Michigan near Death's Door. While the GREEN BAY ADVOCATE of October 16, 1873 confirmed the incident and gave some details, the DOOR COUNTY ADVOCATE of the same date reprinted a story with a letter written by the captain which describes the entire event. It is supplied here in its entirety.

"THE BRIG HAMPTON.-By request we publish the following letter from Captain Lane to the CHICAGO INTER-OCEAN, giving a true account of the loss of the old brig Hampton, well known at this place:-

To the Editor. Sir: As I saw a statement in the CHICAGO TRIBUNE of the loss of the brig Hampton, which is false in almost every particular, the story of Mr. Hatchell to the contrary notwithstanding, I wish to enlighten the readers thereof, and the sailing community in particular. I will now narrate the particulars which are true, and I will warrant that the crew (with the exception of Mr. Hatchell) will attest to the same: We left Racine on Sunday morning, Sept. 20, between 9 and 10 o'clock, bound for Fish Creek, Green Bay, where the vessel was to undergo repairs. We held a fair wind until between 7 and 8 o'clock in the evening, when she was taken aback by a fresh breeze from the north, which obliged us to shorten sail, which we did. The TRIBUNE'S statement says: 'They scarcely knew what to do,' which is a mistake. We knew what to do, and did it-shortening sail; we then put her on the starboard tack, and stood for the land; but the wind being from the northward, and a heavy sea running from S.S.W., we took the heavy sea on the lee beam, which made her roll very heavy, and the water at this time was about two feet deep in the hold and washing all the dirt from aft forward, which was liable to clog the pumps. The wind canted to the N.W., and we went about and stood to the northward, so as to get the sea after us as much as possible, in order to relieve her of the water; but the pump, when we came to start it, was clogged. We got it clear several times, but it would clog again. After seeing the water was gaining on us, and no prospects of clearing the pump, we stood for the land again. By this time there was a heavy sea running from N.N.W., and the vessel was rolling very heavy, and the water gaining in the hold. She looked as though she might roll over. We got the boat ready for a launch, and had got the stern on the rail (the boat being on deck), and were getting the bows on, when, by some misunderstanding or excitement, the stern was shoved off, and the boat was swamped- our hopes were gone in that quarter. Being in fear lest the vessel should roll over, we cut the spars out of her (not by Mr. Hatchell's orders, however, for I cut the main rigging myself). The next thing we did was to relieve her of the anchors and chains - that was not done by Mr. Hatchell's orders- and I doubt whether the idea came into his head until the order had been issued. The next thing we did was to burn torches, and also to construct a raft, to escape death if possible. Mr. Hatchell's story that I begged of him to use his inge- nuity to save the crew, and did not know how to build a raft, etc., is all saloon talk around a good warm stove. We all took hold, every man excepting the steward, Barns, and my son, 16 years of age. They were keeping the torches going, while we worked. The story that Mr. Hatchell stood by with an ax to keep the men from launch- ing the raft, is false-for at the time we built the raft we had no ax, it being lost in cutting away the forerigging; and furthermore, there was not a man on board who showed the least sign of rebellion, or refused to do what he was ordered by Mr. Hatchell or myself. There was as good discipline as at any other time. Some of them, it is true, were anxious to launch the raft, but after talking with them they agreed that it would be safer to hold on until the vessel was about sinking altogether. Mr. Hatchell was quite sure that the vessel would not sink with the anchors, chains, etc., off, and told me when I was hurrying up about the building of the raft that he should not need it, and stuck to the idea until she went from under us. I told him we had better make it, as I would rather be glad twice than sorry once. If we did need it, we would have it. That is how he built the raft alone. Our floating on the raft for twelve hours is true; but when you come to the shirt part of it, Hatchell divesting him of his shirt etc., it is all talk. The facts are these: I had held a board with an oil coat on it for two hours, in the morning (relieved by George Williams), as long as there were any prospects of attracting the attention of any passing vessel; but at the time we sighted the Jo Vilas, *Mr. Hatchell had been making a change in his clothing, and wringing out his wet clothing that was in a bag, and some one proposed to put up something white, as it might be discerned sooner than the oil coat. Hatchell, coming across the old shirt, handed it out, and George Williams split it up the back and tied it on, while I held the board, and took my turn holding it up first, and was relieved by George Williams. Mr. Hatchell neither put the shirt on the board nor took his turn holding it up. I have made the above statement to do justice to all concerned, and to give credit to those who deserve it; but the idea that Mr. Hatchell did it all and balance of us looked on is a mistake. I doubt very much, when Mr. Hatchell told his story that he expected it would ever appear in print. The* INTER-OCEAN's *account of the loss of the Hampton was a truthful, fair one. THEODORE LANE, MASTER, BRIG HAMPTON."*

The *Hampton* was lost five years, almost to the day, after she ran aground (and was thought to be a total loss) on Whale Back Shoal. She was owned by Captain Lane and William Selleck of Chicago. She was built on Lake Ontario and launched May 4, 1845. At that time she was the largest on the lakes. The *Hampton* measured 173.63 tons and hailed from Racine Door County Advocate, October 1,1868. List of Merchant Vessels of the U.S., 1867, p. 83.

74) *Meridian*, #16408, Schooner, Stranded October 23, 1873.

The *Meridian* ran aground on Sister's Reef in Green Bay and was expected to be a total wreck. She was the victim of a heavy gale. A dispatch from Milwaukee, dated November 1, stated that the propeller *Oconto* had arrived with word that the *Meridian*, ashore on Sister Island, was breaking up and had been abandoned. According to the List of Merchant Vessels of the U.S., 1867, the *Meridian* measured 184.84 tons with a length of 120.3 feet and a beam of 23 feet. She was built in 1848 at Black River, Ohio, was owned by J. Downey and hailed from Chicago. GREEN BAY ADVOCATE, October 30, November 6, 1873. List of Merchant Vessels of the U.S., 1867, p. 135. Herman G. Runge Collection of the Milwaukee Public Library/Wisconsin Marine Historical Society.

75) *Illinois*, #12082, Schooner, Stranded October 29, 1873.

The *Illinois* ran ashore and sank in a gale near Smith's Pier in Baileys Harbor. An attempt was made to salvage the vessel, but without success. A dispatch from Milwaukee, dated November 1, stated that the propeller, *Oconto*, arrived with word that the schooner, *Illinois* was ashore two and a half miles south of Baileys Harbor. In the List of Merchant Vessels of the U.S., listings for 1867, she measured 85.60 tons and hailed from Chicago. DOOR COUNTY ADVOCATE, May 3, 1873. GREEN BAY ADVOCATE, November 6, 1873. List of Merchant Vessels of the U.S., 1867, p. 92.

76) *Denmark*, #6129, Schooner, Stranded October of 1873.

The *Denmark* was driven ashore in Hedgehog Harbor, "near the Door." She was an old vessel and was thought to be uninsured. A dispatch from Milwaukee, dated November 1, that stated that someone from the propeller *Oconto* reported that the *Denmark*, which had gone ashore near Death's Door, had gone to pieces in a gale. The crew was saved, although according to other reports two crewmen were "badly crippled" by exposure to the elements. According to the List of Merchant Vessels of the U.S., the schooner measured 169.37 tons and hailed from Chicago. CHICAGO TRIBUNE, November 2, 7, 1870. DOOR COUNTY ADVOCATE, November 6, 1873. GREEN BAY ADVOCATE, November 6, 1873. List of Merchant Vessels of the U.S., 1867, p. 46.

77) *G. Mollison*, Schooner, Foundered November 6, 1873.

The *Mollison* was reported sunk with all hands near Ahnapee. She hailed from Chicago. She is not listed, as such in the <u>List of Merchant Vessels of the U.S.</u> DOOR COUNTY ADVOCATE, November 27, 1873.

78) *Octavia*, #18911, Schooner, Stranded May 2, 1874.

The *Octavia* ran aground north of the Kewaunee pier. She had taken on a cargo of 100 cords of wood for Joseph Wallender. Just before dark, she attempted to set sail but the wind died away. The vessel was carried northward by the ground swell. Her captain was unfamiliar with the area and dropped anchor but not in time to prevent her from grounding herself on the stony shoal just off the village limit. She was 800 feet from shore with her stern to the beach, listing to the starboard. Her hold filled with water. The cargo of wood was thrown over the side with the hope that she could be refloated but the effort was unsuccessful. Most of the wood was recovered. The captain went to Manitowoc for a tug and it was thought that if good weather prevailed she could be pulled off. Later, it was reported that the *Octavia* was stripped and abandoned. The *Octavia* was a three masted schooner and hailed from Chicago. Her hull was said to be 26 years old. According to the <u>List of Merchant Vessels of the U.S., 1867</u>, the *Octavia* measured 135.86 tons. KEWAUNEE ENTERPRISE, May 12, 19, 1874. <u>List of Merchant Vessels of the U.S.</u>, 1867, p. 147.

79) Unnamed Fishing Vessel, Foundered November 12, 1874.

This vessel, albeit small and hardly noteworthy, was the source of one of the Door Peninsula's best reported ghost stories. The account of her loss is reported here, complete.

"DROWNED—On Thursday morning of last week two fishermen, John Halley and Henry Root, left Washington Harbor, in a sailboat, on a fishing expedition in the Bay. About noon a heavy gale sprung up accompanied by a blinding snow storm. As night approached, and no tidings of the fishermen were received, alarm

for their safety was felt by their friends on the Island and the steam tug Katie Gaylord *was sent in search of them. She cruised about the Bay for several hours and returned without any tidings of them. The next morning the oars, rudder and a sail belonging to a sailboat were washed ashore on the Island which led to the belief that the boat had capsized and that both men were drowned, as the sailboat was heavily ballasted with stone, sufficient to sink her at once, when she filled with water. About the time the gale sprung up a large vessel was seen in the Bay and our informant thinks there is a bare possibility that the missing men may have been picked up by the crew of the vessel, and taken to some port. Halley had a family living on the Island. Root was some 18 or 20 years old and we learn has parents living in this city."* —Green Bay Advocate, November 19, 1874

The tale became more interesting with the publishing of this story, over a year later, in the Sturgeon Bay Expositor, February 4, 1876:

"A WASHINGTON ISLAND MYSTERY Lights floating over the Waters of the Harbor near where it is supposed two men were drowned, and the circumstances connected therewith, as related to us by Mr. E.W. Steward of Washington Island. It will be remembered that in the fall of 1874, two men Halley and Root went out in their fisherman's boat and never returned. The oars, net boxes, etc. coming ashore made it evident they were drowned during a terrible snow storm which arose soon after they went out. This occurred on Thursday, November 12. Some weeks previous to this, on Sunday evening, Halley had an altercation with a neighbor, who struck him with a stone on the head, injuring him so severely that he was partially insane at the time he went out in the boat. It is supposed by the people on the Island, that had it not been for Halley's partial insanity, the unfortunate men would have weathered the storm and returned safely to shore. Soon after this disaster, a mysterious light was seen moving along near the ice on Thursday evening, followed again on Sunday evening. These lights appeared during the whole

winter regularly on Thursday and Sunday, and occasionally during the summer, and have been seen every Thursday and Sunday night during the present winter. The light usually has the appearance of being at the mouth of the Harbor, about a mile to a mile and one - half away. It usually has the appearance of a lantern moving along, about as a man would carry it, sometimes moving along four or five miles, but usually passing back and forth over a space of about a mile near the bluff at the mouth of the Harbor. Sometimes it will appear to flare up and look as large as a bushel basket, and again it will rush along at railroad speed for a mile or two. The light is usually pure white with never a halo. Wm. Betts pursued the light one night last winter. He left his house for the purpose, but he was unable to get any nearer than apparently one half to one fourth mile from it, when he went fast the light moved faster and as he slackened his pace the light would follow suit. Finally it turned and moved off toward St. Martin's Island, and led him onto such poor ice that he could not follow it further. Now the mystery about this is; its appearing on Thursday and Sunday nights, the one day of the week on which Halley was hurt and the other on which he and his companion were drowned, and its being seen in winter mainly when atmospheric lights were not produced by natural causes. Nearly every person on the Island has seen it several times, and many have seen it dozens of times, and there is no doubt of its regular appearance as above stated."

A letter to the DOOR COUNTY ADVOCATE from a Washington Island correspondent stated, "The mysterious lights of which so much has been said, still make their semi-weekly appearance on the Bay. They baffle all investigation, and until the reporter of a Chicago paper can be induced to come up and interview them, we fear the origin of these erratic 'Wills-o'-the-Wisp' will remain in the darkness. They are a profound source of wonder to our most intelligent islanders." —Reprinted in the GREEN BAY ADVOCATE, March 9, 1876.

80) Unnamed Vessel, Schooner, Stranded November 20, 1874.

She was reported ashore on Spider Island, laden with lumber. DOOR COUNTY ADVOCATE, November 26, 1874.

81) *Morning Star,* Small Schooner, Stranded November 26, 1874.

She was reported ashore at "Walker's Place," near Escanaba full of water and loaded with a cargo of fish. She was was the property of J. Day and Bro. of Green Bay. CHICAGO TRIBUNE, December 2, 1874. DOOR COUNTY ADVOCATE, December 3, 1874.

82) *Sea Gem,* #22582, Schooner, Stranded November 26, 1874.

The *Sea Gem* was driven ashore at Ahnapee in a gale. She was owned by Jonah Richards of Manitowoc. The *Sea Gem* was stripped and abandoned until spring. The List of Merchant Vessels of the U.S., 1867, lists her as a 103.21 ton schooner out of Manitowoc. KEWAUNEE ENTERPRISE, December 1, 1874. List of Merchant Vessels of the U.S., 1867, p. 175.

Part 2:
Vessels lost between 1875 and 1890

83) *E.G. Grey,* #7305, Schooner, Stranded May 3, 1875.

The *Grey* had been laying at Casco pier, where she had been loaded with wood, when a storm sprang up. Her crew tried to sail her to a safe zone, but could not keep her clear of the shore. She struck a submerged rock and filled with water three quarters of a mile from the pier. Later that day, the crew was taken off in a small boat with some narrow escapes. The *Grey* became a total loss. The cargo of 100 cords of wood belonged to Mr. L. Colby. The vessel measured 118.49 tons according to the <u>List of Merchant Vessels of the U.S.</u> for 1867. CHICAGO TRIBUNE, May 4, 1875. KEWAUNEE ENTERPRISE, May 13, 1875. <u>List of Merchant Vessels of the U.S.</u>, 1867, p. 49.

84) *Cleveland,* #4330, Bark, Stranded Mid-June, 1875.

The *Cleveland* was reported ashore, stripped and abandoned, on the rocks at Pilot Island. The CHICAGO TRIBUNE reported, "Mr. A.G. Van Schaick, of this city, received a dispatch yesterday, announcing that the bark *Cleveland* was ashore on the rocks at Pilot Island near the entrance to Green Bay. The tug *Escanaba*, of Menominee, was sent to her aid, but did not succeed in pulling her off. Being full of water, she was stripped and abandoned, her value being too small to warrant any large expense in attempting to rescue her." The vessel was owned by Ludington, Wells and Van Shaick of Chicago and was used to haul lumber from Menominee, Michigan. She was built as a side wheeler in 1851 before being converted to a passenger boat for commerce between Chicago and Green Bay. (A story in the MENOMINEE HERALD reported her ashore, stripped and abandoned, at Plum Island.) The *Cleveland* measured 230.59 tons and hailed from Chicago. CHICAGO TRIBUNE, June 15, 1875. DOOR COUNTY ADVOCATE, June 24, 1875. GREEN BAY ADVOCATE, July 1, 1875. <u>List of Merchant Vessels of the U.S.</u>, 1867, p. 37.

85) *Orlando*, Sloop, Stranded August 6, 1875.

The *Orlando* was wrecked at Little Harbor near the mouth of the bay. The vessel was anchored - the crew being ashore, picking up logs- when a storm came up, dragging her towards shore. The crew reboarded her and threw out more anchors, with little effect. The crew then tried to sail the *Orlando* into deeper water, but large logs thrown against her hull, stove her in and sank her several rods from shore. Mr. Yngve Dreutzer, one of the occupants, was severly injured about the leg. The other crew members suffered minor injuries. The sloop became a total wreck, having been broken up by subsequent storms. The sails and rigging were saved, however. No vessel by this name is listed for this region in the List of Merchant Vessels of the U.S. DOOR COUNTY ADVOCATE, August 12, 1875.

86) *Ella Doak*, #8205, Scow-Schooner, Stranded August 5, 1875.

The *Ella Doak* was wrecked in a severe gale at Hedgehog Harbor in Death's Door. She was the property of Captain John Doak of Ahnapee and was uninsured. The vessel was partially laden with stone for the Ludington pier when she was wrecked. She had been in command of Captain Conger at the time. The KEWAUNEE ENTERPRISE reported, "Capt. J.R. Doak touched this port on Monday enroute from Ludington to Hedgehog Harbor. The *Ella Doak* which stranded at the latter place on the night of the 5th will be got off the beach and brought here for repairs. It is the captain's intention to make a two master of her. He has finished the contract for furnishing stone for the harbor at Ludington, and taken a similar contract to supply the harbor of Frankfort, Michigan."

The *Doak* had been wrecked and salvaged so often that when she went ashore at Hedgehog Harbor, few people believed it was permanent. DOOR COUNTY ADVOCATE correspondent, Chris Daniel, reported that he found her high and dry where she had been beached. One of her spars had been cut down and all of her rigging removed. One of her sides had been stove in and her hold was filled with logs and driftwood. The ADVOCATE lamented her end as the loss of "first class news." James Tufts took the job of overhauling the *Doak* and by July, 1876 had raised the vessel and put her on ways in preparation for a general overhaul. The work was temporarily suspended, however. John Doak, owner of the vessel reported that work would soon begin on her rebuild. Her final demise was confirmed in the List of Merchant Vessels of the U.S., 1876.

In September, 1872, the *Ella Doak* struck a bar and capsized while attempting to leave Port Washington with a load of brick. She stranded broadside on the beach north of the pier and witnesses stated that the following day the waves were sweeping completely over her. On November 15, 1872, she ran aground at Ahnapee where she had been loading posts. Two days later, while trying to deliver those posts at Kewaunee, she struck against the pier damaging both pier and vessel. She was finally towed off by the tug *Hagaman*. Damages amounted to $700. The *Doak* went ashore on South Manitou Island, October 27, 1873 and at Sheboygan, November 26, 1874. The DOOR COUNTY ADVOCATE reported, "She is bound to maintain her right to the title of 'Queen of the Beach'". The ADVOCATE reported earlier (November 5, 1874) that "The 'everlasting scow, *Ella Doak*,' was how the MILWAUKEE NEWS puts it." On July 13, 1873, the *Ella Doak* gained the distinction of being the first large vessel to enter Ahnapee Harbor. It was reported that "there was general jubilating over the occurrence."

When the *Ella Doak* was launched in May of 1868 the CHICAGO TRIBUNE proclaimed, "Captain Doak's new scow schooner was launched at Pentwater on the 23d ult., and christened the *Ella Doak*. She is 85 feet long, 21 feet wide and 5 feet deep and will be rigged with three masts, carrying a topsail. It is expected that she will carry 80,000 feet of lumber on a draught of only four and a half feet of water." The *Doak* registered 75.04 tons and hailed from Ahnapee according to the List of Merchant Vessels of the U.S., 1876. A picture of the *Ella Doak* can be found in the MANITOWOC HERALD NEWS, Dec. 23, 1933. CHICAGO TRIBUNE, June 4, 1868. CHICAGO TRIBUNE, September 7, 1872. DOOR COUNTY ADVOCATE, September 12, November 21, 28, 1872. KEWAUNEE ENTERPRISE, July 15, 1873. DOOR COUNTY ADVOCATE, August 19,

November 18, 1875. Reprinted from the AHNAPEE RECORD by the GREEN BAY ADVOCATE, August 26, 1875. KEWAUNEE ENTERPRISE, August 28, 1875. DOOR COUNTY ADVOCATE, December 10, 1874. DOOR COUNTY ADVOCATE, August 3, November 16, 1876. List of Merchant Vessels of the U.S., 1876, p. 73.

87) U.S. Grant, #25199, Tugboat, Burned September 4, 1875.

The *Grant* had been laying at the dock at the straight cut in Green Bay harbor, when she caught fire that afternoon. No one was sure how the fire started. Some thought the blaze may have started in the fuel in the hold. Only the fireman, Com. Thomas, was on board at the time, the other crewmen being on the dock at the time. They discovered the blaze and Thomas was awakened and helped from the tug. A grand effort was made to fight the fire and the steam yacht, *Denessen*, came down the river with a crew of men to help fight the fire. When it was realized that nothing could be done, the *Denessen* towed the tug a short distance and grounded her bow in the reeds and scuttled her. Her hull was a total loss and her boiler and machinery were badly damaged. She was owned by her captain and his brothers, A.B. and P.F. Thrall. The *Grant* was rated B-1 and was valued at $7,000 according to her underwriters. She was insured for $4,000. It was expected that she would be abandoned to her insurance company. The loss of the tug was considered a great one to the Thralls as well as the harbor. Later that month, the Thrall brothers settled with the insurance company. The *Grant* was towed up the river to Green Bay where her owners took out the machinery. The boiler and engine of the tug were only slightly injured. The hull itself was considered worthless except for the iron in it. The List of Merchant Vessels of the U.S., for 1876 describes the *U.S. Grant* as a steam screw tug of 17.54 tons, registered at the port of Green Bay and listed as wrecked. GREEN BAY ADVOCATE, September 9, 30, 1875. DOOR COUNTY ADVOCATE, September 16, 1875. List of Merchant Vessels of the U.S., 1876, p. 358.

88) John Webber, #12970, Schooner, Stranded October 5, 1875.

The *Webber* sank at Escanaba. Having loaded with iron ore, she was towed out and anchored but that night she sprung a leak. Her captain raised anchor and tried to run her aground and was able to get the bow on the bank in twelve feet of water. Soon after going on, she sank. The drop off was very fast and the *Webber's* stern settled in 40 feet of water. The crew just barely got out of the cabin. The Buffalo Courier reported,

"Only a day or two since we had something to say about the safe arrival of the schr John Webber *at Escanaba, after her owner, Mr. Peter Wex of this port had about given her up for lost. He had hardly recovered from the joy he felt at her safety, when the many uncertainties of risking a venerable craft on the lakes at this season of the year were made apparent to him, and he is once more disconsolate. Yesterday, about dinner time, Mr. Wex received a private telegram from Capt. John Carroll of the* Webber, *dated at Escanaba, stating that the schooner had sprung a leak, and he had to beach her...."*

Her captain figured she was broken in two, but nothing would be known until she was raised. Her insurer sent Capt. William Benton from Milwaukee to survey the situation. The following week the tug *Leviathan* went to work on raising the *Webber* with a steam pump and the assistance of a diver. The scene drew a large crowd. The *Webber* was briefly abandoned by the *Leviathan* to rescue the schooner *Crosswaithe*, ashore at North Bay. A great storm blew through the area the following week doing much damage to shipping. (A description is given in the Escanaba Tribune of October 23, 1875.) The bad weather ripped off the battens the diver had placed over the hatches. The hull had settled two feet deeper into the bottom than when she was first surveyed and the deck was starting to break up. The Tribune, in its November 18, 1875 issue, announced "The schooner *John Webber*, ashore at this place, was abandoned by the wrecking tug *Leviathan* last Sunday. Her hull has commenced to break up." Elsewhere, in the same issue was a small item, "We understand that Sandy Thomas has purchased what remains of the schooner *John Webber*." The *Webber* remained on the government lists for several years thereafter. Her owner may have had hopes of raising her and returning her to service.

The *John Webber* was one of several vessels blown ashore in a storm on Lake Erie, the previous year. She was raised and towed to Buffalo harbor where she was allowed to settle to the bottom and sit for five months. In April of 1875 she was raised with much effort, rebuilt and returned to service.

The *John Webber* could have been named for any number of people. A likely possibility is the Honorable John Weber, New York state representative, residing in Buffalo, New York. The List of Merchant Vessels of the U.S. for 1876 lists her as a schooner of 152.09 tons and hailing from Buffalo, New York. CHICAGO TRIBUNE, November 8, 14, 1874. CHICAGO TRIBUNE, April 10, 12, October 7, 8, 9, 22, November 12, 1875. BUFFALO COURIER, October 6, 1875. ESCANABA TRIBUNE, October 16, 23, 1875.

89) *Monitor*, #90409, Schooner Lost In October of 1875.

A small item in the October 30, 1875, ESCANABA TRIBUNE, stated that the *Monitor*, a schooner owned by John Rogan, was lost in an October storm. The List of Merchant Vessels of the U.S. for 1876 describes her as a small schooner of 10.89 tons and hailing from Escanaba, Michigan.

90) *Bronson*, Schooner, Stranded October 25, 1875.

The *Bronson* was reported ashore at North Port in two feet of water. The stern was damaged and the rudder was broken. —DOOR COUNTY ADVOCATE, November 4, 1875. According to the MARINETTE EAGLE, the *Bronson* and her scows were blown ashore in a severe gale. —Reprinted by the GREEN BAY ADVOCATE, November 11, 1875. Her ultimate disposition is not indicated. The List of Merchant Vessels of the U.S. for 1867 and 1876 report only one vessel in the Great Lakes named *Bronson*: the *Alvin Bronson*, #399, 192.31 tons, hailing from Detroit.

91) *Sea Bird*, #22276, Schooner, Stranded October 26, 1875.

The AHNAPEE RECORD reported, "We are informed that the schooner *Sea Bird*, Capt. Bateman from Chicago to Buffalo, with 18,000 bushels of wheat sprung a leak Monday night and came to anchor off Horn's Pier in 18 feet of water. During the storm she dragged her anchor and finally went ashore. Latest advices state that she will probably go to pieces. The crew escaped. The vessel is owned by W.P. Ingraham of Buffalo." —Reprinted by the GREEN BAY ADVOCATE, November 4, 1875. The KEWAUNEE ENTERPRISE, October 30, 1875, reported that the *Sea Bird* was not badly damaged initially. Though hard aground, she was still okay and a tug boat was working on releasing her. In its November 4, 1875 issue, the DOOR COUNTY ADVOCATE announced that the vessel had gone to pieces. The grain in her hold had become saturated and swelled causing her decks and bottom to burst. Although the scows *Lady Ellen* and *Whisky Pete* had been engaged to take off water damaged wheat from the wreck, local people scooped up what grain they could. A month later the ADVOCATE stated, "The pork crop of this vicinity was increased several thousand pounds in weight. The wheat aboard was the direct cause of this."

The *Sea Bird* sank twice before and was easily raised and returned to the trade both times. Once, on April 9, 1868, she sank the same evening that her counterpart, the steamer SEA BIRD was destroyed by fire with great loss of life.

According to the List of Merchant Vessels of the U.S., the schooner measured 284.32 tons and hailed from Buffalo. CHICAGO TRIBUNE, April 11, 1868. GREEN BAY ADVOCATE, November 4, 1875. KEWAUNEE ENTERPRISE, October 30, 1875. CHICAGO TRIBUNE, November 17, 1875. DOOR COUNTY ADVOCATE, December 2, 1875. List of Merchant Vessels of the U.S., 1876, p. 241.

92) *William Case*, #26643, Schooner, Stranded November 1, 1875.

The *Case* went ashore on Plum Island in about three feet of water. An early November storm completely turned her around and raised her out of the water. DOOR COUNTY ADVOCATE, November 4, 1875. .List of Merchant Vessels of the U.S., 1871, p. 279.

93) *Queen City*, #20519, Paddle-Wheel Steamer, Burned November 22, 1875.

The *Queen City* burned off Ford River, Michigan. She was bound for winter quarters at Escanaba when a fire in the stove spread to the ship. The crew was unable to control it and had to abandon their vessel. They launched the ship's small boat and rowed to Indian town, about ten miles south of Escanaba.

The *Queen City* was built about 1855 for John Fitzgerald who ran her on the Fox River. She was later purchased by Neff & Leach of Green Bay, who ran her on the Wolf river between Oshkosh and Gill's Landing. Captain John Jacob and later Isaac Stephenson owned her before she was finally purchased by Captain Alfred Taylor. Taylor had her rebuilt and in the spring of 1875, put her on the Green Bay to Escanaba route. The ESCANABA IRON PORT, in its October 6, 1877 issue reported, "a firm of Chicago divers are try- ing, in the interest of the insurance companies, to recover the engine, boiler and other machinery of the steamer *Queen City,* which was burnt off the west shore between Ford River and Cedar River about two years ago." The steamer measured 110.66 tons and hailed from Escanaba. The 1876 List of Merchant Vessels of the U.S. confirms that she was wrecked. Reprinted from the GREEN BAY GAZETTE, by the DOOR COUNTY ADVOCATE, December 2, 1875. GREEN BAY ADVOCATE, November 25, December 16, 1875. CHICAGO TRIBUNE, November 27, 1875. List of Merchant Vessels of the U.S., 1876, p. 346.

94) *Daisy*, Schooner, Stranded September of 1876.

The captain of the schooner, *Venture,* reported seeing a small schooner ashore at Stoney Creek, going to pieces. She was later identified in a CHICAGO TRIBUNE article and was described as a total loss. The ESCANABA TRIBUNE, September 16, 1876. The CHICAGO TRIBUNE, September 20, 1876.

95) *G.R. Roberts*, #10210, Schooner, Stranded September 25, 1876.

The *Roberts* blew ashore at the head of Big Sister Bay. The mate explained to a reporter from the ADVOCATE that they had tried to drop anchor but it fouled in the chains. Her master, Capt. Grey, ordered the other anchor dropped but not in time to prevent her from hitting bottom. The crew was able to remove the sails and rigging. With a heavy gale blowing out of the northwest, the vessel went to pieces on the rocks and became a total loss. —DOOR COUNTY ADVOCATE, September 25, 1876. The CHICAGO INTER-OCEAN listed her as the *G.H. Roberts*, a total loss, valued at $1,000.She registered 82.17 gross tons and hailed from Chicago. She was owned by her captain and M. Johnson of Milwaukee. Reprinted from the GREEN BAY ADVOCATE, January 11, 1877. CHICAGO TRIBUNE, October 3, 1876. List of Merchant Vessels of the U.S., 1876, p. 97.

96) *Ormsby*, #19428, Tugboat, Burned October 7, 1876.

The *Ormsby* was destroyed by fire near Escanaba. Two weeks before, she had been blown ashore. Her crew was living on board, caring for the vessel until she could be rescued and left her only to go to town for provisions. While they were gone, she was thrown on her beam's end by a heavy sea. She then caught fire.

The *Ormsby* was owned by Charles Lawton of De Pere. She had formerly run as a ferry steamer between Green Bay and De Pere until her last season when she was employed to tow logs to Fayette. The loss was estimated at $6,000. She was insured for $3,000 by Kimball & Libby of Green Bay. In February of 1877, the machinery from the vessel was sold at an auction in Escanaba to E. Sorenson of De Pere, for $600. There were no other bidders. Sorenson had held the mortgage on the craft. The *Ormsby* registered 25.42 gross tons and hailed from the port of Green Bay. GREEN BAY ADVOCATE, October 19, 1876. GREEN BAY ADVOCATE, March 1, 1877. List of Merchant Vessels of the U.S., 1876, p. 342.

97) *Jessie Jewell*, Schooner, Foundered December 8, 1876.

The *Jessie Jewell* was thought to have been lost in the great storm that blew through the area that day. On board were Captain Frank Perry and his nephew. No trace was ever found of her, and, with her hull being ballasted with pig iron, it was thought that nothing ever would be found. She hailed from Escanaba. She is not listed in the List of Merchant Vessels of the U.S. for either 1867 or 1876, and may have been too small to document. ESCANABA TRIBUNE, March 31, 1877.

98) *Eliza*, Schooner, Foundered April 28, 1877.

The *Eliza* was dismasted and sunk in a storm while laying at anchor. She was owned by Charles Stevenson of Little Sturgeon. Two vessels by this name were registered for the Great Lakes area in the List of Merchant Vessels of the U.S. for 1876: #8248, schooner of 30.03 tons hailing from Chicago, and #36126, sloop of 170.79 tons, hailing from Bangor, Michigan. DOOR COUNTY ADVOCATE, May 3, 1877. List of Merchant Vessels of the U.S., 1876, p. 70.

99) *Physic*, Schooner, No Apparent nature or date of loss.

The *Physic* was sunk near Schjoth's Dock. Capt. George Wead was negotiating to buy and raise the vessel. The vessel was not listed in the 1867 or 1876 List of Merchant Vessels of the U.S. DOOR COUNTY ADVOCATE, May 17, 1877.

100) *Samuel L. Mather*, #23925, Schooner, Foundered August 17, 1877.

The *Mather* was sunk in a collision with the schooner *Mary Copley* on Lake Michigan. She had set sail from Escanaba that day, bound for Cleveland with 1,000 tons of iron ore. When she collided in the dark with the *Copley*, the *Mather* sank instantly in 180 feet of water barely giving the crew time to save themselves. The *Mather's* captain stated later the night was not unusually dark and the *Copley's* lights could be seen with little difficulty. The captain's wife and mother were on board at the time and only by the coolness of the mate who launched the small-boat were they saved. The schooner went down so fast that they were only fifty feet away when it sank. The *Copley* had her head gear ripped off but was otherwise undamaged.

The following day, the *Mary Copley* was seized by a Federal Marshall at Detroit. The day after that the marshall was sued for trespass on the ground that the seizure was made in Canadian waters and furthermore was invalid because it was made on a Sunday. The matter was later settled out of court with the owners of the *Copley* agreeing to pay $5,000.

The *Mather* was built at Vermillion, Ohio, in 1870 and measured 530 tons. She was valued at $20,000 and was owned by C.P. Minch and others of Cleveland. CHICAGO TRIBUNE, August 21, 23, 1877. ESCANABA TRIBUNE, August 25, 1877. List of Merchant Vessels of the U.S., 1876, p. 236.

101) *Bill Morse*, #2862, Tugboat, Lost or abandoned prior to 1877.

The tug was lying sunk in the Oconto River. In late October of 1877, a scow loaded with lumber was snagged and sunk by striking the old hulk.—Reprinted from the OCONTO REPORTER by the GREEN BAY ADVOCATE, November 1, 1877. The *Bill Morse* measured 10.58 gross tons and originally hailed from Buffalo, New York. List of Merchant Vessels of the U.S., 1876, p. 296.

102) *Dick Somers*, #6136, Schooner, Stranded November 19, 1877.

According to the ESCANABA IRON PORT, the *Somers* left that port that same day with 550 tons of iron ore. When in the vicinity of Poverty Island, she encountered a heavy sea and was driven ashore. Within three days, she would break "all to pieces." It was further explained that she had sprung a leak and if she hadn't gone ashore, she would have sunk in deep water. Captain N.P. Hines and his crew escaped and were taken back to Escanaba on a sailboat by Sandy Thomas.

The following spring the contract for salvage was awarded to Church and Hill of Chicago with work beginning in early April. After three weeks of effort, the expedition returned to Chicago with their schooner, *Experiment*, loaded with the *Somers'* anchors, chains, capstan, windlass, pumps, blocks and iron work. The hull of the vessel was said to be gone except where it was covered with iron ore. One of the salvors, Frank Hill told the CHICAGO TRIBUNE that wreck was in fourteen feet of water but a few rods from the light on the southern end of Poverty Island and the ore was easily recoverable. Later expeditions were sent to salvage the ore which was valued at $6 per ton and by the end of October 500 tons of ore were recovered.

The *Somers* was owned by W Weinert of Chicago and B.H. Meyer of the schooner *Aetna*. She built in Milwaukee in 1863 and was insured for $6,000. According to the List of Merchant Vessels of the U.S. for 1876, the *Somers* was a schooner of 332.21 tons, from Chicago. CHICAGO TRIBUNE, November 26, 1877. GREEN BAY ADVOCATE, November 29, 1877. DOOR COUNTY ADVOCATE, November 29, 1877. CHICAGO TRIBUNE, April 18, 1878. CHICAGO TRIBUNE, May 4, 1878. CHICAGO TRIBUNE, June 3, 14, October 26, 1878. List of Merchant Vessels of the U.S., 1876, p. 61.

103) *Dan Sickles*, #35780, Scow-Schooner, Capsized May 4, 1878.

The *Sickles* capsized about two and a half miles out from Sherman Bay and drifted ashore where she settled on her beam's end in sixteen feet of water, five miles north of the ship canal and a mile off shore. She was bound for Milwaukee with cordwood from Detroit at the time and was in the command of Louis Gardes. The scow was owned by Grange, King and Degner at the time she was wrecked although the CHICAGO TRIBUNE later reported, "At Milwaukee, Monday, William Degner sold his one quarter interest in the capsized scow *Dan Sickles* to C.A. Augustus for $50, and now doesn't care a fig what becomes of her." It was several days before the tug *Leviathan* arrived on the scene and was able to salvage the cargo and everything else of value except one pump, a towline and the small anchor which were lost overboard. The vessel itself was deemed unworthy of salvage. Although the newspapers describe her as a scow, the List of Merchant Vessels of the U.S. for 1876 lists the *Sickles* as a schooner of 65.57 tons hailing from Milwaukee. CHICAGO TRIBUNE, May 7, 8, 9, 13, 15, 1878. DOOR COUNTY ADVOCATE, May 9, 1878. GREEN BAY ADVOCATE, May 16, 23, 1878. List of Merchant Vessels of the U.S., 1876, p. 57.

104) *Hunting Boy*, #95258, Schooner, Stranded October 12, 1878.

The *Hunting Boy* was driven ashore between the harbor piers at the lake end of the Sturgeon Bay canal. She was loaded with sand. The vessel became a total loss and was stripped of her sails. She was owned by E.B. Graham of Fish Creek. She was blown up with a charge of dynamite in July of 1880. The *Hunting Boy* was a schooner of 55.16 tons and hailed from Manitowoc, according to the List of Merchant Vessels of the U.S. for 1876. Captain Graham nearly lost another schooner, the *Rover*, three weeks before at Sturgeon Bay. The DOOR COUNTY ADVOCATE, October 17, November 7, 1878. List of Merchant Vessels of the U.S., 1876, p. 123.

105) *Daniel Lyons*, #6780, Schooner, Foundered October 18, 1878.

The *Lyons* was sunk in an early morning collision with the schooner *Kate Gillett*, three miles due east of Capt. C.L. Fellows' pier at Foscoro. The *Gillett* was tacking safely to starboard but suddenly hove to port, into the path of the *Lyons*. The mate of the *Lyons* tried to avoid the approaching *Gillett*, but before the helm could answer, the *Gillett* sliced halfway through the deck of the *Lyons*' starboard side, just aft of the main mast, and poking her jib boom through the main sail of the *Lyons*. Fifteen minutes elapsed before the vessels parted. When the *Gillett* was pulled off, the *Lyons* sank stern first in eighteen fathoms of water. The crew barely had time to retrieve their personal belongings and launch the small boat before she sank head foremost. They were taken on board the *Gillett,* which was only slightly damaged. The vessel's main topmast, with the fly attached, was sticking out of the water twenty feet. The mizzen mast, which was unstripped, was visible in the water. (The vessel was originally thought to be the schooner *Trinidad*, but that report was quickly corrected by a letter to the editor from C.L. Fellows, himself. The DOOR COUNTY ADVOCATE dates are not confirmed. Other newspapers had some coverage of the collision although some details conflict.) The *Lyons* had a cargo of 20,000 bushels of wheat which was partially covered by insurance. The vessel was insured for $10,000 and was a total loss. Total value of vessel and cargo was placed at $25,800. At one time Chicago diver Frank Hill was negotiating with the insurance companies, but no effort was ever made.

The *Daniel Lyons* had been in command of Captain M.M. Holland and owned by Lyons & Goble of Oswego, New York. She was built in 1873 by one of her present owners, George Goble. The List of Merchant Vessels of the U.S. for 1876 lists the *Daniel Lyons* as a schooner of 317.98 tons. CHICAGO TRIBUNE, October 21, 23, 26, 1878. KEWAUNEE ENTERPRISE, October 25, 1878. GREEN BAY ADVOCATE, October 31, 1878. List of Merchant Vessels of the U.S., 1876, p.57.

106) *Two Kates*, #24980, Scow-Schooner, Foundered October 25, 1878.

The *Two Kates* foundered four miles off the canal after colliding with another vessel during a gale. After the collision the masts were showing. It was expected that she would be raised, however water in this area may have been too deep for diving technology of the time. This scenario is suspiciously similar to that of the *Daniel Lyons* (No. 120). The vessel was actually registered as the *Two Katies*. She was a three masted scow-schooner of 73.48 tons and hailed from Racine, according to the List of Merchant Vessels of the U.S. for 1876. DOOR COUNTY ADVOCATE, October 31, 1878. List of Merchant Vessels of the U.S., 1876, p. 263.

107) "The Gunpowder Wreck" reported November 14, 1878.

No specific location or date is available for this vessel. The GREEN BAY ADVOCATE ran this article in the November 14, 1878 issue;

"A Curious Find On Chambers Island. -We learn that recently Mr. L.J. Day, in the course of his business on Chambers Island in the north end of Green Bay, made rather a remarkable discovery. He found secreted under an old pile of slabs and refuse from the mill, not far from a hundred kegs of gunpowder, that must have lain there for many years. It was water soaked and worthless. Nothing positive is known as to how it came there, but it was remembered that about 20 years ago a vessel was wrecked on or near Chambers Island, on which was a large quantity of gunpowder. It

is inferred that this powder was saved from the vessel and secreted here, but by whom, or why it was never removed, cannot be told to this late day."

108) *E.M. Davidson*, #8879, Schooner, Stranded October 18, 1879.

The *Davidson* was driven ashore on Pilot Island. Captain William Morris and his crew were able to reach Escanaba where a telegram was sent requesting the services of the Milwaukee tug, *Leviathan*. The tug *McClellan* was instead dispatched and would have pulled on the stricken vessel if she hadn't been leaking so badly. In the mean time, the *Davidson* was subjected to storms from the west and south. The *Leviathan* arrived on the scene in late October and was prepared to pump out and salvage the hull but autumn storms prevented total success of the project. Before another serious salvage attempt could be launched the hull became encased in 100 tons of ice and nothing more could be done. The vessel was stripped and abandoned with hopes that she could be salvaged in the spring of 1880. She was inspected by the tug *Welcome* in April of 1880. It was found that her bottom was ripped off. The firm of Wolf & Davidson, owners of the tug, *Leviathan*, had the vessel libeled for $8,000 for work done the previous fall, adding to the $300 suit against the schooner for sailor's wages. When the *Davidson's* owners could not pay, Wolf & Davidson became the new owners.

A salvage tug commenced work on the vessel August 16th and plans called for the building of a false floor to help keep her afloat for the trip to the ship yard. The effort was abandoned the following month. The vessel was thought to have gone to pieces in the great gale of October 16, 1880. The schooner, *Oak Leaf*, reported that when they went through the Death's Door straits, the *Davidson* was pounding away on the rocks. When the *Oak Leaf* came back through the straits after the storm, the *Davidson* had completely disappeared. The schooner measured 281 tons and was built at Bay City, Michigan in 1871. The <u>List of Merchant Vessels of the U.S.</u> for 1876 described the *Davidson* as a Schooner of 281.83 tons hailing from Chicago. Chicago Tribune, October 20, 21, 24, 28, November 20, 22, 29, 1879. Door County Advocate, October 30, 1879. Door County Advocate, April 15, September 23, 30, October 28, 1880. List of Merchant Vessels of the U.S., 1876, p. 65.

109) *Mariner*, #16401, Schooner, Stranded November 11, 1879.

The *Mariner* was driven aground in Sherman Bay near the Horn & Joseph pier. She was attempting to leave the pier at the time with a load of posts and ties when she fell victim to a heavy gale from the southeast. When she hit bottom, her captain and crew of six were able to save themselves. The cargo which belonged to Horn & Joseph washed ashore and was saved. She hailed from Chicago and was owned by Captain Fred Kaehler. The Chicago Tribune reported, "The loss to her owner is about $2,500 and it is scarcely necessary to add that the vessel was not insurable." She was abandoned. Schoffield & Co. bought the anchors and chains salvaged from the vessel. They paid three cents a pound for the "junk." The *Mariner* measured 112.88 net tons. She was built in Milwaukee in 1852 and was rebuilt in 1871. Chicago Tribune, November 12, 1879. Door County Advocate, April 15, November 13, 27, 1879. List of Merchant Vessels of the U.S., 1876, p. 175.

110) *Ida H. Bloom*, #12134, Schooner, Stranded November 15, 1879.

The *Bloom* ran aground and pushed a rock through her bottom a mile below the Clay Banks pier and 1,000 feet off shore with nine feet of water surrounding her. Her captain, Patrick Murphy wrote to Milwaukee Tug Company for a tug and steam pump but company officials, mindful of a northeaster then blowing decided to wait. She was loaded with a cargo of ties and wood. The vessel was later declared a total loss and was abandoned later that month. Captain Murphy, known in Milwaukee maritime circles as "Paddy the Lawyer" sold the *Bloom* where she was. He was later reported to be in trouble for affixing his partner's name to the sales receipt without his permission. James Tufts purchased it for $175 and attempted to salvage it. It was later reported stripped and abandoned. The *Bloom* measured 88.20 tons and hailed from Milwaukee. Door County Advocate, November 20, 27, 1879. List of Merchant Vessels of the U.S., 1876, p. 124.

111) *Warren,* #26223, Schooner, Stranded November 21, 1879.

The *Warren* ran ashore at Baileys Harbor while trying to set sail with a cargo of wood. She was pulled out to the end of the pier but was leaking so badly that she was permitted to sink. The *Warren's* captain requested the assistance of the tug *Leviathan,* but was unwilling to pay what the tug's owners considered a reasonable fee. She was to be stripped and abandoned. George Bennett of Baileys Harbor completed the wrecking of the schooner in late December of 1879, having taken off all sails and cordage. She hailed from Manitowoc. The *Warren* was built in Chicago in 1848 and was one of the oldest vessels afloat on the lakes at the time. According to the List of Merchant Vessels of the U.S. for 1876, the *Warren* measured 76.67 net tons. Chicago Tribune, November 29, December 18, 1879. Door County Advocate, December 4, 1879. Door County Advocate, January 8, 1880. List of Merchant Vessels of the U.S., 1876, p. 272.

112) *Free Democrat,* #9310, Schooner, Stranded December 13, 1879.

The *Free Democrat* hit a boulder on the east side of Baileys Harbor, punching a big hole in her bottom. She was loaded with 60 cords of wood which had been salvaged from the schooner *Warren,* lost there the previous month and was lost not far from the *Warren.* The crew members of the stricken vessel were rescued by the schooner, *Cuba* and taken to Chicago. The vessel was owned and sailed by Captain Jacob Muehlhauser of Chicago and was considered old and of little value. She was declared a total loss. George Bennett of Baileys Harbor completed the wrecking of the schooner in late December of 1879, having taken off all sails and cordage. The List of Merchant Vessels of the U.S. for 1876 describes the *Free Democrat* as a schooner of 40.60 tons hailing from

Manitowoc. CHICAGO TRIBUNE, December 18, 1879. DOOR COUNTY ADVOCATE, December 25, 1879. GREEN BAY ADVOCATE, January 1, 1880. (According to the GREEN BAY ADVOCATE story, the vessel sank on Saturday, December 20, 1879.) List of Merchant Vessels of the U.S., 1876, p. 95.

113) *Negaunee*, #18469, Schooner, Foundered September 19, 1880.

The *Negaunee* collided with the schooner *E.M. Portch* between Ahnapee and Kewaunee and went to the bottom "presumably with all hands." Later, the crew appeared to be safe. The *Portch* was abandoned with a hole stove in her bottom but her cargo of cedar ties kept her afloat. Her crew rowed to shore safely and the vessel was later salvaged by the tug, *Thomas Spear*. The accident occurred about eight miles off Grimm's pier. The *E.M. Portch* was loaded with ties; the *Negaunee* was loaded with coal from Buffalo. Both were south bound, one on a starboard tack, the other on a port tack. In the dense fog, the *Portch* rammed the *Negaunee*, cutting into her quarter, damaging her mizzen rigging and stoving in her bulwarks ten feet down to the deck and breaking her cabin. The vessels separated from each other immediately and lost sight of each other. The *Portch* lost her head gear and started leaking forcing her crew to abandon her in their small boat. They rowed to Ahnapee safely. When the fog cleared the next day, the *Portch* was located by the tug S*pear*. Both masters claimed to have sounded their foghorns and it was thought that the matter would be taken to court. The List of Merchant Vessels of the U.S. for 1876 listed the *Negaunee* as a schooner of 640.71 ton, hailing from Cleveland. DOOR COUNTY ADVOCATE, September 23, 30, 1880. KEWAUNEE ENTERPRISE, September 24, 1880. List of Merchant Vessels of the U.S., 1876, p. 199.

114) *Thomas Spear*, #145216, Tugboat, Burned September 24, 1880.

The *Spear* burned to the water line off Carlton. Two scows she had been towing were cut loose and were picked up by the tug, *John Gregory*. The fire was assumed to have started in a pile of slabs in the forward section of the boat. By the time it was discovered the fire was beyond control and the crew was forced to abandoned the vessel. The *Spear* had left Two Rivers in command of Capt. E.F. Burnham bound for Ahnapee with the two scows in tow. Just before noon she caught fire off Sandy Bay, eight miles south of Kewaunee. The fire started in the oil room and wood pile and was quickly beyond control. One of the crewmen singed his hair and whiskers badly when he tried to get the pony engine in the oil room to work. He was driven back by the flames. Captain Burnham ordered the scows cut loose and headed the vessel for shore. He and the crew retreated from the flames to the pilot house. When they could no longer bear the heat, the vessel was stopped and the captain and crew abandoned her for the yawl. They saved only the clothes on their backs. Some were not even able to save their coats. The tug's books and papers were lost as well as the captain's wallet and money.

After the *Spear's* crew departed, the schooner *Rand* came along side and remained with the wreck for some time, looking for its crew in the water. Captain Larson of the *Rand* thought he could have even put out the fire and salvaged the vessel had the weather not worsened. A newspaper article declared, "The *Spear* now lies sunk in eight feet of water near Sandy Bay. The *Spear* was owned by Spear Bros. of Sturgeon Bay and was insured for $8,000 which was all she was worth." According to the DOOR COUNTY ADVOCATE, efforts were being made to salvage the engine and boiler from the wreck where she laid in the sand at Carlton, five miles south of Kewaunee. In May of 1881, Capt. Williams of Manitowoc purchased the tug for $1,700. He intended to convert her into a steam barge and had a dredge scow working on her for removal to a Manitowoc shipyard. The hulk was reported lying 400 feet north of the Sandy Bay Pier. In June of 1882, George Roberts and James Ross began the work of raising the engine from the tug. A monstrous "horse" or lift frame, was erected on each side of the hull holding a powerful "stump puller" for straightening the wreck. Once it was straightened they planned to use jack screws to raise the vessel. James Ross had purchased the engine and machinery from the *Spear*, and the following summer, continued the task of removing it from the wreck. It was said to be a difficult job. In July of 1884 efforts were renewed to raise the engine and boiler for the *Spear*. George Roberts of Ahnapee was again in charge of the operation. Halver Johnson purchased the wreck and by August of 1887 succeeded in raising the boiler from the wreck. The boiler was six feet by twelve feet and was completely filled with sand. Johnson was looking for a barge to transport it to Manitowoc. By July of 1888, Johnson and Louis Albertson of Two Creeks succeeded in salvaging the machinery from the vessel. Albertson told a KEWAUNEE ENTERPRISE reporter that the boiler was very large and was good as new and the engine, shaft and wheel were in fairly good condition. The hull was so badly burned that it was useless.

The *Thomas Spear* had only been built that season and with the machinery from the tug, *Home*, installed in her, was launched in early May of 1880. The *Spear* had twin engines and measured 85 feet in length 16 feet, 9 inches across the beam and a 10 foot draft. GREEN BAY ADVOCATE, May 6, 1880. DOOR COUNTY ADVOCATE, May 6, September 30, October 20,1880. KEWAUNEE ENTERPRISE, October 1, 1880. KEWAUNEE ENTERPRISE, May 20, 1881. DOOR COUNTY ADVOCATE, May 11, 1882. KEWAUNEE ENTERPRISE, June 23, 1882. DOOR COUNTY ADVOCATE, August 2, 1883. KEWAUNEE ENTERPRISE, July 4, 1884. KEWAUNEE ENTERPRISE, August 12, 1887. KEWAUNEE ENTERPRISE, July 27, 1888.

115) *William Livingstone, Jr.*, #80411, Tugboat, Foundered October 4, 1880.

The *Livingstone* sank in 42 fathoms of water off Cana Island when her shaft broke and twisted the deadwood opening a fourteen inch hole to the lake. The crew escaped to the safety of the two barges she was towing until they were picked up by the propeller *Favorite*.

Capt. John Nicholson was going on watch about noon when he discovered the engine had stopped working. He heard water rushing in below. Upon investigation it was learned that the shaft had broken inside somewhere. Efforts were made to plug the hole with blankets which were quickly pushed out by the water pressure. All efforts to bail with two syphons, a pony pump, and water buckets proved useless. The first mate struggled in the hold with the rising water level until it was nearly up to his neck. About 3 p.m. the rising water put out the fires in the boilers and Nicholson gave the order to abandon ship. All hands took their personal belongings and escaped to the barge *Mauntee*, the first of the *Livingstone's* two barges. About 3:30 p.m. the tug *Favorite* was spotted nearby and hailed down. She dropped her towline and took the sinking tug in tow and started for the beach. When the *Favorite* took the *Livingstone* in tow the stricken vessel had only gone a short distance before she gave a forward plunge and settled lower in the water. She righted herself but soon gave a backward lurch and sank stern first. The *Livingstone* measured 291 tons and was uninsured. Her other tow at the time was the barge *Advance*. The tug was valued at $30,500 and had been recently purchased by the Peshtigo Co.

The William Livingstone
Photo courtesy of the Marinette County Historical Society

At the time the *Livingstone* was considered one of the most powerful tugs on the lakes. The CHICAGO TRIBUNE bragged,

" *She was built by the Port Huron Dry Dock Co. in 1874 and received unusual care and attention both in workmanship and materials. The best selected oak from Canada was used, and she was heavily planked. Her keel is a solid one, composed of five pieces of oak twelve inches by fourteen inches in width and depth.*

The bottom is concave, and frames nineteen inches from centre to centre; every plank and frame is thoroughly bolted through and she has knees under every deck beam. The cabin is a model of elegance, some of the state-rooms being fitted up with body-Brussels carpet, marble washstands, steam heaters, etc. There are two large boats and other lifesaving apparatus aboard of her, and in fact her appointments in all respects are of the most complete description...The Livingstone *has no equal on the lakes in point of speed, power, and strength and fittings and furnishings. "*

The List of Merchant Vessels of the U.S. for 1876 lists the *Livingstone* as sailing from Detroit. CHICAGO TRIBUNE, November 11, 1878. From an account in the MARINETTE EAGLE, reprinted by the GREEN BAY ADVOCATE, October 14, 1880. DOOR COUNTY ADVOCATE, October 7, 14, 1880. DOOR COUNTY ADVOCATE, June 30, August 4, 1881. DOOR COUNTY ADVOCATE, June 15, 1882. List of Merchant Vessels of the U.S., 1876, p. 362.

116) *Ardent*, #563, Schooner, Stranded October 12, 1880.

The *Ardent* was blown ashore at Hedgehog Harbor after her anchor chain snapped. She was loaded with wood and bark which were saved. The vessel was stripped and abandoned. The List of Merchant Vessels of the U.S., for 1876 describes the *Ardent* as a schooner of 57.44 tons hailing from White Lake, Michigan. DOOR COUNTY ADVOCATE, October 21, 1880. List of Merchant Vessels of the U.S., 1876, p.22.

117) *Josephine Lawrence*, #12976, Schooner, Stranded October 16, 1880.

The *Lawrence* was driven ashore at Baileys Harbor during the "big blow." She found the bottom near the schooner, *Pauline*, about half a mile east the range lights. (The *Pauline* was later salvaged.) Captain Boyd had taken along his wife and child for the voyage and the family narrowly escaped drowning. The vessel was abandoned and worked her way down into the sand to such an extent that only a small part of her hull was visible.

Eight years before, in August of 1872, the *Lawrence* was "run down" by the steam propeller *Favorite*. The schooner filled with water and capsized but was kept afloat by her cargo of wood. She was righted and towed to Manitowoc for repairs.

The *Josephine Lawrence* measured 88.13 gross tons and hailed from Milwaukee. She was officially dropped from the government list in 1881. CHICAGO TRIBUNE, August 20, 1872. DOOR COUNTY ADVOCATE, October 21, November 11, 1880. List of Merchant Vessels of the U.S., 1881, p. 113.

118) *Ebenezer*, #7518, Schooner, Stranded October 16, 1880.

The *Ebenezer* was "totally wrecked" at Mud Bay during the "big blow." She was loaded with stone at the time. Nothing but the sails and rigging could be saved. The vessel was considered very old and was a total loss. The vessel was owned by Ephraim parties. According to the List of Merchant Vessels of the U.S., the *Ebenezer* was a schooner of 119.67 tons and hailed from Chicago. She was one of a number of area vessels sailing under this name. DOOR COUNTY ADVOCATE, October 21, 1880. DOOR COUNTY ADVOCATE, June 30, 1881. List of Merchant Vessels of the U.S., 1876, p. 66.

119)*Perry Hannah*,#11178,Schooner, Stranded October 16, 1880.

The *Hannah* was driven ashore at Jacksonport in the "big blow." She lodged in the center of the approach to Reynold's pier in eight feet of water. The vessel had been taking on hemlock ties from the pier at the time and most of the ties were blown back on the shore. She did $2,500 of damage to the pier. The schooner, which was owned by John Long of Chicago, was abandoned. A small item in the the GREEN BAY ADVOCATE reported only that "the *Perry Hannah* is sunk between the piers at Jacksonport." The schooner was later reported to have been hauled along side the pier where her remaining cargo could more easily be recovered. The schooner *Felicitous* was brought in to salvage whatever possible from the wreck. No vessel named *Perry Hannah* is entered in the List of Merchant Vessels of the U.S., There is, however, the *Hannah Perry* of 219.69 tons and hailing from Chicago. DOOR COUNTY ADVOCATE, October 21, November 4, 1880. GREEN BAY

ADVOCATE, October 21, 1880. List of Merchant Vessels of the U.S., 1876, p. 112.

120) *Reciprocity*, #21185, Schooner, Stranded October 16, 1880.

She became water logged off Two Rivers in the "big blow of 1880" and went ashore at Foscoro where she went to pieces. The crew barely escaped with their lives. The vessel was owned by Captain E.D. Wilson. The KEWAUNEE ENTERPRISE reported, "The crew of the schooner *Reciprocity* abandoned her and got ashore at Two Creeks. The vessel passed here and went ashore at Stoney Creek, where she is a total wreck." According to the List of Merchant Vessels of the U.S., the schooner measured 224.73 tons and hailed from Chicago. DOOR COUNTY ADVOCATE, October 21, 1880. KEWAUNEE ENTERPRISE, October 22, 1880. List of Merchant Vessels of the U.S., 1876, p. 224.

121) Unnamed Scows, Stranded October 16, 1880.

The two scows were separated from their escort tug while on their way from Two Rivers to Ahnapee. The two scows were under the tow of Spear's tug *Martin* when the tug's hawser wrapped around her propeller. As they were attempting to untangle themselves, the big storm of 1880 blew upon them. The scows were both blown ashore at Ahnapee and went to pieces at a loss of $3,000. The *Martin* was able to limp into Ahnapee harbor. DOOR COUNTY ADVOCATE, October 21, 28, 1880.

122) Unknown Steambarge, Foundered October 16, 1880.

Sunk ten miles north of Two Rivers. The vessel's masts could be seen sticking out above the lake. DOOR COUNTY ADVOCATE, October 28, 1880

123) *E.C.L.*, #7294, Schooner, Stranded October 20, 1880.

The *E.C.L.* went ashore at Sister Bay and went to pieces. The schooner was in the process of setting sail from the Bay when a head wind sprang up and forced her to drop anchor. Her captain left to get a tug but the vessel was blown ashore later in the day and began to break up.

Captain C.H. Oellerich of Milwaukee, owner of the vessel, reported her laying near Henderson's Pier badly listed to starboard with her deck nearly underwater. He considered the hull to be in good condition. The wrecking tug *Leviathan* attempted to pump out the vessel and raise it, but the water in the hull could only be lowered six inches. It was thought that a diver could patch the hull allowing the vessel to be raised without much difficulty. Wolf and Davidson had purchased her for $800 with the intention of raising her, however she was abandoned in the summer of 1881, and stripped of her "outfit." Her new owners hoped that the sale of the rigging would compensate for the loss of the vessel. The DOOR COUNTY ADVOCATE reported September 15, 1881 that the schooner had broken up in the storm of September 10th. In the fall of 1881, a Norwegian family of nine, needing housing, cut the deck around the deck house and floated it ashore. When they no longer needed it, the deck house was passed on to another family. The *E.C.L.* was registered in the 1876 List of Merchant Vessels of the U.S. as a bark of 248.92 tons hailing from North Port, Michigan. DOOR COUNTY ADVOCATE, November 25, 1880, December 2, 1880. DOOR COUNTY ADVOCATE, March 14, 21,1881.List of Merchant Vessels of the U.S., 1876, p. 63.

124) *Mary Newton*, #90112, Tugboat, Burned November, 1880

The *Newton* burned to the water's edge at Red River. Captain Asabel Hart, engineer William Toseland and the fireman were all in their bunks asleep when fire started and barely escaped with their lives. The engine had been taken apart and the vessel was laid up at the Red River pier. The fire was believed to have started from a stove pipe. The loss was valued at $2,500. The tug's owner, W.C. Bailey of Green Bay, had $1,500 fire insurance. The *Mary Newton* registered 35.84 gross tons and mustered 30 horsepower. GREEN BAY ADVOCATE, November 18, 1880. List of Merchant Vessels of the U.S., 1876, p. 335.

125) *Trinidad*, #24621, Schooner, Foundered May 11, 1881.

The *Trinidad* foundered 10 miles off Ahnapee while carrying coal from Port Huron to Chicago. She was found to be taking on water while off the canal. The pump didn't work and by 5 p.m. it was realized that the hull was settling in the water. Up to this time the crew had made no preparations to escape and the captain and crew of seven were forced to abandon ship in the life boat. They no more than cut loose the small boat before the *Trinidad* "lurched heavily" and slid below the surface dislodging its foremast as it sank. The vessel was 13 years old and insured for $8,000. The cargo was insured for $3,210. The *Trinidad* had a capacity of 20,000 bushels of grain and was owned by Holt and Balcon of Oconto. Originally, she had been thought to be three miles east of Clay Banks but was later reported to be 15 miles east of Ahnapee. A mast was found sticking out of the water six feet. The other mast could be seen bottom end up. The tug *Kitty Smoke* went to the site and found 114 feet of water. It was located 3 1/2 miles due east of Clay Banks and 12 miles from Ahnapee.

The Trinidad was one of the hundreds of vessels built during the post Civil War ship building boom. When she made her first appearance in the harbor of Chicago, the TRIBUNE observed,

"It was our pleasant duty to inspect the handsomely built fore-and-aft schooner "Trinidad," which reached here yesterday with a cargo of 400 tons of pig iron from Oswego. The keel of this truly fine specimen of marine architecture was laid in May, at the yard of the well known ship-builder William Keefe, Esq., at Grand Island on the Niagara River. and successfully launched on the 14th of September. She is the property of Messrs. John Keller and A.B. Merriman, of Oswego, New York. The following figures show her dimensions: length of keel, 138 feet, or over all 142 feet 3 inches;

depth of hold, 11 feet; breadth of beam, 26 feet; measures 358 tons new style; cost $30,000; has a carrying capacity 18,500 bushels of grain through the Welland canal, or 20,000 bushels to Buffalo, and classes A.1, for seven years. She is wire-rigged—the rigging being furnished by Robert Gaskin, of Kingston, and the outfit by P. Stuart of Oswego. Her masts are towering and massive, and measure as follows: Foremast, 88 feet; mainmast, 90 feet; main-boom, 66 feet, and foreboom, 54 feet. She spreads 2,200 yards of the best cotton canvas. She is fastened in the most substantial manner. Her planking, which is entirely of white oak, is all edge-bolted through and through, and forelocked, giving her great strength. She has extra heavy knees under every beam all well bolted through and through, and forelocked. She has timber heads aft on the quarter, which is seldom seen on a canal vessel. She is also supplied with all the latest improvements. She has a spacious cabin, which is neatly fitted up. It is 20 x 22 feet, and contains the dining room and five state rooms besides a 'spare' room. The Trinidad *is in command of Captain J.W. Horton, a thorough seaman and perfect gentleman. We wish her many profitable voyages."*

The List of Merchant Vessels of the U.S. for 1876 lists the *Trinidad* as measuring 333 tons, hailing from Oswego, New York. CHICAGO TRIBUNE, November 14, 1867. DOOR COUNTY ADVOCATE, MAY 19, August 3,1881. List of Merchant Vessels of the U.S., 1876, p. 262.

126) *General Q.A. Gilmore*, #20543, Schooner, Stranded June 19, 1881.

The schooner *General Q.A. Gilmore* ran ashore on Gull Island reef. The vessel was loaded with coal at the time. The cargo was salvaged and the ship was abandoned to the lake. This little schooner should not be confused with the *J.E. Gilmore* (No. 202), which coincidentally went ashore only a few miles away at Pilot Island.

The *General Q.A. Gilmore* was once proclaimed the fastest schooner working the limestone trade out of the port of Cleveland. She measured only 51.64 tons and hailed from Lorain, Ohio. She was built in Black River, Ohio, in 1867 and was named for General Quincy A. Gillmore, a leading figure in the Army Corps of Engineers and a distinguished Civil War veteran. (Note: General Gillmore spelled his name with two "L"s. DOOR COUNTY ADVOCATE, June 23, 1881. List of Merchant Vessels of the U.S., 1884, P. 136. CLEVELAND HERALD, April 27, 1872.

127) *Ebenezer*, Schooner, Stranded Mid-June of 1881.

This small "trading schooner" was one of several vessels by that name lost on the shores of Door County. She ran on the beach at Sherman Bay while trying to navigate through a fog. Nothing but the sails and rigging could be saved. The vessel was considered very old and was a total loss. This *Ebenezer* was undocumented. DOOR COUNTY ADVOCATE, June 25, 1881.

128) *Garibaldi*, #10212, Schooner, Stranded July 15, 1881.

According to the ESCANABA IRON PORT of July 23, 1881, the "little schooner" sprang a leak while on her way through the lower bay. She was run aground on the Portage Island shoals and was described as badly broken up. She was bound for Fayette with a cargo of bricks. The List of Merchant Vessels of the U.S. for 1876 listed the *Garibaldi* as a schooner of 15.96 net tons and registered in Racine, Wisconsin. Reprinted by the DOOR COUNTY ADVOCATE, August 4, 1881. List of Merchant Vessels of the U.S., 1876, p. 97.

129) *Jennibell*, #12975, Schooner, Stranded September 17, 1881.

This widely recognized schooner capsized in "Death's

Door" in a southern squall. The *Jennibell* was carrying green wood and hemlock bark out of Egg Harbor and was abreast of Plum Island when the accident occurred. The incident was witnessed by Captain Burnham of the tug *Gregory*, who went to assist. The tug rescued all sailors and took the vessel in tow. Rough water caused her to sink when in the vicinity of Chambers Island due to weight of the green wood. The vessel was commanded by Captain Jacobson and owned by Captain Christianson of Milwaukee. J.J. Barringer owned the cargo. Attempts were made to raise her but she had to abandoned owing to the fact that her anchors were over board.

George O.Spear, the owner of the *Gregory*, demanded payment from Jacob and C. Christianson, owners of the *Jennibell*, for services rendered, amounting to about $600. This was refused where upon suit was begun in the United States District Court for the recovery of the amount. The schooner's owner filed a counter suit for $3,000, the value of the vessel. On November 8th and 9th, 1882, the litigants appeared before Judge Hamilton, who took the depositions of both sides and then several witnesses, G.M. Markham appearing for G.O. Spear, the libelant, and G.D. Van Dycke for the respondents, Jacobson and C. Christianson. The arguments were made in the District Court at Milwaukee. When the case came to trial in late February, 1885, Captain F. C. Burnham appeared in court to give further testimony on behalf of his employer, George Spear. The decision was made in favor of Spear who won at least a small portion of what he claimed against the wreck. Owners of the schooner were dissatisfied and were preparing to take the case back to court, however nothing more was heard about it.

In the mid 1960s, Frank Hoffman, of Mystery Ship fame, located the *Jennibell* and intended to raise the hull for use as a museum (which he later did with the schooner *Alvin Clark*). Members of his group attempted to raise her on their own. They brought a barge and crane on the sight, and strung cables underneath the hull in a two cable cradle. As the vessel was being lifted off the bottom, the hull sagged in the center and broke in two. The *Jennibell* was listed in the 1876 List of Merchant Vessels of the U.S. as a schooner of 132.82 tons. While spelling of the name varies from book to book and from paper to paper, the List of Merchant Vessels spells the name with two E's, two N's, two L's, one I, — one word. One book even listed it as the "*Jane Bell*", and while there was indeed a vessel by that name that sailed on the bay for a short time, it ultimately moved to another part of the Great Lakes. DOOR COUNTY ADVOCATE, September, 22, 1881. DOOR COUNTY ADVOCATE, November 16, 1882. DOOR COUNTY ADVOCATE, February 26, 1885. William Eckert, personal interview, June 14, 1986. List of Merchant Vessels of the U.S., 1876, p. 138.

130) *D.A. Van Valkenburg*, #6318, Schooner Stranded September 15, 1881.

The *Van Valkenburg* ran ashore on the north side of Whitefish Point three miles south of Jacksonport. Eight of the nine seamen aboard died trying to get ashore. Bodies of the men washed up on the rocks at Cave Point. Thomas Breen, the only seaman to survive, stated that something was wrong with the compass. The *Van Valkenburg* had left Chicago for Buffalo the previous day with a cargo of 30,000 bushels of corn. The vessel hit the rocks about seven p.m. The crew climbed into the ship's yawl and waited for a chance to escape to shore, but after some time the wind increased and changed directions to the Northeast. The wind flipped the yawl over and washed away three men. Two subsequent waves swept off the remaining victims and swept them into the rocks. When Breen awoke on shore he was the only man alive. He wandered, dazed, into Jacksonport and was found by Lincoln Erskine who asked him what was wrong. Breen could only utter something barely intelligible about a shipwreck. A group of townsfolk went down to the shore and found the wreckage.

Killed were: Andrew L. Keith-Master, H.F. Kalloch-First Mate, Robert Keith-Second Mate, Richard Harlow-Steward, Peter Hennesey, George Curtis, and Thomas Keegan. The identity of the eighth victim was not known. All were buried in Jacksonport. Of four seamen interred at Jacksonport, three were re-interred at Chicago. The cook, Richard Harlow, was reburied at Sturgeon Bay.

The *Van Valkenburg* hailed from Chicago. The vessel had been breaking up at the time of the escape and when salvors went to the scene the next day, no sign of the vessel could be found. It was thought that she broke up and floated out into the lake. Portions of the wreck were discovered floating up on shore or just off it later the next day. She was near a rock ledge twenty to thirty feet high. Most of the anchors and chains were recovered. For weeks thereafter local residents used fish nets to gather the cargo of corn that had floated ashore. On one particular day, thirty wagons, loaded with corn, were counted. The vessel's remains could be seen in nine feet of water. Years later, the DOOR COUNTY ADVOCATE stated that the light house on the east end of the Sturgeon Bay ship canal was built after the loss of the *Van Valkenberg* demonstrated the great need for one there.

Oddly enough the *D. A. Van Valkenberg* had been dismasted and driven ashore at Whitefish Bay, two miles to the south in the "Big Blow of 1880" almost eleven months prior to her ultimate demise. The great storm of the previous year did $8,000 worth of damage to the vessel. The *D. A. Van Valkenberg* measured 538.78 tons and was built in 1866 at Tonawonda, New York. She was valued at $16,000 and was owned by Hood Millan of Chicago. DOOR COUNTY ADVOCATE, November 18, 1880. DOOR COUNTY ADVOCATE, September 22, 29, October 13, November 17, 1881. DOOR COUNTY ADVOCATE, February 11,

131) Unnamed Schooner, Capsized September 31, 1881.

The vessel was found capsized off Baileys Harbor. No sign of the crew was found. Shingles, the presumed cargo, were found floating around the wreck. No other information was ever given about the vessel. DOOR COUNTY ADVOCATE, October 6, 1881.

132) *Granite State*, #10815, Steambarge, Stranded October 3, 1881.

The *Granite State* was bound from a Canadian port to Chicago with a load of cedar. While passing through the Mackinac Straits, she pounded on a rocky shoal and by the time she reached the Sturgeon Bay ship canal, she was taking on water so fast, it was decided that she should be beached to prevent her from sinking in deep water. The steamer was run ashore at Clay Banks. The tugboats, *Kitty Smoke* and *Leviathan* tried to salvage the vessel, but before an effective rescue could be made, autumn storms broke her back and made a mess of her. She was abandoned by her owners, S.J. Russel and Philo Chamberlain. The loss was estimated at $5,000. Three weeks later, the ship broke apart in a storm. Portions of the deck and cabin floated ashore. A law suit for seaman's wages amounting to $208.25 was filed against the owners by Owen Flynn and other members of the crew. In February of 1882 the ship's machinery was sold in Milwaukee by Federal Marshals to pay off the crew's wages. O.S. Richardson bought the engine and boilers where they were for $700. Supplying the schooner, *Bessie Boalt* and a diving rig, he directed the salvage of the equipment. Sending down a diver, Captain Falcon, Richardson spent $1,000 on the operation and by September of 1882 succeeded in recovering the machinery. The engine was lashed to the side of the *Boalt* and taken to

The steambarge, Granite State
Photo courtesy of the Great Lakes Marine Collection
of the Milwaukee Public Library/Wisconsin Marine Historical Society

the Spear shipyard where it was hoisted up, onto the schooner for shipment to Chicago. It was estimated that the sale of the machinery would bring $4,000.

In October of 1885, owners of the *Granite State* started a lawsuit against A.W. Lawrence for $15,000, the value of the steamer. The owners blamed Lawrence for not rescuing the vessel before autumn storms broke her up. The *Granite State* measured 428. 82 tons with 256 horsepower according to the List of Merchant Vessels of the U.S. of 1876. Door County Advocate, October 6, 1881. Door County Advocate, October 20, 1881. Door County Advocate, January 12, February 23, September 14, 28, 1882. Door County Advocate, October 29, 1885. List of Merchant Vessels of the U.S., 1876, p. 318.

133) *Shank*, Schooner, Stranded early October of 1881.

The *Shank* went ashore at Ahnapee (now Algoma) and became a total wreck. Her master turned her over to the insurance companies. The Milwaukee daily newspapers mistakenly reported her ashore at Kewaunee. The *"Shank"* was not listed as such and may be the *Isaac L. Shanks*, a small schooner of 25.94 tons hailing from Chicago. Kewaunee Enterprise, October 7, 1881. List of Merchant Vessels of the U.S., 1876, p. 127.

134) *Little Johnny*, Scow-Schooner, Capsized October 15, 1881.

The *Little Johnny* was bound for Bay View with a load of 8,500 bricks when she capsized and drifted ashore at North Point and went to pieces. The little scow had set sail for the canal from Ahnapee (now Algoma). When a rising sea forced her back she turned back for Ahnapee. She was unable to enter the harbor and after the anchor was dropped the vessel careened over. Captain William Dingman and his crew escaped in the small boat. The Kewaunee Enterprise, of October 28, 1881, had only this small item about the wreck: "In large headlines a Milwaukee Daily displayed the fact that the scow *Little Johnny* went on the beach at Ahnapee the other day and was totally wrecked. That marine editor doesn't know that the only important thing about the *Little Johnny* is the legend which she bears on her stern." The *Little Johnny* was apparently too little to be listed in the Federal listing. Door County Advocate, October 27, 1881.

135) *Melita*, #91309, Schooner, Stranded October 17, 1881.

The *Melita* went ashore when she missed Citizen's pier while trying to dock. The pier was just north of Ahnapee. She was sitting safely on a sand bottom and was thought to be recoverable. The schooner was listed in the 1884 List of Merchant Vessels of the U.S. as a craft of 57.65 gross ton, built in Manitowoc in1881. Door County Advocate, October 27, 1881. List of Merchant Vessels of the U.S., 1884, p. 208.

136) *Lewis Day*, #15410, Schooner, Stranded October 23, 1881.

The *Lewis Day*, was a three masted schooner that went ashore on the southeast reef of Plum Island. The vessel was sailing at a "fair rate of speed" when she missed stays and ran on the rocks. Captain David Clow and his crew were rescued by the schooner *G.D. Norris*. The wind was not blowing hard at the time but heavy winds developed from the northeast by the following morning. The *Day* pounded until she started taking on water and by the time the tug, *Leviathan*, arrived the schooner had gone to pieces. All sails, rigging, and anchors, etc. were salvaged. The vessel and cargo were uninsured and were a total loss. She was bound from Cedar River for Chicago with a load of cedar. Eli P. Royce of Escanaba, owner of the cargo of cedar, sent his schooner, the *Oak Leaf*, to salvage any of the cargo that might be recoverable. The vessel was later burned. The *Lewis Day* had been built by Captain Clow at Chamber's Island in 1868 and was built with wooden pins, or trunnels, instead of steel spikes and rivets. She was originally bark rigged and measured 150 feet in length, 31 feet across the beam, and 11.5 feet in depth. The List of Merchant Vessels of the U.S., 1876 lists her as measuring 381.89 tons, home ported at Chicago. CHICAGO TRIBUNE, June 2, 1868. DOOR COUNTY ADVOCATE, October 27, November 17, 1881. ESCANABA IRON PORT, November 5, 1881. List of Merchant Vessels of the U.S., 1876, p. 160. Arthur and Evelyn Knudsen, A Gleam Across the Wave: The Biography of Martin Nicolai Knudsen, Lighthouse Keeper on Lake Michigan, p. 61.

137) *Pierrepont*, #19759, Schooner, Foundered November 26, 1881.

The *Pierrepont* sank between the pilings at the lake side entrance to the Sturgeon Bay ship canal and broke up.

The vessel had been moored along the outside pier and was stove in by a pier fender. She filled with water and sank in seven feet of water. The schooner was loaded with merchandise for M. Cochems of Sturgeon Bay, $400 worth of iron bars for E.S. Minor, and considerable freight for J.J. Barringer of Egg Harbor. A steam pump and tug were brought in to raise the ship but the hole was so large that the diver was unable to patch it. The vessel was abandoned to the insurance company, Orient Insurance Co., who thought they could raise it and take it to Manitowoc for rebuilding. The owners of the tug, *Lawrence*, took the contract to move the hulk for $1,500 and on December 10, 1881 pulled on her till they snapped their hawsers. The wreck had been moved about a foot. The next day, heavy winds out of the south sent waves crashing over her to such an extent that the deck washed out and the hull started to break apart. As the wreck was going to pieces, Louis Bavry and others saved the spars and standing rigging. The sails and light rigging were saved by the insurance company and placed in storage at the canal house. By mid-December, no trace of the vessel could be seen, and it was thought that she had been washed out into the lake by heavy seas. After the wreck had broken up, government engineers ordered the insurance company to remove any vestige of her to prevent any damage to the north pier. A portion of the *Pierrepont* floated into the canal where it remained on the bottom, halfway between the blacksmith shop and the mouth of the canal. The schooner became a menace to navigation, and in April of 1882, the tug, *Gregory*, towed her two miles from the canal and let her settle in shallow water.

Years later when government dredges were deepening the channel in the canal, an anchor and a few bars of iron from the ship were scooped up. The *Pierrepont* was owned by Chipman and Roesser and hailed from Sanilac, Michigan. She measured 153 tons and was built at Sackett's Harbor in 1853. DOOR COUNTY ADVOCATE, March 10, December 1, 8, 15, 22, 29, 1881. DOOR COUNTY ADVOCATE, April 20, July 22,

138) *Julia Smith*, #12979, Schooner, Stranded November 27, 1881.

The *Smith* was driven aground at Ahnapee during a storm. She was bound from Jacksonport's Hibbard's pier with a load of cord wood for Milwaukee. She attempted to come to anchor off of Ahnapee but when her anchors did not hold, she ran ashore south of the bridge pier. The crew was rescued by the scow-schooner, *Sea Star*. It was reported that the vessel's sails, rigging and portions of the hull became "twisted and mixed up in an inextricable mass and little or nothing can be saved." The schooner was declared a total loss. The cargo of wood drifted ashore and was picked up on the beach. The *Julia Smith* was owned by Fred and Ernest Paetz of Milwaukee and was registered in Kenosha, Wisconsin. She measured 69.47 tons. DOOR COUNTY ADVOCATE, December 1, 8, 1881. List of Merchant Vessels of the United States, 1876, p. 149.

139) *Northern Queen*, Steam Propeller, Stranded
140) *Lake Erie*, Steam Propeller, Foundered November 29, 1881.

The *Northern Queen* was driven ashore at Manistique while trying to enter the harbor there, bringing a bad end to a bad day.

The *Queen* and her sister ship, the *Lake Erie*, had left Chicago, steaming together in tandem for what their owner, the New England Transportation Co., thought would be an added measure of safety. Fifteen miles east southeast of Summer Island, the *Queen* accidentally collided with her sister, sending the *Lake Erie* to the bottom. The *Queen* was able to rescue the *Erie's* crew and set a course for Manistique. As she was entering the river there, she struck a shoal and broached. The following March the tug

Winslow was sent from Detroit to salvage the steamer, which had become a danger to vessels entering the harbor. The tug's captain, Martin Swain, surveyed the situation and decided the wreck was "not worth taking a hold of" and the *Northern Queen* was abandoned. Swain reported "the deck and deck frames and all above were all gone and the hull full of sand." By May of 1882, the hull was nearly across the channel allowing only 26 feet of passage. She was laying 100 feet inside the harbor piers in 16 feet of water with four feet of water over one end and six feet of water over the other. Salvors thought a $5,000 salvage project would remove the hulk, otherwise the government engineers were prepared to dynamite it. In early June of that year, the hull was raised and moved out of the way. Door County Advocate, December 8, 1881. Reprinted from the Escanaba Iron Port by the Green Bay Advocate, March 23, 1882. Door County Advocate, May 11, 1882. Green Bay Advocate, June 8, 1882.

141) *Ben Drake*, #2143, Tugboat, Abandoned June 22, 1882.

The *Drake* had been steaming down the Peshtigo River when her propeller apparently whipped up a board and drove it through the hull. The tug quickly sank in nine feet of water. A canvas was pulled over the hole and the tug was lifted to the surface and taken to Sturgeon Bay where she was drydocked. An examination revealed that she was completely rotten below the water line. One crewman explained that one could kick a hole through the planking almost anywhere. The vessel was found to be in such a shocking condition that it was immediately abandoned and work was started on removing all equipment. Within the month all of her power drive including engine, boiler, shaft and wheel were taken out in preparation for installation in a new hull. The *Ben Drake* was taken to the bone yard and abandoned.

The *Drake* continued to cause problems. She was laying on the bottom of the bay near the city wharf in Sturgeon Bay. On November 21, 1884 she damaged the schooner *Richard Mott* which had run upon her wreckage. A portion of her hull was set adrift and came ashore below the ferry landing in the city. The *Drake* was built in 1864 in Brooklyn, New York, and was last registered at Chicago. According to the List of Merchant Vessels of the U.S. for 1884 she measured 47.37 tons and her machinery, when she had any, generated 72 nominal horsepower. DOOR COUNTY ADVOCATE, July 20, 1875. DOOR COUNTY ADVOCATE, June 29, 1882. DOOR COUNTY ADVOCATE, November 27, 1884. List of Merchant Vessels of the U.S., 1884, p. 290.

142) *May Queen*, #90809, Schooner, Foundered December 2, 1882.

The *May Queen* was a small schooner that had been in tow of the tug, *J.F. Dayan*, at the time of her sinking. The vessel sprung a leak and went down so fast that Captain Thor Anderson and his two crewmates could not clear the lifeboat from davits in time and found themselves floundering in the water. The *May Queen* sank in eight fathoms off Ingallston, twelve miles north of Menominee. She had been overloaded with salted fish and the vessel and cargo, which were valued at $1,500, had no insurance to cover either. Immediately after she sank, the *Dayan* came around and rescued the crew. Weeks later, packages of fish started washing ashore at Chambers Island. The following spring, the tug went out looking for the wreck. Bad weather interrupted the search, but the *May Queen* was ultimately found by a fisherman. Efforts were made to lift the schooner, however there is no statement of her recovery. The *May Queen* was only seven years old and was owned by John Linquist of Menominee. She was built by Captain E.B. Graham, measured 13.03 tons and hailed from Green Bay.

Door County Advocate, October 12, November 2, December 14, 1882. Reprinted from the Marinette Eagle by the Green Bay Advocate, December 28, 1882. Door County Advocate, July 3, May 17, May 10, 1883. List of Merchant Vessels of the U.S.,1876, p. 189.

143) *Home*, #11210, Tugboat, Abandoned Autumn 1882. The *Home* was purchased from Detroit parties. She saw much business towing barges in the Baileys Harbor - Two Rivers area before being taken to the Spear shipyard where her engines and boilers were removed and installed in the tug, *Thomas Spear*. The hull was converted into a hoisting barge and used for lifting logs lost around the lake shore. Her owners decided that the design was not suitable for that use and a new, small, sidewheel tug was built to accommodate the *Home's* hoisting engine. The old hull was abandoned. She was the property of G.O. Spear of Sturgeon Bay.

The List of Merchant Vessels of the U.S., for 1882 describes the *Home* as a tug of 84 tons and registering 37.80 tons. She hailed from Milwaukee. Chicago Tribune, September 4, 1879. Door County Advocate, January 8, February 26, May 6, 1880. List of Merchant Vessels of the U.S., 1876, p. 320. List of Merchant Vessels of the U.S., 1882, p. 252.

144) *M.R. Hunt*, #91251, Steambarge, Burned January 10, 1883.

The *M.R. Hunt* had been frozen in at the Green Bay harbor the previous fall and was later hauled from the channel to the beach near the mouth of the Fox river. About 7 p.m. on January 10th, a bright light was seen north of the city. It proved to be the *M.R. Hunt*...in flames. Being so far from the city, she was distant from help and was totally consumed by the fire. Nearly all of her "fit out" was on board. Arson was suspected. She was owned by J. McDonnell and was valued at $10,000. Only $4,000 was covered by insurance. The *M. R, Hunt* measured 99.53 gross tons and only recently had been registered at Green Bay. Green Bay

ADVOCATE, January 18, 1883. List of Merchant Vessels of the U.S., 1880. List of Merchant Vessels of the U.S., 1881. List of Merchant Vessels of the U.S., 1882 , p. 265.

145) *Prince Albert*, #150182, Scow, Stranded May 2, 1883.

The *Prince Albert* was driven ashore near the lighthouse at the entrance to Green Bay harbor. She was loaded with wood for J.J. Tracy, all of which was lost. The vessel was still there weeks later and it was assumed that she would prove a total loss. The scow had at one time been owned by J.J. Barringer of Egg Harbor. The *Prince Albert* was built at Egg Harbor in 1879 and was a small vessel registering only 22.83 gross tons. DOOR COUNTY ADVOCATE, May 10, 31, 1883. List of Merchant Vessels of the U.S., 1884, p. 230.

146) *Monitor*, Schooner, Stranded October 31, 1883.

The *Monitor* was bound for a lower lake port with a load of iron ore when she was overwhelmed by an autumn storm and driven ashore near Manistique. It was thought that she would be a total wreck but the tug *Leviathan* was on her way to help. A later dispatch from Cheboygan, Michigan, dated November 4, 1883, stated that the *Monitor*, ashore near Seul Choix Point, had gone to pieces and was a total loss.

The List of Merchant Vessels of the U.S. for 1884 lists two possible vessels; #50397, scow schooner of 105.85 tons from Milwaukee, #16650, scow schooner of 307.95 tons from Sheboygan, Wisconsin. DOOR COUNTY ADVOCATE, November 8, 1883. KEWAUNEE ENTERPRISE, November 9, 1883. List of Merchant Vessels of the U.S., 1884, p. 212.

147) *Banner*, #2582, Scow-Schooner, Stranded November 4, 1883.

The *Banner* ran ashore just south of the breakwater at Sturgeon Bay and went to pieces.

The vessel, while attempting to set sail, broke its rudder forcing Captain John Stokes to steer with the sails. The vessel had been bound for Racine but she was brought about near Ahnapee and headed for the canal. About midnight, Stokes found the canal but in the darkness missed the entrance, and hit the shore south of it. Stokes and his crew reached shore safely but the ship was broken up by the sea. The cargo of fifty-five cords of wood was saved by its owner, F. Paarmann, who had initially loaded it at Clay Banks. There was no insurance on the *Banner*. It was owned by partners, O.M. Nelson of Sturgeon Bay, and Mary Schultz of Racine, who had purchased it only a week before, for $1,200. It was the *Banner's* first voyage in service to her new owners. According to the List of Merchant Vessels of the U.S. for 1876, the *Banner* measured 74.95 tons and hailed from Holland, Michigan. Door County Advocate, November 8, 1883. Kewaunee Enterprise, November 9, 1883. List of Merchant Vessels of the U.S., 1876, p. 27.

148) *Maria*, #91096, Schooner, Stranded November, 1883.

This small vessel had just taken on a load of cord wood at Hedgehog Harbor, when she was blown on the beach. Rigging, sails, and cargo were all saved and taken ashore. The *Maria* was owned by Captain John Saveland. She measured 8.6 tons and was built in Milwaukee in 1878. She was registered at Grand Haven, Michigan. The schooner had a length of 33.7 feet, with a beam of 12.3 feet and a 3.8 foot depth of hold. Door County Advocate, May 29, 1884. List of Merchant Vessels of the U.S., 1884, p. 197.

149) *Minnie*, #16464, Steambarge, Burned December 3, 1883.

Owners of the *Minnie*, Hagen and English Co., had her brought to Fowles Shipyard in Fort Howard (West Green Bay) for repairs. Engineer James Dunlap and his wife slept on board that night and shortly after 11 p.m. were awakened by smoke and flames. They barely escaped the cabin alive. Dunlap lost all of his clothes and $90. An alarm was sounded for the fire department and the Fort Howard fire company arrived with their fire engine but no hose. The firemen could only join the gathering crowd of onlookers and watch as the fire enveloped the ship. The hose was delivered to the scene an hour and a quarter after the firemen arrived, by which time the ship was completely destroyed. Dunlap had made an appeal to the Green Bay fire company for help but the company's engineer, Mr. Lison had no authority to take the steamer into Fort Howard without that fire company's permission. The fire was thought to have been started by a lamp bursting. The *Minnie* was valued at $12,000 but was insured for only $8,000. She had originally been a sidewheel steamer used on the Detroit river between Bear Creek, Canada, and the Peninsula furnace in Detroit. The sidewheeler was brought to Green Bay, in 1877, lengthened, strengthened, and modified to a steam propeller at the cost of $6,000. She registered 226.56 tons. GREEN BAY ADVOCATE, December 6, 1883. List of Merchant Vessels of the U.S., 1871, p. 190.

150) *H. Witbeck*, Tugboat, Foundered December 26, 1883.

The *Witbeck* broke away from her mooring and went to pieces in Sturgeon Bay.

The vessel's owner E.S. Minor and Captain David Ramage found that a strong lake bound current had torn her away from her moorings and left her in the middle of the Sturgeon Bay harbor of refuge. When her engineer Thomas Swaty came down to inspect her that morning he discovered that her upper works were gone and only her bow showed above the surface of the water. The tug's hull seemed to be in good condition until a southerly blow pounded her to bits against the north pier. Minor gave up hope for the *Witbeck* and two days later Ramage and Alex Laurie began the week-long task of salvaging the engines and boiler. The hull washed away.

The *Witbeck* broke up on almost the exact spot where the schooner *Pierrepont* broke up several years before. Coincidentally, E.S. Minor lost financially from both vessels, on this occasion losing 800 pounds of fish. Also lost were thirty fishing nets belonging to John La Fond, a business associate of Minor's. The vessel was valued at $3,000 but was insured only against loss by fire. The boiler and one of the engines salvaged from the wreck found a future powering the machinery of a flour mill in Forestville.

The *H.Witbeck* was built in Oshkosh in 1869 as the *Kearsarge*, but was later lengthened sixteen feet and brought to Green Bay. At one time she had been seized by Green Bay authorities for having allowed sparks from her smoke stack to set fire to the widow Tank's house. DOOR COUNTY ADVOCATE, January 3, 1884. DOOR COUNTY ADVOCATE, November 19, 1885.

151) *Louisa*, #15420, Scow-Schooner, Foundered October 26, 1884.

The *Louisa* sank at Manistique, Michigan where, while trying to enter the harbor, she struck the west pier and broke in two. She was expected to go to pieces. The scow was considered old and soft having been built in 1868. She registered 192.82 gross tons, was rated B2 by the insurance companies and was insured for $2,000. The List of Merchant Vessels of the U.S., for 1884 confirms that she was wrecked and was to be dropped from the register. Reprinted from the ESCANABA IRON PORT by the GREEN BAY ADVOCATE, October 30, 1884. List of Merchant Vessels of the U.S., 1884, p. 189.

152) *North Star*, #18117, Schooner, Abandoned June of 1884.

The GREEN BAY ADVOCATE, in a June 26, 1884 item, reported that the vessel's owners, Hagen and English, ordered everything of value taken from the sunken schooner. The hull was to be removed from its resting spot in the Fox River and taken out of the way and deposited in an unstated location.

Five years before, the schooner had been blown ashore at Little Sturgeon Bay. With her keelson broken and a number of timbers displaced, she was considered unworthy of salvage and her owner, a Captain Ferris, abandoned her to the insurance company. A local salvage company contracted with her new owners to salvage the vessel, and the tugs *Gregory* and *Piper* attempted, without success, to pull her off the rocks. She sat in Little Sturgeon for two years before she was purchased by Hagen and English and rebuilt. The <u>List of Merchant Vessels of the U.S.</u> for 1876 describes the *North Star* as a schooner of 139.84 tons registered at Chicago. DOOR COUNTY ADVOCATE, November 27, 1879. DOOR COUNTY ADVOCATE, March 11, April 29, 1880. GREEN BAY ADVOCATE, July 14, 1884. <u>List of Merchant Vessels of the U.S.</u>, 1876, p. 203.

153) *Christine Nilson*, #125293, Schooner, Stranded October 24, 1884.

The *Nilson* ran aground on Baileys Harbors outer reef. The schooner had left Escanaba the day before, bound for Chicago with a cargo of 575 tons of pig iron. She sailed down the bay, through the Sturgeon Bay ship canal and, upon entering the lake slammed into an autumn gale. Captain N.A. Hammer ordered her brought about for the safety of Baileys Harbor. As the vessel came into the harbor in a snow storm, she drifted too far to the north. An attempt was made to swing the craft eastward and run outside the reef but the effort was futile and the schooner struck hard on the reef and began to fill with water. When the anchor was dropped, the *Nilson* swung about and her stern struck the reef. She sank almost immediately in two and a half fathoms of water and started to break up. Hammer and her crew of eight abandoned the wreck for the safety of the small island. The personal belongings of the crew were later recovered. The vessel was insured for $8,000 and the cargo for $12,000.

Captain Rounds of the wrecking tug, *Etna*, went to Baileys Harbor to superintend the salvage of the vessel. It was generally believed that salvage of the vessel was unlikely due to the stormy weather. The schooner, *F.H. Williams*, was brought to the scene in mid-November, with a full wrecking outfit and began removing the pig iron from the *Nilson*. Salvors hoped that once the wreck was unloaded, she could be buoyed up with cedar ties until she could be dry docked. They later concluded that her bottom was gone when three steam pumps, working in unison, could only lower the water in the hold an inch or two over hours of pumping. Efforts to save the cargo were successful and by early December 250 tons of pig iron were salvaged. Efforts to save the hull were abandoned till spring. Weeks later the DOOR COUNTY ADVOCATE reported, "During one of the recent heavy northeasterly blows, the mizzen mast of the schooner *Christina Nelson* [sic] was blown down which indicates that the craft is gradually breaking up, the wind and ice being too much for the hull even though this is under water. The spar has fallen toward the main mast, and it is the opinion of some that the stern and cabin have been crushed in with the ice leaving nothing but the keelson which was insufficient to hold the weight of spar and standing rigging." A year later, in January of 1885, the foremast and bowsprit were standing above the water. Much of the pig iron which had been left on deck was also shoved over the side by ice and was also thought to be a total loss.

The *Nilson* was owned by Mrs. J. Lindgren of Chicago.

The List of Merchant Vessels of the U.S. for 1884, lists her as a schooner of 311.36 tons, registered at Chicago. She was built in Manitowoc in 1871. DOOR COUNTY ADVOCATE, October 30, November 13, December 4, 1884. DOOR COUNTY ADVOCATE, January 15, 29, 1885. KEWAUNEE ENTERPRISE, October 31, 1884. List of Merchant Vessels of the U.S., 1884, p. 95.

154) *Whiskey Pete*, Scow, Stranded prior to 1885.

This vessel was mentioned only in passing in an August 13, 1885, DOOR COUNTY ADVOCATE story about the *Ellen Couture*. The ship was run aground at Horseshoe Bay and was later the victim of a collision with the *Couture*. Nothing else was located about her ultimate disposition.

The *Whiskey Pete* was built in Ahnapee in 1875. CHICAGO TRIBUNE, May 26, 1875.

155) *Ellen Couture*, Schooner, Stranded August 4, 1885.

The *Couture* had been moored in wait for a cargo at the pier in Horseshoe Bay when a strong north wind came up. First mate J.H. Gumm recommended they leave the vessel tied up where she was, which was done. The mooring lines parted and the ship went ashore striking the old scow, *Whiskey Pete*, and breaking up. The crew was saved but the ship was a total loss. Captain Duffy was in command. DOOR COUNTY ADVOCATE, August 13, 1885.

156) *Lily Hamilton*, Schooner, Foundered August 21, 1885.

The *Hamilton* was bound for Milwaukee when she sank in heavy seas twenty miles southeast of Cana Island. The crew just barely escaped in the ship's yawl when she went down. They had to keep the small boat before the sea for six hours before they were finally picked up by the tug, *J.C. Perrett* and delivered to Milwaukee. The schooner was owned by Malston Bank of Owen Sound and was valued at $6,000 and was uninsured. She was loaded with a cargo of

680 pounds of salt for John Plankinton at Milwaukee. The *Hamilton* measured 264 tons. She was not listed in the 1876 or 1884 <u>List of Merchant Vessels of the U.S.</u> DOOR COUNTY ADVOCATE, August 27, 1885.

157) *Cecelia*, #5548, Schooner, Stranded September 8, 1885.

The *Cecelia* was anchored off shore from Jacksonport attempting to wait out a storm. Her anchors did not hold and she was thrown upon the beach "decks to." Prior to the storm she had been loading wood at Reynold's pier and hit the shore just south of that spot. All of her rigging and equipment were stripped. Captain B. Smith thought her back was broken and she would be a total loss. Nonetheless, he went to Chicago for a wrecking outfit but no one would take the job for much less than the vessel was worth. He returned a week later unsuccessful and quite certain that the *Cecelia* would stay where she was. A later unsuccessful effort was made to release the schooner.

The *Cecelia* was wrecked twice before on the same shore. She was owned by Chicagoan Captain John Long who also lost the schooners *Yankee Blade*, *Perry Hannah* and *Pilgrim* on the same reef all in the previous ten years.

The *Cecelia* was valued at $4,000. She was built at White Lake, Michigan, in 1868 and measured 175.82 tons according to the <u>List of Merchant Vessels of the U.S.</u> for 1884. DOOR COUNTY ADVOCATE, September 10, September, 17, 1885. <u>List of Merchant Vessels of the U.S.</u>, 1884, p. 91.

158) *Emma Leighton*, #8186, Schooner, Stranded, September 8, 1885.

The *Leighton* had been moored at Porth's pier at Rowley's Bay when a storm blew her ashore. She was swept through seven cribs. The schooner, *Belle*, moored along side of the *Leighton* was also damaged. The <u>List of</u>

Merchant Vessels of the U.S. for 1884 describes the *Emma Leighton* as a scow-schooner of 82.36 tons. She was built in Port Huron, Michigan, in 1867 and hailed from Milwaukee. DOOR COUNTY ADVOCATE, September 17, 1885. List of Merchant Vessels of the U.S., 1884, p. 120.

159) *Japan*, #12761, Schooner, Stranded October 19, 1885.

The *Japan* had been loading wood at Garret Bay when a gale sprang up and caught her unprepared. She was unable to get away and pounded until she filled with water and broke up in the waves. Captain C. Gunderson remained on board in an effort to save his ship but had to abandon her. She was owned jointly by him and C.A. Sirhorn and was taking on board 120 cords of wood they had purchased from Louis Neman of Ellison Bay.

A news article reprinted from the MILWAUKEE WISCONSIN by the GREEN BAY ADVOCATE raises some confusion about the facts. The WISCONSIN article is probably in error on some points but gives some interesting information, nonetheless.

"Captain Sirhorn took the old schooner Japan *to Green Bay in the fall of 1886 to load a cargo of wood for S.F. Gunderson and Cyrus A. Barker, two Chicago dealers. The man who owned the wood declined to deliver it until he had been paid for it, and Capt. Sirhorn, rather than submit to a tedious delay, paid $419.75 of his own money. While the vessel was being loaded the wind shifted to the northward and began to blow a gale, and she was driven on the rocks, where she pounded to pieces in a short time. Barker and Gunderson declined to reimburse the captain for his expenditure because the wood was not delivered, and he brought suit for the amount. Yesterday a jury returned a verdict for the entire amount, with interest, in his favor."*

The List of Merchant Vessels of the U.S. for 1884 lists

99

the *Japan* as a schooner of 191.88 tons. She was built at Milan, Ohio, in 1853. DOOR COUNTY ADVOCATE, October 22, 1885. GREEN BAY ADVOCATE, May 24, 1888. List of Merchant Vessels of the U.S., 1884, p. 165.

160) *John Spry*, #75599, Side-wheel Steamer, Burned Early November of 1885.

The *Spry* had stopped at Wrightstown to unload eleven tons of flour and middlings* and continued down the river to a dock three miles north of the village to spend the night. The crew turned in early. About 8 p.m., engineer Rasmussen smelled smoke and aroused everyone just in time to save their lives. The fire started near the boiler or smoke stack and spread quickly until the little steamer was consumed down to the water's edge. Some of the crew members were left with no choice but to jump into the river to save themselves. The crew was forced to walk back to Wrightstown. The *Spry* was built in 1866 for F.B. Gardener as a shallow draft tug. In 1884 she was purchased by A.J. Cointe, fitted out for freight and passengers, and put to work on the Fox River route between Green Bay and Fond du Lac. She measured 55.46 tons according to the List of Merchant Vessels of the U.S. for 1884. *Coarsely ground wheat mixed with bran. GREEN BAY ADVOCATE, November 12, 1885. DOOR COUNTY ADVOCATE, November 19, 1885. List of Merchant Vessels of the U.S., 1884, p. 322.

161) *Tornado*, #145037, Tug, Burned July 3, 1886.

The *Tornado* had been tied up at the dock at Red River where her captain, Louis Legot, hoped to spend the July 4th holiday with his family. Only the engineer, August Genneisse, was on board at the time. Fire was discovered sometime between 11 p.m. and midnight and made such rapid headway that the flames couldn't be beaten back. Genneisse escaped with severe burns. The fire was thought to have started in the boiler area where a large number of slats were kept.

The tug was valued at $5,000 but was insured for $4,000 with the A.A. Warren Insurance Agency of Green Bay. The vessel was a total loss and it was decided that considering the work load requiring the tug, she should be abandoned to the insurance company. Her owners, Leathem & Smith, later purchased the engine and boiler back from the underwriter and the hulk was towed to the Leathem Smith shipyard where the machinery was lifted out. The hull was burned for its iron in January of 1891.

The *Tornado* was built at Red River in 1872. She measured 22.58 tons with a length of 56 feet, a depth of seven feet and a beam of twelve feet. DOOR COUNTY ADVOCATE, July 8, 1886. DOOR COUNTY ADVOCATE, January 31, 1891. List of Merchant Vessels of the U.S., 1884, p. 351.

162) *F.J. King*, #9299, Schooner, Foundered September 16, 1886.

The *F. J. King* was bound for Chicago with a cargo of iron ore from Escanaba. Having departed from that Michigan port about 1 p.m. on the 15th, she made good time in agreeable weather until the following morning when strong southeast winds made the schooner "labor hard" and buck the wind and waves. The vessel was found to be leaking and, although the schooner was just off the canal, orders were given to bring the *King* around and head her for North Bay where, hopefully, she could be run aground in a protected area. Captain William Griffin was unfamiliar with the entrance. The vessel, in her leaking condition, drew eleven to twelve feet of water and he feared that she may run aground in an exposed situation trying to enter Sturgeon Bay.

By the time the *King* reached the south point of North Bay, the wind died but prevailing waves made her roll violently and as the water in the hold rose faster than the pumps could handle, it was decided the vessel should be abandoned. A sail was spotted and hailed. The vessel, the schooner *La Petite,* headed for the sinking *F.J. King.*

The crew of the *King* grabbed their belongings and climbed into the ship's longboat, Captain Griffin being the last to leave, and pulled oars towards the approaching *La Petite.* As they rowed away, "twenty-eight minutes after the pumps ceased working the noble craft went down head first, a loud explosion following as the confined air rushed through the companionway, some of the captain's papers being blown fifty feet or more heavenward." Exactly twenty-four hours after she sailed from Escanaba, the schooner sank in twenty-five fathoms, four to five miles off North Bay. Soon after the crew of eight and Captain Griffin pulled along side the *La Petite* which delivered them safely to a wharf in North Bay. From there they were taken, by stage, to Sturgeon Bay, where Captain Griffin gave his story to the ADVOCATE.

Captain William Sanderson, keeper of the Cana Island lighthouse, wrote to the Milwaukee customs house explaining that the mastheads of the *King* could be seen sticking out of the water some six miles away, and as they were directly in a shipping lane, they should be removed. Before anything could be done, a storm did the work.

The *F.J. King* was an old vessel having been built in Toledo, Ohio in 1867. She registered 280.55 gross tons. DOOR COUNTY ADVOCATE, September 23, 30, October 14, 1886. List of Merchant Vessels of the U.S., 1884, p. 125.

163) Unnamed Flat Scow, Burned October 9, 1886.

This unidentified barge caught fire and burned off the Sturgeon Bay ship canal. She was in tow of the steam barge *T.H. Smith* and was loaded with 10,000 dry cedar ties for Chicago parties. When the ties caught fire the Sturgeon

Bay life saving crew threw off 400 ties and tried to scuttle the craft, but the cargo burned so rapidly that the scow rose too rapidly to allow water to flow into the burning hulk. Loss on the scow and her cargo amounted to $2,500. There was no insurance. KEWAUNEE ENTERPRISE, October 15, 1886.

164) W.L. Brown, #80767, Steamer, Foundered October 21, 1886.

The *Brown* sank in foul weather while on her way from Escanaba to De Pere with 550 tons of iron ore. When the vessel was off Peshtigo, the engineer reported that the ship was making water very fast just forward of the boiler, due, it was thought, to her wrenching in the storm. Her captain, F. W. Spafford sounded the pumps forward and found four inches of water. By this time water was running over the floor to the firehold. The pumps were manned, a distress signal was displayed, and the lifeboats were made ready. Captain Spafford decided to run her aground on Peshtigo reef, but ten minutes later the rising water extinguished the boiler fires. Her signal of distress was seen by Captain Henry Tufts of the tug *John Leathem* which was bound for Menominee from Sturgeon Bay.

The crew of the *Brown* couldn't wait for the tug to arrive and took to the life boats. Moments later she sank to 78 feet with a loud explosion. Accounts reported that "as she went down, the hatches blew off, the top of the cabin floated away and a dismal farewell moan or shriek arose from the steam whistle, the rope of which must have become fouled. She appeared to break in two. The point where she went down is about a mile and a quarter off Peshtigo Reef." The crew of fourteen was safely rescued by the *Leathem*. The *Brown* was an old boat, but had been thoroughly rebuilt in 1879 and was thought to be seaworthy. It was speculated that improper loading of the heavy cargo caused a severe strain on her seams in bad weather. She was rated B-1. Two years before her loss she received a new engine, and just a year before received a new boiler.

The following June, salvors began the search for the wreck. Originally, the vessel was thought to be unsalvageable due to the great depth of 78 feet which was an extreme challenge for the diving technology of the time. Captain P.F. Williams of Manitowoc, was given the diving job at $25 per day.* He later declined because his assistant refused to work with him. Williams sold the diving outfit to William Marshall who intended to take the job.

It was a Detroit diver, Frank Dwyer, who with his mentor, George W. Martin, began the work of salvaging the ship's machinery. Martin, like the other divers before him was concerned about the depth. Nonetheless, the job began with the hatches being blown off with electrically fused dynamite. Numerous storms made the work difficult, but by the end of July, 1887, the *Brown* gave up her anchors and chain. Within a week, the boiler was also recovered. Once everything of value was taken, the hulk was left to become just another piece of junk on the bottom of the bay.

About 85 years later, she was located again, this time by diver Frank Hoffman. The *Brown* is still a popular diving sight.

The *W. L. Brown* was originally built as the *Neptune* and was owned by the National Iron Company of De Pere. She measured 336 tons, was valued at $33,000 and insured for $18,000. The cargo was valued at $2,500.

*Although steam driven air pumps were available, many diving contractors used a hand operated pump. Pumps could be set up to keep two divers at thirty feet, or one diver at sixty feet. The diver's fee is also interesting. About this time $25 was almost as much as an ordinary seaman made in a month. DOOR COUNTY ADVOCATE, October 28, 1886. DOOR COUNTY ADVOCATE, June 4, July 9, 16, 23, 30, August 6, 1887. GREEN BAY PRESS-GAZETTE, August 21, 1974. List of Merchant Vessels of the U.S., 1885,

165) *Quickstep*, #20567, Schooner, Stranded October 6, 1886.

The schooner *Quickstep* is often seen in ship losses, in part, because there were several vessels by this name. This particular "*Quickstep*" ran on a rock near the inlet of Detroit harbor on Washington Island in the fall of 1886. The vessel was badly broken and her owners, which included Captain John P. Jessen, decided they could only save the rigging. It was the third time in eight years that she ran aground on Washington Island. No explanations have been given for the name, "Quickstep." It may have come from a Civil War infantry march order corresponding to today's "doubletime." The *Quickstep* was built at Bay de Noquette, Michigan in 1868 and registered 65.70 gross tons. DOOR COUNTY ADVOCATE, October 28, 1886. List of Merchant Vessels of the U.S., 1884, p. 231.

166) *Detroit*, Schooner, Foundered November 3, 1886.

The *Detroit* was outbound from Escanaba with a cargo of iron ore for Cleveland when she sank. The vessel settled in 125 feet of water off Summer Island outside the passage. Her captain and crew escaped in the ship's lifeboat and rowed to Summer Island. The captain continued on to Mackinac via Manistique. The *Detroit* was built in Canada as the *Mary Battle*. She had been declared "too soft to carry ore." ESCANABA IRON PORT, November 11, 1886.

167) Unknown Vessel, Foundered November 4, 1886 off Poverty Island.

This is probably the *Detroit*. The wreck was reported by Captain Hart of the propeller *Moore*. The crew escaped in the yawl. This vessel, however, was reported bound for Chicago with iron ore from Escanaba. The DOOR COUNTY

168) *Union*, #25046, Schooner, Stranded November 10, 1886.

This little vessel is the subject of conflicting news accounts. According to the DOOR COUNTY ADVOCATE, she sprang a leak off Eagle Harbor, filled with water, rolled over and drifted ashore where she went to pieces on the jagged rocks off the south point. She was bound for Green Bay, with cord wood. The owners, Nels Zinc and Nels Jepsen were on board at the time and had to be rescued by fishermen. The vessel was insured.

According to an article in the GREEN BAY ADVOCATE, the *Union* capsized off Sister Bay the afternoon of Nov. 10, 1886. There was a terrible gale blowing at the time. The crew was left in a dangerous situation for four hours before they were rescued by the crew of the schooner, *Foam*. Most of the cargo was lost. Damage to the vessel was unknown. Captain Price was listed as master.

The *Union* was built in Sheboygan in 1867 and hailed from Washington Island. She measured 41.35 gross tons, with a length overall of 59 feet, a beam of 15 feet and a 6 foot depth of hold. DOOR COUNTY ADVOCATE, November 18, 1886. GREEN BAY ADVOCATE, November 18, 1886. List of Merchant Vessels of the U.S., 1884, p. 358.

169) *Sea Star*, #22356, Scow-Schooner, Stranded November 4, 1886.

The vessel was loading wood at the Clay Banks pier when heavy seas began to slam the hull against the pier. A portion of the pier gave way and an effort was made to pull the ship away from the pier. This was successful but the captain and a crewman were stranded on the wreck. The Sturgeon Bay life saving crew was sent for. Rescuers shot a lifeline out to the stranded vessel and with great difficulty got the two men off. The *Sea Star* drifted ashore and became a total wreck shortly thereafter. The craft was owned by Captain C.L. Fellows. She was valued at $3,000. There was no insurance. The *Sea Star* was built at Irving, New York in 1855. She measured 95.48 tons and had a length of 91 feet, a beam of 23 feet, and a depth of 8 feet.

DOOR COUNTY ADVOCATE, November 11, 1886. KEWAUNEE ENTERPRISE, November 12, 1886. List of Merchant Vessels of the U.S., 1884, p. 248.

170) *Emerald*, #36340 and

171) *Florence M. Dickenson*, #24109, Schooner-Barges, Stranded November 17, 1886.

The *Emerald* and the *Florence M. Dickenson* and their fellow consorts, the barges *Lillie May* and *George W. Bissell* in tow of the propeller *Chief Justice Field*, were bound from Toledo for Manitowoc and Milwaukee laden with coal. The entourage was overtaken by an easterly gale when off the Sturgeon Bay ship canal. The *Dickenson* began to leak and soon parted her towline. The *Field* continued on her course with the stricken barge following as best she could with shortened sail. By this time the craft had three to four feet of water in the hold and coal was clogging the bilge pump. At dawn the following morning the *Dickenson* found herself near Kewaunee and the captain, Thomas Robinson, knowing he could not keep his ship off the beach much longer, steered along the shoreline toward the harbor. Two hundred yards off the north pier, the vessel struck a rock and started to break up. The crew lowered the ship's yawl with one man in it and before the remaining five crewman and the cook could board, the boat was swept away from the crumbling wreck by a wave. James McDonald, the lone occupant of the row boat and youngest member of the crew, drifted up against an old abandoned pier where he climbed out and hung on in the wind and spray for several hours until rescuers could get to him. The other crew members, one by one, jumped into the water, clinging to wreckage, hoping it would carry them to safety. Captain Robinson was carried towards the harbor where he was rescued. Mate Louis Todd, and crewman Henry Demar were washed ashore benumbed by cold but still alive. Crewmen Jerry Jeren, Arthur Bouvins, and the cook, Mary Waters, were drowned in the surf.

Residents, who had gathered in hundreds on the beach to watch the developing events and help when they could, sent for the Two Rivers lifesaving crew. That crew was already involved in the rescue of a shipwreck near that port. The Sturgeon Bay lifesaving crew was then contacted and arrived on the scene at 6 p.m., seven hours too late.

An hour after the *Dickenson* struck the rock she had broken to pieces, littering the shore and harbor with wreckage. She was the largest of the fleet of four barges and was loaded with 706 tons of coal.

As the *Dickenson* was about to meet her end, the *Chief Justice Field* came about and headed north, possibly to help the ailing barge, but the propeller could make no headway through the storm and cast adrift the three remaining consorts before heading east across the lake. The *Emerald*, *Lillie May*, and *Bissell* quickly anchored as best they could in the gale. Shortly thereafter, the *Emerald*, badly leaking and a mile off shore, raised a flag of distress. She rode out the storm for two hours until 11 a.m. when she cut loose her anchor and allowed herself to be swept toward shore. Just before the *Emerald* touched bottom, her crew of six, having seen the destruction of the *Dickenson*, launched their yawl and rowed for the safety of Mashek's pier, a quarter of a mile away. Unable to row towards the pier, against the storm, they headed their craft for the beach and were instantly capsized by a breaker drowning all but one crewman. The sole survivor, mate William Cowdy, held onto the bottom of the overturned yawl, several times being washed off, and each time swimming back and regaining his grasp. The other crewmembers, Captain Alex Gorham, brothers, Louis and Mike Pontak, William Alberts and the cook, Maggie Clark, were all drowned. The following day a coroner's inquest ruled that the Blanchard Navigation Co. failed to equip the *Emerald* with lifejackets and a lifeboat of appropriate size.

The *Chief Justice Field* found the safety of Manitowoc harbor and returned the next day to pick up the surviving barges *Lillie May* and *George Bissell*. A lifesaving crew rowed out to check on the vessels. The *May* was in good condition but the *Bissell* was leaking and out of provisions and this was provided before both vessels were towed to Manitowoc.

For months, coal from the two wrecks washed ashore. Two months after the disaster, the KEWAUNEE ENTERPRISE reported "Those who have considerable coal on hand, washed ashore from the barge *Dickenson* and which was picked up along the beach are selling the same at $3.00 a ton and quite a number in the city are burning the coal in their wood stoves." Even a year later the ENTERPRISE reported, "The heavy storm on the Lake Sunday, washed a large amount of coal ashore from the ill-fated barge *Dickenson*, which went to pieces a little north of the harbor last fall. Several tons of coal have been picked up by parties here nearly every day this week."

While little was left of the *Dickenson*, the *Emerald* sat upright in a salvageable condition and remained a constant reminder of the story. The ENTERPRISE reported:

"Last Sunday evening while coming out of the Union Church, a number of those who attended the services discovered a bright light on the spars of the schooner Emerald, *which lies on the beach south-east of the church. At first it was thought to be a ghost and some of the more timid ones were no little horrified at the sight, but it soon*

leaked out that the light was a lantern which had been placed on the top of the spar by some boys who walked out to the vessel on the ice during the daytime. Some of those who saw it did not get 'onto' the joke until the next day and spent a very sleepless night in consequence."

The following spring the *Emerald* was purchased, raised, and repaired for under $3,000. She was valued at $10,000 and the DOOR COUNTY ADVOCATE described her as 147 feet long, 33 foot beam and 9 to 11 foot depth. . ."She was the largest carrier working out of Sturgeon Bay up to that time. . .[and] was built for hauling and with the exception of stanchions and masts she was completely open below decks."

The barge was put back in service and continued to serve for many years. By 1899 her upper works were dilapidated and she was cut down for use as a stone carrier by her new owners, Leathem & Smith. As of 1903 she was left in Sturgeon Bay's "boneyard" of old ships and would have ended her days as a dock or breakwater but was reactivated for a few more shipments of stone. On October 29, 1903, loaded with stone, the *Emerald* was sheltering at Kewaunee harbor where she had made maritime history almost twenty years before. Despite the barge's leaking condition, her escort, the tug, *John Leathem*, took her in tow for Ludington, Michigan. Water in the bilge gained steadily and in mid-lake the vessel was so waterlogged, the two crewmen on board signaled to be taken off. Minutes after they climbed aboard the tug, the *Emerald* rolled over, dumping her cargo of stone to the bottom of the lake. She was cast off and abandoned.

The next day the schooner *Vega* sighted a derelict vessel floating upside down about 35 miles off Frankfort, Michigan. She was unpainted on the bottom with red topsides—like the *Emerald*. The *Emerald* was built in

Saginaw, Michigan in 1869 and measured 286 tons. When she came out she was considered the very model of a well built barge, with the traditional schooner bow and a squared or scow stern. An early story boasted of her being "edge bolted throughout, rail 6 x 15 inches, bilge keelsons the same, hook scarfed, 3-inch skin, heavily timbered, and 'all oak' save the deck and cabin."

The *Florence M. Dickenson* was built in Cleveland in 1855 and measured 390 tons. She had a 180 foot length, 27 foot beam and a 10 foot hold. CHICAGO TRIBUNE, June 18, 1869. KEWAUNEE ENTERPRISE, November 19, 1886. KEWAUNEE ENTERPRISE, January 28, March 11, October 28, 1887. DOOR COUNTY ADVOCATE, September 3, 1887. DOOR COUNTY ADVOCATE, May 3, 1903. KEWAUNEE ENTERPRISE, November 6, 1903. List of Merchant Vessels of the U.S., 1884, p. 118 and 130.

172) *James Reid*, #10234, Tug, Burned June 12, 1887.

The *Reid* had just come in to Sturgeon Bay with two scows in tow when her captain, John Cusick, smelled smoke and upon investigation discovered that the forward cabins were on fire. William Larkins and Sylvester Schwartz were sleeping in the forecastle immediately below the compartment which was on fire. Both men barely escaped with their lives. Schwartz severely burned his hands.

Captain Cusick started directing activities. However, due to the fact that the oil room was part of the burning compartment, the flames spread uncontrollably. The *Reid* had been preparing to go through the Sturgeon Bay bridge at the time. Bridge tenders heard Cusick sound the fire alarm and within minutes, they said, the tug was in flames from stem to stern. Cusick ordered the tug abandoned. When the tug had been pulled away from the barges the crew of thirteen escaped to the forward barge, leaving behind all of their personal belongings. The burning hulk was pushed up on a shoal near the Spear mill where she burned to the waterline.

In October of 1887 the *Reid* was towed from her spot near the Spear mill to the upper mill where work was begun removing her engine, shaft and wheel. Two weeks later, the *Reid*, having been stripped of anything of value, was taken in tow by the tugs *Lawrence*, and *Spalding* and towed to deep water in Green Bay and scuttled. The *James Reid* was originally built as the *General Burnside* at Sandusky, Ohio, in 1867. She was owned by D.N. Runnels of Port Huron, Michigan, who was leasing her to Cusick. She measured 90 feet in length, 17.4 feet at the beam, and 8.7 feet in depth. DOOR COUNTY ADVOCATE, June 18, October 1, 15, 1887. List of Merchant Vessels of the U.S., 1884, p. 319.

173) *Frank D. Barker*, #9165, Schooner, Stranded October 3, 1887.

The *Barker* was bound light from Manistee, Michigan to Escanaba for a load of iron ore when she ran aground on Spider Island in "thick weather." The tug, *Spaulding*, attempted to pull her off without success and her master, Captain Lynch, ordered her stripped and abandoned. Further efforts were made by John Leathem to haul her off and he nearly succeeded. The stern was left in 14 feet of water, with the bow in six feet. E. S. Minor bought the wreck where she was for $1,700 and salvage efforts continued. Near the end of October, the wrecking crew was almost drowned when the vessel was blown backward swamping the cabin. Leathem declared he could rescue the vessel at anytime if only he had a few good days of good weather. Nature did not cooperate, and it was decided that the *Barker* would have to be left for the winter.

In November, high seas pushed the schooner adrift. She swung around in the gale, capsized and broke apart in "mountain high" waves on the rocks of Spider Island. She was laying on the west side of the south end of the island in a northeast-southwest direction. The anchors had been set out to keep her from floating away. The portside had been ripped off leaving nothing but the frames. E. S. Minor had lost an estimated $5,000 with the destruction of the vessel. The *Frank D. Barker* was built in Clayton, Ohio, in 1867. She measured 137 feet in length, with a 26 foot beam and an 11 foot hold. Door County Advocate, October 8, 15, 1887. Door County Advocate, November 24, December 15, 1888. List of Merchant Vessels of the U.S., 1885, p. 140.

174) *Blazing Star*, #2868, Schooner, Stranded November 12, 1887.

The *Blazing Star* was lumber laden and Chicago bound from Manistique when she ran aground on Fisherman's shoal near the wreck of the *I.N. Foster*. The foremast hand, John Burke was steering a course laid down by the captain and, though he could see the wreck and the shoals, did not deviate from the course. In an effort to free the vessel, the crew threw overboard, the deckload of lumber and part of the cargo from below deck. The more the ship rose in the water, the further it was pushed upon the rocks. Her owner and master, Captain Comerford, and his crew abandoned the vessel. Comerford had only purchased the ship the previous spring. According to the Escanaba Iron Port, the wreck was total and it looked as though she had been "deliberately sold to the underwriters." The crew rowed to Pilot Island where they secured passage to Chicago on a steambarge. She was valued at $8,000 and was soon declared a total loss.

Just two weeks before she ran aground, the *Blazing Star* earned a bad reputation when she passed within 100 yards of Axel Stone, sole survivor of the wreck of the steamer *Vernon*, never pausing to rescue him. At the time she was sailing in broad daylight with good weather and clear visibility.

In early December, Leathem and Smith made an attempt to salvage the *Blazing Star* and successfully placed their barge along side and their famous centrifugal pump on board. The weather quickly deteriorated and both barge and pump had to be abandoned (although both were later retrieved). By the time salvage efforts could be renewed, the ship's entire bottom was broken up putting her beyond recovery. The *Blazing Star* was built in Manitowoc in 1873 and measured 279 tons with a length overall of 137 feet, a 26 foot beam, and a 10 foot depth hold. DOOR COUNTY ADVOCATE, November 19, 1887. GREEN BAY ADVOCATE, November 24, 1887. DOOR COUNTY ADVOCATE, June 9, 1888. List of Merchant Vessels of the U.S., 1885, p. 87.

175) Unknown Scow, Stranded November 20, 1887.

Newspaper accounts describe a scow carrying a load of logs in tow of the tug *Spear*. She was bound from De Pere to Menominee. Laboring in a heavy sea, she broke her line and went ashore at Red Banks. DOOR COUNTY ADVOCATE, November 26, 1887.

176) *Sophia Lawrence*, #115870, Scow, Stranded November 21, 1887.

The *Lawrence* had taken on a cargo of wood at Thorpe's pier in Egg Harbor. As she left the harbor, her bow sprit was carried away leaving her disabled. The craft was headed for Kirtland's pier but she was driven ashore on the south side of the harbor. The hull broke in two amidships minutes after she struck. Her fast demise suggested that she had outlived her usefulness. The crew was able to reach shore safely and the cargo of wood was later saved. The *Lawrence* was a small hooker, measuring 20 tons and was built in Menominee in 1882. DOOR COUNTY ADVOCATE, November 26, 1887. List of Merchant Vessels of the U.S., 1884, p. 251..

177) *Fleetwing*, #9883, Schooner, Stranded September 26, 1888.

The *Fleetwing* was loaded with lumber and outward bound from Menominee. Trying to find Death's Door passage, her captain mistakenly sailed in to Garrett Bay and went aground. The tug *Spalding* went to assist but after getting their pump on board had to flee from an incoming gale. When the *Spalding* returned, it was discovered the *Fleetwing* was coming apart. The cargo of lumber was saved. The vessel was valued at $14,000 and was owned by Wells, Ludington, and Schaick.

In late November of 1888, Captain Cox of the tug *Nelson*, inspected the wreck and stated that the hull was split in two in the middle and that "the only thing of value about it is the old iron."

The *Fleetwing* was built at Manitowoc in 1867 by the Burger Boat Co. and hailed from Chicago. She measured 320 tons, had a 136 foot length, 28 foot beam, and an 11 foot depth of hold. DOOR COUNTY ADVOCATE, October 6, December 1, 1888. R.L. POLK MARINE DIRECTORY, 1884, p. 56. List of Merchant Vessels of the U.S., 1888, p. 325.

178) *Robert Noble*, #110577, Steambarge, Stranded November 7, 1888.

The *Noble*, loaded with a cargo of cedar, was bound for Arthur Bay, ten miles north of Menominee, when a lamp in the cabin exploded setting the interior on fire. According to the engineer, the steamer was north at some distance from shore when the explosion occurred. The door leading to the engine room was open at the time and the engineer, seeing the flames, set up the fire hose, but couldn't contain the fire. He was unable to get back into the engine room to stop the boat and the vessel being under such headway, burned that much more fiercely until she was totally engulfed. The cook, Barney O'Reilly, was in the galley at the time and was almost lost in the fire. With great difficulty, Captain William Anger, O'Reilly and crewmen William Jacobs and Joseph Hampton lowered the lifeboat and rowed to the nearest shore and walked to Menominee. According to the engineer, the crew lost all clothing and even the ship's papers. While there was no estimate given for her value, she was insured for $3,000.

According to an article from the MENOMINEE HERALD, while the *Noble* was burning, after the crew abandoned her, a fisherman, Louis Garbosky, boarded her and took sails, towline tackleblocks and one anchor chain.

Fishermen towed the burning vessel to shore where she sank in four feet of water ten miles north of Menominee. She was declared a total loss. The engine and boiler were

The steamer, Robert Noble
Photo courtesy of the Wisconsin Maritime Museum, Manitowoc, Wisconsin

recovered, and purchased by C.T. Emms of Menominee. They were later taken to Fowles shipyard in Fort Howard and placed in the steamer *Menominee and Marinette.*

The *Robert Noble* was well known in the Sturgeon Bay area where she had been built in 1883 by Robert Noble and J. Johnson. She spent her first years as a ferry, carrying passengers, wagons and stock back and forth across Sturgeon Bay. In 1887 she was purchased by her current owners, A.W. Lawrence and George Spear and converted into a freight carrier.

The *Noble* measured 74 tons with a length overall of 74 feet, a beam of 23 feet and 4.6 foot depth of hold. DOOR COUNTY ADVOCATE, November 10, 1888. GREEN BAY ADVOCATE, December 6, 15, 1888. DOOR COUNTY INDEPENDENT by the GREEN BAY ADVOCATE, February 21, 1889. List of Merchant Vessels of the U.S., 1888, p. 325.

179) *H.S. Hubbell*, #95699, Steam-Propeller, Burned November 12, 1888.

The *Hubbell* had been engaged in the lumber trade between Manistique, Michigan, and Chicago. She was following her normal routine when she caught fire and burned twenty miles off Poverty Island. Her crew was driven to the life boats without a chance to save their personal belongings. They were later rescued by the steamer *New Orleans.*

The *Hubbell* was the property of John Sprang. She measured 398.76 gross tons with 325 horsepower. She had been built at Lorain, Ohio, only six years before. ESCANABA IRON PORT, November 17,1888. List of Merchant Vessels of the U.S., 1884, p. 313.

180) *Erastus Corning*, #7239, Schooner, Stranded May 27, 1889.

This large schooner was outward bound from Escanaba loaded with iron ore when she ran aground on the west side of Poverty Island. The point at which she ran ashore is so steep that when the stern settled to the bottom, the bow was out of the water with the vessel almost standing on end. As sailing ships of this time and era go, she was quite large at 204 feet in length and was the largest ship wrecked in the Bay up to that time. The keeper of the Cana Island Light received the contract to strip her. Captain Bartley took an agent of the underwriters out to look at her. He stated that it was "no use bothering with her" and did not think it would be worth "fishing" the ore out of her.

On June 5, 1867, the *Erastus Corning* was involved in a fog enshrouded collision that sent the bark, *Clayton* to the bottom of Lake Huron in fifty fathoms of water. By "superhuman exertions" on the part of Captain Locke of the *Corning*, the *Clayton's* crew was safely rescued.

The *Corning* was built in 1867 and launched on April 24th of that year in Tonawanda, New York. She was originally rigged as a barkentine—square sails on the foremast and fore-and-aft rigs on the main and mizzen masts. She carried 5,300 yard of canvas. Her main mast measured 152 feet from the deck, her keel was 201 feet with an over all length of 216 feet. Her prodigious length was matched with a beam of 35.3 feet and a 14.5 foot depth of hold. She measured 832.43 tons, and was rated for 53,000 bushels of corn. She was built at a cost of $75,000.

Erastus Corning, after whom the ship was named, was a financier, railroad developer and founder of Corning, New York. He is the Corning in Corning Glassworks and Corningware. The Corning family is well represented on the Bay shore. The schooner *Ida Corning* rests in the shallows of Sturgeon Bay. CHICAGO TRIBUNE, June 17, 1867. CHICAGO TRIBUNE, June 10, 1868. DOOR COUNTY ADVOCATE, June 1, 1889. Reprinted from the ESCANABA IRON PORT by the DOOR COUNTY ADVOCATE, June 29, 1889. ESCANABA IRON PORT, June 22, 1889. List of Merchant Vessels of the U.S., 1888, p. 108.

181) *James Garret*, #13875, Schooner, Stranded May 30, 1889.

As the *Garrett* had approached V & C Mashek's pier in Lily Bay, Captain Smith ordered the anchor dropped and the anchor cable payed out as they came in. When they discovered they were too far out with too little cable, a line was secured to the end of the cable and the vessel was brought up to the pier. According to the mate, Charles Donley, the crew spent 20 hours loading the vessel with 200 cords of wood. A "heavy northeaster" arose and Smith ordered everyone to their bunks to wait it out. As the weather grew worse, efforts were made to haul the schooner out to deeper water, but the line snapped, leaving the *Garrett* to drift on to the beach. The cord wood which was the property of the Masheks, was almost all saved. Fifty-five cords were taken on board the schooner *Lizzie Metzner* which also rescued the ship's sails and "outfit." Efforts to save the ship, itself, had been postponed due to the stormy conditions which lasted for several days and finally broke up the hull. The following March, another storm pushed the remnants of the *Garrett* closer to the pier before sweeping her out into the lake.

The *Garrett* measured 260 tons with a length of 138 feet, a beam of 27 feet and 9 feet of depth. She was built in Sheboygan in 1867 and hailed from Milwaukee. DOOR COUNTY ADVOCATE, June 1, 1889. Reprinted from the MILWAUKEE WISCONSIN by the DOOR COUNTY ADVOCATE, June 15, 1989. DOOR COUNTY ADVOCATE, April 12,1890.

182) Unknown Fishing Vessel.

According to a Chicago newspaper, two fishermen were picked up by a vessel 12 hours after their fishing boat capsized and sank off the Sturgeon Bay ship canal. The local marine reporter was unable to find any other accounts of missing fishing boats. DOOR COUNTY ADVOCATE, June 22, 1889.

183) *Kittie Laurie*, #14317, Schooner Stranded August 9, 1889.

The *Laurie* was bound for Ephraim from Ellison Bay when she accidentally went aground between Eagle Harbor and Little Sister Bay. Two weeks later, the KEWAUNEE ENTERPRISE on August 30, 1889 reported "The small coasting schooner, *Katie Laurie* [sic] which ran ashore two miles north of Ephraim, Wisconsin, on the 9th inst. has gone to pieces." The DOOR COUNTY ADVOCATE reported in January 1891 that the *Laurie* was still aground and breaking up then.

The *Kittie Laurie* was built in 1872 by Robert Laurie but was owned by Captain Nicholi Anderson. She measured 39 feet in length with a 12 foot beam, 5.6 foot depth of hold and was registered at 13 tons. She was uninsured. DOOR COUNTY ADVOCATE, August 17, 1889. List of Merchant Vessels of the U.S., 1888, p. 162.

184) *Batchelder*, Tug, Burned, November 14, 1889.

The *Batchelder* was gathering logs from a broken raft off Red River, Wisconsin when she caught fire. The crew barely escaped with their lives before the vessel capsized and sank. She was valued at $6,000 and was insured for $3,500 and was a total loss. The cause of the fire was unknown, but it was believed to have started near the boiler and reached such intensity that controlling the flames was impossible. The tug was reported to have sunk in deep water shortly after. The crew came to Green Bay in a small boat. The job of gathering the logs was given to the tug *Chandler*. The *Batchelder* was owned by the Island Lumber Co. for the purpose of towing logs from Menominee. The engine, shaft and wheel, shoe and boiler were salvaged by Capt. John Walker of Chicago and taken to port for placement in a new hull. After it was salvaged from the wreckage, the boiler was lost through the ice and

120

The Erastus Corning as she appeared with barkentine rigging.

Photo courtesy of the Great Lakes Marine Collection of the Milwaukee Public Library/Wisconsin Marine Historical Society

in November of 1890 efforts were made to recover it a second time. It was hauled to the surface and lashed to the side of the schooner, *I.N. Foster* but had to be cut loose when the vessel encountered a northeast gale off of Squaw Island. Conflicting accounts place it in fifty and sixty feet of water. It was stated that no further efforts would be made to recover the boiler. While the List of Merchant Vessels of the U.S. does not describe a *"Batcheldor"* or *"William Batcheldor"*, etc., the *Webster Batchellor* (#80766) might be a possibility. (Both news accounts and the List of Merchant Vessels occasionally made errors of this type.) The *Webster Batchellor* was a steam tug of 45.95 gross tons, measuring 68 feet in length, 15 feet at the beam in 7 feet in depth. She was built in Grand Haven, Michigan in 1880. DOOR COUNTY ADVOCATE, November 16, 1889. GREEN BAY ADVOCATE, November 21, 1889. DOOR COUNTY ADVOCATE, November 15, 29, 1890. List of Merchant Vessels of the U.S., 1885, p. 375.

185) Unknown Fishing Vessel, Foundered November 16, 1889.

This small fish boat sank on its way from St. Martin Island to Washington Island with a load of hay. The vessel's owner, a Mr. Allen, his son and a hired hand had been aboard. Apparently they were taking on water. Witnesses following a mile behind said they saw the three throw out the hay, make sail, and run for the beach. The boat sank before it reached shore. The two men were found near a bale of hay and, it was thought that they floated to shore with it but were too exhausted to drag themselves from the water. The boy presumably went down the the boat. Reprinted from the MILWAUKEE WISCONSIN, November 26, 1889 by the DOOR COUNTY ADVOCATE, November 30, 1889.

186) *Z.Y.M.C.A.*, #5990, Schooner, Capsized August 24, 1890.

The *Z.Y.M.C.A.* was bound from Charlevoix to Chicago with a load of bark and wood when she overturned. The vessel was said to be overloaded and was unable to rebound from the waves. The seven men on board escaped in the yawl and were subsequently picked up by the schooner, *Jessie Phillips*, while on its way to Thomson, Michigan, just south of Manistique. The accident occurred an estimated seven miles from the western shore. The ship was kept afloat by her cargo of bark. Reports described her floating near the Manitou Islands and Frankfort, Michigan. She was reported 30 miles east of Kewaunee by the captain of the schooner, *Naiad*. At the request of the vessel's owners, the tug *Leathem* was sent out to look for the *Z.Y.M.C.A.* The tug returned the same day having found the cabin, parts of the deck and other wreckage. It was thought that her deck was broken up by the sea allowing her cargo of bark to float free and the hull to go "to the bottom like a stone." The *Z.Y.M.C.A.* was built in 1869 in Manitowoc. She had a tonnage of 189 with a 123 foot length and 28 foot beam. There was no insurance on the ship or the contents. Captain A.M. Elliot was master and owner. The name, "*Z.Y.M.C.A.*" stands for "Zealous Young Men's Christian Association." DOOR COUNTY ADVOCATE, August 30, 1890. KEWAUNEE ENTERPRISE, August 29, September 12, 1890.

187) *A.S. Piper*, #105898, Tug, Burned October 14, 1890. This small tug caught fire and burned at the upper mill pier in Sturgeon Bay while her crew was ashore. The tug, *Mosher* pulled the *Piper* away from the pier before nearby lumber piles could ignite. She drifted ashore. Fire started in a pile of slabs near the boiler. She was a total loss. The *Piper* was owned by Captain John Walker and was valued at $3,000. She was insured for $2,000. The tug was built in Milwaukee in 1880 and measured 21.11 gross tons with a length of 54 feet, and a beam of 12 feet. In April of 1904,

she was reported still sunk at the head of the bay. The burned hulk had been shifted so that it nearly reached the channel. DOOR COUNTY ADVOCATE, October 18, 1890. DOOR COUNTY ADVOCATE, April 23, 1904. List of Merchant Vessels of the U.S., 1888, p. 260.

188) *Clara*, Schooner, Abandoned June of 1892.

Having been damaged in the fall of 1890 "by contact with Green Island" in a storm, the schooner was finally hauled out at the Philbrook shipyard at Menekaune in June of 1892. No one would assume financial responsibility for her and she was left on the ways. When the yard was abandoned, the owners didn't know what to do with her. They could break up the hull, or for $100 return her to the water and send her adrift. She became a shelter for tramps of Marinette-Menominee. On December 30, 1892, she was pulled out on the ice on the river opposite the Menominee River Coal and Dock Co. and was abandoned there. By April, 1893, she was still lying in the river below the bridge. The List of Merchant Vessels of the U.S. names several vessels by this name. Two likely are #125616, a sloop of 10.98 tons built in Chicago in 1877, and, more probably, #125400, a scow of 28.44 tons built in Sheboygan, Wis., in 1875. DOOR COUNTY ADVOCATE, June 18, 1892. DOOR COUNTY ADVOCATE, January 7, April 29, 1893. List of Merchant Vessels of the U.S., 1884, p. 96.

189) *Nevada*, #13021, Steambarge, Foundered November 15, 1890.

The *Nevada* was the subject of one of the most unique court cases in the history of Wisconsin's maritime law.

The steam barge was bound for Sheboygan with 1,500 tons of coal from Buffalo. Somewhere in mid-lake, the vessel was found to be leaking and, according to the crew, taking on water faster than the pumps could manage. A signal of distress was sounded on the whistle and sometime

The Schooner Z.Y.M.C.A.
Photo courtesy of the Great Lakes Marine Collection
of the Milwaukee Public Library/Wisconsin Marine Historical Society

later the steamer *Manchester* came along side and the *Nevada's* crew climbed on board. The *Manchester* took the stricken vessel in tow, but owing to the fact that the *Nevada* was sitting low at the stern, she did not tow well and snapped her tow line. Only the ship's compass was salvaged.

The *Nevada* floated about off Kewaunee, and at one point

The steamer Nevada coming into harbor.

Photo courtesy of the Great Lakes Marine Collection
of the Milwaukee Public Library/Wisconsin Marine Historical Society

was even checked out by a passing schooner. That vessel, finding no one about, abandoned the steamer to her fate. No further help was forthcoming and about 10 a.m. the next morning she plunged to the bottom about five miles southeast of Kewaunee, three miles off shore.

Despite the fact that she had been rebuilt the previous winter and given a high insurance rating—A2-Inland Lloyd's—she was considered an unlucky ship. According to the KEWAUNEE ENTERPRISE, November 21, 1890, "some doubt is expressed if she ever made a cent for her owners." Her cargo of coal was valued at $3,000, but the *Nevada*, herself, was valued at $40,000 and was fully insured by Smith, Davis & Co. of Buffalo. She was owned by her captain, William H. Landgraf, and several other maritime businessmen from Sandusky, Ohio.

Almost three years to the day after the *Nevada* sank, her former chief engineer, John A. Schurg, and first mate, Captain James Goodman were arrested on a federal indictment of willfully sinking their ship for $1,500, a hanging offense. The indictment was handed down by a Chicago grand jury. The insurance company was represented by C.E. Kramer, a Chicago attorney specializing in maritime law.

The case was later dropped at the discretion of the U.S. district attorney because the witnesses were too scattered and so much time elapsed since the incident occurred that he felt it would be impossible to secure a conviction. The KEWAUNEE ENTERPRISE stated that the story had drawn much attention "for the reason that but one case of the kind had occurred on the Great Lakes in the history of navigation, and for the further reason that the only punishment known to the law for the offense is death." Ironically, 37 years and fifteen or so miles away, the steamer *Lakeland* sank under similar circumstances. The *Nevada* was built at Bay City, Mich., only eight years before her demise, and measured 186 feet in length, 30.8 feet at the beam, and 12 feet in the hold. She displaced 791 tons. KEWAUNEE ENTERPRISE, November 21, 1890, KEWAUNEE ENTERPRISE, November 17, 24, 1893, December 15, 1893. KEWAUNEE ENTERPRISE, June 8, 1894. The List of Merchant Vessels of the U.S., 1884, p. 335.

Part 3:
Vessels lost between 1891 and 1910

190) *G.A.R.* #85969, Tug, Burned September 17, 1891.

The *G.A.R.* had spent the night tied up at her pier in Green Bay harbor and was on her way out about 5 a.m. when fire was discovered. The flames spread so rapidly that the crew could do little more than abandon ship. They were picked up by the tug, *Stewart Edwards*. The craft burned to the waterline. She was laying about a mile inside the "cut".or channel dredged through Grassy Island. The vessel was owned by A. Roulette and Capt. P. Roulette, who later recovered the engine, boiler, wheel and shaft from the burned and sunken hulk. The *G.A.R.* was built in 1887 at Fish Creek and was registered at Milwaukee. She measured 45 feet in length, 11.9 foot beam and a six foot hold. "*G.A.R.*" undoubtedly refers to the Grand Army of the Republic, a Civil War Veterans group not unlike the Veterans of Foreign Wars (V.F.W.). DAILY STATE GAZETTE, Sept. 17, 1891. The DOOR COUNTY ADVOCATE, September 19, 1891. GREEN BAY ADVOCATE, September 24, 1891. DOOR COUNTY ADVOCATE, March 12, 1892. List of Merchant Vessels of the U.S., 1888.

191) *Transit*, #24231, Schooner, Foundered September 23, 1891.

The *Transit* was bound for Milwaukee with a cargo of lumber, when Captain Elias Oleson decided to pull into Kewaunee harbor for the night. Unknown to the captain was the fact that the north pier had been lengthened but the pier head light had not yet been moved to the end of the pier. In the darkness, the *Transit* sailed directly into the pier tearing a gaping hole in her bow. Before she could be brought around, the ship quickly water logged and drifted on to the rocks a thousand feet north of the pier.

Captain Oleson evacuated the ship's crew and valuables into the yawl and rowed to shore. Oleson later examined the wreck and deemed her unworthy of salvage. She was subsequently stripped of anything usable. The hulk was towed off the beach by the steam barge *William Rudolph* and taken in to the harbor where her deck was pried off and the 90,000 board feet of hardwood lumber removed. She was then raised between two scows, towed out into the lake and cut loose. She later drifted ashore and broke up.

In January of 1897, owners of the *Transit*, Elias and Peter Oleson, filed a claim against the government for $2,650 — their estimated value of the vessel.

The *Transit* was built in Manitowoc in 1854 and measured 92 tons. KEWAUNEE ENTERPRISE, September 25, November 6, 1891. KEWAUNEE ENTERPRISE, January 15, 1897. List of Merchant Vessels of the U.S., 1884, p. 269.

192) *L.C. Butts*, #15850, Schooner, Stranded October 29, 1891.

The *Butts*, a double decked schooner laden with coal, was in tow of the *Niagara* for Escanaba when she started taking on water during an autumn storm. Her captain, fearing she would founder, ran her ashore on the east side of Washington Island. The *L.D. Smith* brought a steam pump to her, but she pounded on a rock, driving it through the hull and raising the deck six feet amidship. The crew escaped to shore safely. The ship was stripped of her equipment and within a week she broke in two. In January of 1892, large quantities of coal began to wash ashore on Washington Island, and by March, 200 tons had been gathered on the beach. About that time, local parties removed the mizzen-mast, that being the only thing left other than some rigging. It was hoped that the coal could be sold locally, but if a buyer could not be found it would be taken to Milwaukee or Chicago. The balance of the 1,250 tons of coal was washed away.

In 1922, the DOOR COUNTY ENTERPRISE reported that wreckage of the old schooner could still be seen off shore from the Nor Shellwick property on Washington Island.

The *L.C. Butts* was built in 1872 at South Saginaw, Michigan. She was valued at $14,000, insured for $10,000 and registered 730 gross tons. DOOR COUNTY ADVOCATE, November 7, 14, 1891. DOOR COUNTY ADVOCATE, March 12, 19, 1892. DOOR COUNTY ADVOCATE, January 26, 1922. List of Merchant Vessels of the U.S., 1888, p.162.

193) *Myra*, #91709, Tug, Burned October 30, 1891.

This craft caught fire at the Lime Kiln wharf at Little Sturgeon and was a total loss. She was small—50 tons burden—and was owned by a Menominee firm for hauling lime. There was no insurance. She was valued at $600.

The *Myra* was built in 1884 in Menominee and measured 52 feet in length, 14 feet in beam, and 3.9 feet in depth. DOOR COUNTY ADVOCATE, October 31, 1891. List of Merchant Vessels of the U.S., 1888, p.314.

194) *Forester*, #37181, Scow-Schooner, Stranded October 28, 1891.

The *Forester* ran afoul off Pilot Island. In a flowing, graceful script, lighthouse keeper Martin Knudsen wrote in his log book, "A schooner stranded this evening on the S.W. end of this island at 9:40...She is the three mast scow *Forest* [sic] of Chicago." The crew spent the night trapped on board the wreck until Knudsen, and his assistants, Thomas Avery and G.M. Hansen could help them ashore the next day. At the captain's request, the assistants retrieved the anchor chain and pump from the wreck. The following evening a southern gale threw the hulk off the rocks wrecking her stern. The crew continued to stay as guests of the lighthouse staff for a week. By mid-January, the vessel started to break up. Her equipment was left on the island to be recovered in the spring.

In December of 1894, Knudsen cut off the scow's cabin for use as a winter hut on Detroit Island point.

For a three-masted vessel, the *Forester* was small, measuring only 55.31 gross tons. She was built in Cleveland, Ohio in 1868. Door County Advocate, November 7, 14, 1891. Door County Advocate, January 16, 1892. Journal of the Lighthouse Station at Porte Des Morte, on Pilot Island, October 28, 29, 1891, November 5, 14, 15, 26, 1891, April 20, 1893, December 14, 1894, July 21, 1898. List of Merchant Vessels of the U.S., 1884, p. 131.

195) *Ross*, Steam Yacht, Stranded November 15, 1891.

If this was indeed a Federally documented vessel, it may possibly be the *E.P. Ross*. The Federal list only refers to two other vessels by this name, both of which were on the eastern seaboard. The *Ross* broke her mooring lines in a gale and went ashore in Sawyer Harbor. She was described as being high and dry on the beach, near the "Brown Mill." Some time later, high winds carried her away from the beach at Idlewild. She soon sank in eight feet of water. Years later the boiler was removed and sold to an area farmer. A later report said the *Ross* sunk at the foot of Spruce Street in Surgeon Bay.

The *E.P. Ross* was a steam propeller driven craft of 28.12 gross tons, built in 1874 in Buffalo, New York. Door County Advocate, January 9, 1892. Door County Advocate, March 29, 1902. Door County Advocate, December 3, 1904. List of Merchant Vessels of the U.S., 1884, p. 302.

196) *Sarah R. Shipman*, #115120, Tug, Burned November 15, 1891.

This small tug burned in the port of Escanaba and became a total loss. She was built in Green Bay in 1871 and was insured for $2,500. The *Shipman* measured 17. 6 gross tons, with a length of 50 feet, a beam of 11.6 feet and a depth of 6 feet. Reprinted from the ESCANABA IRON PORT by The DOOR COUNTY ADVOCATE, November 21, 1891. List of Merchant Vessels of the U.S., 1888, p. 328.

197) *Newsboy*, #18086, Schooner, Stranded November 17, 1891.

The *Newsboy* ran upon Fisherman's Shoal near where the *Blazing Star* was wrecked. The crew barely escaped with their lives. They retreated from the ship's "apartment" or cabin to the forecastle and from there to the chain locker. Two local sailors, Captains Nels Peterson and Ole Christianson had made an initial attempt to rescue the crew but were driven back by the breakers. When the schooner crew raised more signals of distress the two tried again and were swamped. The rescuers were then rescued by the crew. Christianson and Peterson and the seven crewmen huddled in the chain locker for two days before being rescued by the tug, *Monarch*. The *Newsboy* was loaded with 54,000 bushels of corn all of which was lost.

Martin Knudsen of the Porte Des Morte lighthouse on Pilot Island reported that the schooner was "twisted like a corkscrew (by the force of the sea) within 24 hours of stranding." The vessel ended up with her stern high in the air and her spars all broken off. In January it was reported that "the *Newsboy* had been split in two from stem to stern, and it looks as if some one had cut her deck-beams so effectively has the job been done."

The KEWAUNEE ENTERPRISE wrote this post script to their story on the *Newsboy*:

"Her late mishap recalls the palmy days of sailing vessels on the Great Lakes as she was one of the fastest vessels that ever traversed the lakes, and some of her runs to Buffalo and some of her round trips, were made on what

was 'good steamboat time' in the years of her prime."

In a letter to the DOOR COUNTY ADVOCATE, Lighthouse keeper, Martin Knudsen cited the loss of the *Newsboy* demanding a lifesaving station in Death's Door which ultimately led to the establishment of the Plum Island Coast Guard Station.

The "outfit" or rigging and sails were salvaged and shipped to Chicago on the steamer *Ludington.* It was purchased by Captain Sam Neff, presumably, it was thought, for the schooner *Sydney Neff.* Like many of the Great Lakes sailing craft built after the Civil War, the *Newsboy* started her career as a bark—three masted with square sails on all but the mizzenmast. Sailing captains found this ineffective for these waters. By the early 1870s most of the barks had been changed to schooner rigs. In August of 1869 the *Newsboy* was brought to a Buffalo shipyard with a sprung foremast. Her owners took the opportunity to change her to a schooner. CHICAGO TRIBUNE, August 6, 1869. DOOR COUNTY ADVOCATE, November 21, 28, 1891. KEWAUNEE ENTERPRISE, November 27, 1891. DOOR COUNTY ADVOCATE, June 4, 1892. DOOR COUNTY ADVOCATE, January 23, 1893. DOOR COUNTY ADVOCATE, December 29, 1894. List of Merchant Vessels of the U.S., 1888, p. 201.

198) *H.M. Scove*, #95256, Schooner, Stranded December 5, 1891.

The *Scove* went ashore between Detroit Island and Pilot Island in a southerly gale. She was Milwaukee bound with lumber from Pine Lake. In his logbook, lighthouse keeper Martin Knudsen wrote, "The schooner *H.M. Scove* dragged her anchor behind Plum Island and is now on the middle ground flying signals for help. Three schooners are at anchor close by." Efforts were made to salvage her in mid-December but it was discovered that a large hole had been stove in by a rock and whenever pumped out she'd fill in again in twenty minutes. The vessel spent the winter "froze in solid at a point north of Plum Island...and if the ice field happens to go out in a body it will undoubtedly carry the craft with it."

Spring brought renewed salvage efforts by the Leathem Smith Co. Her deckload was removed and a pump put aboard, but the water level in the hull could not be lowered. The salvage attempt was postponed pending the arrival of a new and larger pump from New York and the possible patching of the holes by a diver should the two pumps not work.

The salvage expedition returned again in mid-June. Arriving in the early morning daylight of June 17, they found a scow moored along side the wreck. It was discovered that the crew of the scow that had been plundering the wreck were still asleep in their beds. Some of the lumber from the hold of the *Scove* had been transferred to the scow. The *Scove's* cabin had been partly demolished to allow removal of the cook stove from the galley. The ADVOCATE reported, "Captain Leathem having exhausted his vocabulary of plain English, informed the beach combers that he let them off on the condition that they take the lumber and other property to this port (Sturgeon Bay) and put it on the dock." Efforts to pump out the hull were resumed and quickly abandoned when it was found that three steam pumps could not lower the water in the hold. Four tugs pulled on the schooner for several hours and succeeded only in breaking an eight inch hawser. In September, Martin Knudsen logged the fact that the *H.M. Scove* was breaking up. In March of 1893, the ADVOCATE reported "Every vestige of the old schooner, *H.M. Scove*, ashore in the Door, has now disappeared and the loss is therefore total." A year later the ADVOCATE added this final note to the story of the *Scove*, "Sometime ago the ADVOCATE reported that the *H.M. Scove* had entirely disappeared from view. That was true enough. But those who have to pass the red spar buoy ought to give it a wide berth and keep up under Plum, as all of the bottom, which is loaded down with stone ballast, still remains and a good many ugly timbers are projecting from it and will do damage to ones passing over it."

Two years after the vessel was wrecked, in its December 22, 1894 issue, the DOOR COUNTY ADVOCATE ran a small article that stated, "It is reported that Captain Sam. Thorson got away with $1,000 of his employers' money instead of only $350, as first stated. According to the stories afloat Thorson, who was owner and master of the schooner *H.M. Scove*, took this method of getting even with the people that undertook the job of getting his vessel afloat at the time she went ashore in November 1891. Report has it that Captain Thorson has returned to Norway where he will be able to live in ease and comfort should he so desire." Thorson's sister refuted the story in the next issue of the ADVOCATE.

The *H.M. Scove* was named after Hans Scove, a partner in the Hanson and Scove shipbuilding firm of Manitowoc. She was built in Manitowoc in 1873, registering 305 gross tons. She measured 130 feet in length, with a beam of 26 feet and a depth of 10 feet. Journal of the Lighthouse Station at Porte Des Morte on Pilot Island, December 5, 1891. DOOR COUNTY ADVOCATE, December 12, 19, 1891, DOOR COUNTY ADVOCATE, January 16. April 23, June 25, 1892. DOOR COUNTY ADVOCATE, March 11, 1893. DOOR COUNTY ADVOCATE, February 17, 1894. List of Merchant Vessels of the U.S., 1888, p. 130.

199) *Laurel*, #15409, Scow, Stranded March 12, 1892.

The *Laurel* was blown on the beach at Washington Island. By the following fall she was still aground and the ADVOCATE reported, "The old scow *Laurel* is hanging together wonderfully despite her years. The last southwest wind shoved her up higher on the beach, and made her spars work like a pair of scissors. The owner thinks he will burn her down in order to get the iron, of which there are many tons." The *Laurel* was old having been built in 1852, at Blasten Bend, Ohio. She registered 62 gross tons with a length of 80 feet, a beam of 20 feet and a depth of 5 feet. DOOR COUNTY ADVOCATE, March 12, 1892. List of Merchant Vessels of the U.S., 1888, p. 165.

200) *Roving Star*, #110475, Schooner, Foundered October 1, 1892.

She was loading wood at the pier at Clay Banks when a heavy wind caused the *Roving Star* to strike the bottom breaking her in two. She was built in Egg Harbor in 1881 and had a small capacity of 30 cords of wood. According to the ADVOCATE, she was owned by Chris Braunsdorf of Clay Banks. (The KEWAUNEE ENTERPRISE stated she was captained by Braunsdorf and owned by George W. King.) The *Roving Star* registered 26.38 gross tons. She was 61.5 feet in length, 18 feet at the beam and 3.4 feet in depth. DOOR COUNTY ADVOCATE, October 8, 1892. KEWAUNEE ENTERPRISE, October 7, 1892. List of Merchant Vessels of the U.S., 1888, p. 219.

201) *City of Sturgeon Bay*, #126119, Side-Wheel Steamer, Stranded October 8, 1892.

This steamer broke away from her anchorage and went ashore in a big blow. She had been used as a light ship off Escanaba during a part of the season. The sidewheeler was not a particularly large steamer registering 76.51 gross tons. She measured 80 feet in length, 17 feet across the beam and 4.5 feet in depth. No other information was available on the location of her grounding or her ultimate disposition. She was built at Sturgeon Bay in 1883. DOOR COUNTY ADVOCATE, October 15, 1892. List of Merchant Vessels of the U.S., 1888, p. 273.

202) *J.E. Gilmore*, #13307, Schooner, Stranded October 16, 1892.

Trying to navigate the Death Door straits late at night, the *Gilmore* was running before the wind when the wind suddenly changed and drove her up on the south end of Pilot Island in three feet of water. Lighthouse keeper Martin Knudsen helped the crew to the safety of shore. The ship was subsequently stripped. She was valued at $3,500 with no insurance. By Autumn of 1899 the schooner had become a source of stove wood for the lighthouse crew.

For efforts to aid the crew of the *Gilmore*, Knudsen was awarded a medal from the Life Saving Benevolent Association.

Registered as the *J.E. Gilmore* and later the *James E. Gilmore*, the schooner was built in 1867 in Three Mile Bay, New York. She measured 276 net tons with a length of 137.7 feet, 25.4 feet across the beam, and 11 feet of depth. The *J.E. Gilmore* should not be confused with the *Q.A. Gilmore* (No. 126), another schooner that sailed in this area and was wrecked not far away at Gull Island Reef.

DOOR COUNTY ADVOCATE, October 22, 29, 1892. DOOR COUNTY ADVOCATE, August 4, 1939. Journal of the Lighthouse at Porte Des Morte on Pilot Island, October 17, 1892 and September 22, 1899. List of Merchant Vessels of the U.S., 1885, 170.

203) *A.P. Nichols*, #566, Schooner, Stranded October 28, 1892.

The schooner *A.P. Nichols* had been riding out a fierce gale at anchor in Death's Door when she dragged her anchor and went on the shoal on the northwest side of Pilot Island. Captain Clow, his father, and the crew of six were rescued by lighthouse keeper Martin Knudsen who waded out along the deck of the partially submerged schooner, *Forester*, to within a few feet of the stranded vessel. One by one all aboard jumped into the water and were pulled to the shallows by Knudsen. The keeper sheltered the crew in the station's old fog signal house where he was already housing the crew of the *J.E. Gilmore.* The next day, Knudsen hailed the passing steamer *J.H. Outhwaite* and put the Nichols' captain aboard.

At the recommendation of the Chicago collector of customs, Knudsen was awarded the second degree silver life saving medal.* In his logbook entry for July 29, 1893, the lightkeeper made a terse note, "Keeper received silver medal from gov't for life saving service." On August 7, 1939, for the 150th anniversary of the founding of the lighthouse service, the NBC radio network broadcast a dramatization of Martin Knudsen's rescue of the *A.P. Nichols* crew followed by a speech by the lighthouse keeper, by then retired and living in Milwaukee.

The *Nichols* was purchased by F.H. Van Cleve, a member of the Escanaba Wrecking Co. in December of 1892. However nothing could be done with the hulk and she sat on the rocks of Pilot Island. On October 31, 1893, almost exactly a year after the schooner went aground Keeper Knudsen wrote in his logbook, "An extreme large sea prevails today from the southward and schr. *A.P. Nichols* is completely broken to pieces and partially washed ashore." By January, 1894 no sign was left of the vessel. The *Nichols* was built at Madison Dock, Ohio, in 1861. She was registered at 299.67 gross tons and measured 145 feet in length, 13 feet across the beam, and 11 feet in depth.

*Knudsen was erroneously reported to have received the Congressional Medal of Honor in one or two articles about him including his obituary. His medal stated, "Act of Congress, June 20, 1874."and was therefore, a medal ordained by Congress but was not "the" Congressional Medal of Honor. DOOR COUNTY ADVOCATE, November 12, December 24, and 31, 1892. DOOR COUNTY ADVOCATE, March 11, 1893. DOOR COUNTY ADVOCATE, February 10, 1894. DOOR COUNTY ADVOCATE, August 4, 1939.

Journal of the Lighthouse at Porte Des Morte on Pilot Island, October 28, 29, 30, 1892, July 29 and October 31, 1893. List of Merchant Vessels of the U.S., 1888, p 54. Arthur and Evelyn Knudsen, A Gleam Across the Wave: The Biography of Martin Nicolai Knudsen, Lighthouse Keeper on Lake Michigan, p. 58-63. U. S. Government Printing Office, Medal of Honor Recipients 1863 - 1978, Washington, D.C., 1979, p. 7-10. Edward F. Murphy, Secretary of the Medal of Honor Historical Society, Mesa Arizona, telephone interview, October 13, 1996.

204) *Petrel*, #19665, Schooner, Stranded November 5, 1892.

The DOOR COUNTY ADVOCATE in its November 12, 1892 issue reported, "The little schooner *Petrel* is no more, having become wrecked at Monument Pt. near the mouth of Sturgeon Bay, while laying at Anderson's pier. She was valued at $1,000. No insurance." The schooner was built in 1864 at Pultneyville, New York. She measured 47.71 gross tons, 79 feet in length, 15 feet at the beam, and 5 feet in depth. List of Merchant Vessels of the U.S., 1888, p. 208,

205) *Veto*, #25966, Schooner, Stranded November 15, 1892 (approximately).

The Veto dragged her anchor and went ashore at Egg Harbor. Captain Kirkland and the schooner's crew barely escaped drowning inside. The vessel which hailed from Egg Harbor, was a total wreck. She was built there in 1879 and registered 56 gross tons, measuring 92 feet in length, 16 feet in the beam, and 5 feet in depth. DOOR COUNTY ADVOCATE, November 26, 1892. List of Merchant Vessels of the U.S., 1888, p. 288.

206) *J.K. Stack*, #75805, Schooner, Foundered April 12, 1893.

The *Stack* was one of three vessels wintering at Eagle Harbor in Ephraim. A west wind moved a sheet of ice crushing the little schooner. The other vessels, the *Jenny* and the *Ebeneezer* were also damaged but not so severely that they couldn't be fixed. The *Stack* was owned by Henry Amundson and registered 12.9 gross tons. She was built in Escanaba in 1875. Door County Advocate, April 12, 1893. List of Merchant Vessels of the U.S., 1884, p. 161.

207) *Sassacus*, #22916, Scow, Stranded September 29, 1893.

The *Sassacus*, loaded with cordwood, had originally gone ashore at Jacksonport in a gale. Four sailors on board suffered from exposure before they were rescued by a Jacksonport fishing boat. A week later, a salvage expedition arrived from Sturgeon Bay to recover the vessel. The cordwood was jettisoned to make room for a steam pump. The hull was pumped out and, by the following Sunday, pulled off the shore. While under tow to Sturgeon Bay, the *Sassacus'* towing hawser snapped. Through the day, the seas worsened and at times the vessel was submerged by the waves. The salvage crew on board was taken off moments before the wreck careened, filled with water and rolled over. Two more efforts were made to get her back in tow but she was eventually abandoned. The hulk ultimately washed ashore near at a point between Lily Bay and the canal and became a total wreck. By December of 1896, the weather had pushed the scow so high on shore and so deeply into the sand that the seas had no effect on her.

One story states that the *Sassacus* was valued at $1,000 and owned by George W. Wing of Kewaunee. However, it was Captain William H. McDonald who brought suit against the tug owner for negligence. The Door County Advocate explained that "Captain McDonald has his all invested in the craft and as there is not a dollar of insurance on the vessel, the loss is a particularly severe one on him. She stood him $2,700 at the moment she went ashore."

The case went to circuit court in Sturgeon Bay in January, 1896. When the court decided in favor of the defendants, McDonald renewed the case in Federal District court in Milwaukee. There, the jury decided that because the tow line was the property of the vessel in tow, the tug owner could not be held liable for its parting.

In 1917 the barge *City of Glasgow* blew ashore a number of miles north of the canal in Lily Bay. The DOOR COUNTY ADVOCATE pointed out that she was "right out from where the old *Sassacus* went ashore some twenty years ago, her wreckage being still in evidence on the beach."

The *Sassacus* was built at Oswego, New York, in 1867. She registered 109 gross ton with a length of 94.7 feet, a beam of 22.3 feet and a depth of 6.7 feet. DOOR COUNTY ADVOCATE, October 14, November 11, 1893. DOOR COUNTY ADVOCATE, January 30, 1896. KEWAUNEE ENTERPRISE, February 28, 1896. DOOR COUNTY ADVOCATE, October 11, 1917. List of Merchant Vessels of the U.S., 1888, p. 226.

208) *Margaret A. Muir*, #90459, Schooner, Foundered September 30, 1893.

The *Muir* was bound from Bay City, Michigan, to Chicago with 4,375 barrels of salt. She encountered a wild gale and, being so heavily laden, labored in the high waves which eventually opened her seams according to early reports. She sank in seventy feet of water, approximately three miles from Ahnapee. The crew was able to launch the life boat and escape the sinking vessel. They made land near Ahnapee where they were cared for by the residents.

Her captain, David Clow, was able to relate this story to a reporter from the KEWAUNEE ENTERPRISE.

"When the gale struck us, we were in the middle of the lake sailing southward and westward for the west shore of the lake. The wind continued to blow harder by the hour all

Friday night but our boat did fairly well and frequent trials at the pump showed that no water was coming into her hold. Early Saturday morning the schooner got into the trough of the sea. Huge mountains of water fell on her deck. I do not think she foundered from any water that came through except that which fell on the deck. I rushed aft and began cutting and slashing to get the lifeboat free. We didn't lose a minute's time and had just gotten into the boat when the schooner keeled over and filled our lifeboat with water. Fortunately it was not capsized and we succeeded in bailing it out. We were about four miles from shore and had several narrow escapes from drowning on the way in. In getting through the breakers it seemed as if every man must be drowned, but luck was with us and we all got on the beach in safety. The loss of the Muir *was not caused by any leak. I am certain of that for we tried the pump just before she went down. We were simply engulfed by water and drowned out like rats in a hole."*

The crew lost everything except what they had on and the Captain's dog went down with the vessel. Clow lost $125 which had been left behind in a bureau drawer on board ship. This and other items washed ashore about two miles north of Ahnapee, but the money was lost.

The following summer, the government tug, *Lorena* was called to Ahnapee to remove a submerged obstacle. It proved to be a portion of the hull of the *Muir*. It was disposed of by the tug.

The *Muir* was owned by Muir and Clow and hailed from Chicago. She was valued at $6,000 and insured for $4,000. She registered 347.44 gross tons, measured 128.6 feet in length, 26.2 feet across the beam and 11.5 feet in depth.

KEWAUNEE ENTERPRISE, October 6, 1893. DOOR COUNTY ADVOCATE, October 7, October 21, 1893. DOOR COUNTY ADVOCATE, July 2, 1894. List of Merchant Vessels of the U.S., 1888, p. 180.

209) *Windsor*, #62523, Schooner, Stranded September 30, 1893.

The *Windsor* was cedar laden and Chicago bound when somewhere off Ahnapee she developed a leak. She set off for North Bay but when off Cana Island became helpless. She ran for shore shortly thereafter and hit the rocks where she capsized on a bearing of 135°, approximately 1,200 feet from the island. The crew was unable to reach dry ground through the surf and the lifesaving crew at Sturgeon Bay was sent for.

Owing to the fact that the weather was rough and the distance so great, the lifesaving crew loaded the boat, Lyle gun and other equipment on to wagons which were in turn loaded on to the government tug, *Dionne*, and freighted to the city. Horses were procured and the thirty mile trip begun. The wagons were too wide for the narrow road north to Jacksonport making the journey a difficult one. The lifeboat had been punctured by a tree limb and when a line was shot out to the *Windsor*, strong currents dragged away the line and projectile and would have pulled in the Lyle gun had it not been cut free. Dark of night prevented an accurate shot to the vessel. The surf boat was given some hasty repairs and the lifesaving crew rowed out to the *Windsor* and rescued the crewmen.

One crewman from the *Windsor* was lost just before she hit the shore. His body was found in Mud Bay (now Moonlight Bay) several months later and interred in a local cemetery.

The *Windsor* was valued at $5,000 and insured for $3,000. She was built at Detroit in 1856 and measured 237.84 tons with a length 114. 7 feet, a beam of 30 feet and a depth of 9.4 feet. (See also, *E.P. Royce*, #213.) DOOR COUNTY ADVOCATE, October 7, 1893. List of Merchant Vessels of the U.S., 1888, p. 256.

210) *C.L. Fellows*, Tug, Foundered September 30, 1893.

The *Fellows* had been launched a day before by her owner, Captain C.L. Fellows at Foscoro. She was anchored off shore when a storm came up leaving her to pound on the bottom. Eventually she broke her moorings and sank. The tug had been reconstructed from the hull of the tug, *Tillinghost* of Marinette, and was valued at $3,000. Late reports described her on the shore at Stoney Creek.

By August of 1895, Fellows gave up hope of recovering his vessel and left her to be a total loss. DOOR COUNTY ADVOCATE, October 7, 1893. DOOR COUNTY ADVOCATE, August 31, 1895.

211) *Willard A. Smith*, #80587, Schooner, Foundered October 14, 1893.

The *Smith* had been moored at Anderson's Pier at Horseshoe Bay where she had taken on a load of wood. Her captain, Hans Peterson, had an anchor set to windward in addition to her mooring lines. When a storm came up, the vessel began to pound on the rocks. When the wind changed, Peterson climbed on to the pier and cut the mooring lines only to have the ship swing away from the pier leaving him behind. It became apparent that the *Smith* would not last and the captain, with the assistance of Captain Anderson, launched a small boat to rescue the crew. The two were capsized but were able to reach shore safely. Anderson set out a second time, this time successfully reaching the schooner and rescuing the crew. The schooner pounded to pieces, and with her cargo, became a total loss. Neither was insured.

The *Willard Smith* was a small vessel registering 44.22 gross tons with a length of 65 feet, a beam of 16.6 feet, and a depth of six feet. She was built at Charlevoix, Michigan, in 1875. DOOR COUNTY ADVOCATE, October 21, 1875. List of Merchant Vessels of the U.S., 1888, p. 250.

145

212) *J.A. Travis*, #13862, Schooner, Stranded November 18, 1893.

The *J.A. Travis* was outward bound from Ellison Bay with a load of wood, potatoes and other farm products for Milwaukee. Coming into the lake, she found such heavy seas that Captain Albert Icke ordered her brought about for North Bay. She missed stays and went up on the rocky reef off North Point. Observers on shore sent a message for the Sturgeon Bay lifesaving crew who journeyed north and rescued the five sailors on board. The cargo was lost.

Prior to their being called to Ellison Bay, the lifesaving crew had been up all night for a rescue of the *Rising Star* at Ahnapee. That call proved to be a false alarm.

Captain Icke ordered the vessel stripped of her outfit some of which was sent to Milwaukee and the rest being stored at North Bay. After 41 years on the lakes and the oceans, Icke decided to give up the merchant marine after the wreck of the *Travis*, presumably to devote his time to his pier, store, and cheese factory at Ellison Bay.

The *Travis* was a relatively old vessel but had been rebuilt and was thought to be in good condition. However, within two weeks the main mast had gone by the board and other parts of her above the decks were expected to follow anytime. She was still in the same position off North Bay where the storm had left her. The *J.A. Travis* was built at Pentwater, Michigan, in 1867. She registered 101.28 tons with a length of 106 feet, a beam of 20 feet, and a depth of six feet. KEWAUNEE ENTERPRISE, November 24, 1893. DOOR COUNTY ADVOCATE, November 25, December 9, 16, 1893. List of Merchant Vessels of the U.S., 1888, p. 144.

213) *E.P. Royce*, #8912, Schooner, Stranded November 25, 1893.

The *E.P. Royce* had been brought to Cana Island to salvage the cargo of cedar ties and posts from the wreck of the *Windsor*. When high winds came up, she was driven on the shore just south of Cana Island at Little Harbor. The crew was saved.

The *Royce* was left at the mercy of winter storms and ice. A correspondent from Baileys Harbor wrote to the ADVOCATE that every time an easterly or southeasterly wind came up, cedar in the *Royce's* hull washed out and was carried away. The newspaper proclaimed that "no effort will be made to get either the *Royce* or the *Windsor* afloat again." In spite of the efforts of wind and wave to empty her hull, the *Royce* still contained a sizable quantity of cedar. Observers speculated that the wreck, which was surrounded by ice, would wash out into the lake with the first offshore breeze.

In June, the schooner, *H. Badger*, was able to take the remaining ties off the *Royce* and deliver them to Chicago and by August, Captain Thomas Wilson brought the schooner *D.L. Filer* up to the wreck site to remove the remaining rigging "...masts, topmasts, yards, sails, square sails, blocks and ropes to match besides a lot of other rigging" and brought it to Sturgeon Bay.

The *E.P. Royce* was named for Eli Parsons Royce, an attorney and pioneer resident of Escanaba. She was built at Sac Bay, Michigan, in 1873, measured 249.29 gross tons and was valued at $4,000. She was owned by Martin McNulty of Chicago and was uninsured. The schooner was 124 feet in length, 29 feet at the beam, and 8.8 feet in depth. DOOR COUNTY ADVOCATE, December 2, 16, 1893. DOOR COUNTY ADVOCATE, January 6, February 10, 17, June 9, August 25, 1894. List of Merchant Vessels of the U.S., 1888, p. 97.

214) *South Side*, #115334, Scow-Schooner, Foundered December 9, 1893.

The *South Side* had taken on a cargo of Christmas trees and ties at Newport. Having left that port, she fought rough weather and was forced to take shelter in the lee of Plum Island for several days before heading for Milwaukee. On her way south, the schooner sprang a leak and was taken in to Baileys Harbor where she settled on the bottom. No tugs were still in commission for the season and she was left. A week or so later, the steam barge, *Rudolph*, attempted to salvage the scow but could do nothing and abandoned it.

By the end of January, the *South Side* began to break up and her cargo of ties floated away. Within two weeks she broke in two amidships and the main mast "went by the board."

There are conflicting stories on the scow's ownership. One story has the vessel and ties owned by Theodore Plathner and the trees owned by Captain Morbeck. Still another story explains that the *South Side* was purchased, but not paid for, by Morbeck and the original owners were Johnson & Knudson of Newport.

The *South Side* was built in Milwaukee in 1867. She measured 139.75 gross tons, with a length of 101 feet, a beam of 25 feet, and a depth of 5 feet. DOOR COUNTY ADVOCATE, December 16, 23, 1893. DOOR COUNTY ADVOCATE, February 3, 17, 1894. List of Merchant Vessels of the U.S., 1888, p. 230.

215) *City of Marinette*, Schooner, Stranded May 11, 1894.

The *Marinette* was blown on the beach south of Clay Banks by a northeaster. She was abandoned with her canvas still set and was described as having been left lying on a sandy bottom and was high and dry with damage. The vessel was owned by Chris Braunsdorf.

The following September, the DOOR COUNTY ADVOCATE reported "The old Schooner *City of Marinette*, which is lying on the beach in a water logged condition up at the head of the bay, is going to rack and ruin. The canvas still remains secured to the masts and booms. The *Marinette* was beached early in the summer, shortly after she had been released from the shore on the other side of Clay Banks where she was driven in a northeaster of May." The *Marinette* had also been driven ashore at Ephraim some years before. DOOR COUNTY ADVOCATE, November 26, 1887. DOOR COUNTY ADVOCATE, May 19, September 8, 1894.

216) Unnamed Fishing Vessel, Foundered July 20, 1894.

This vessel was thought to have been lost somewhere in the Bay with Charles I. Martin, a prominent stockman, and two companions. A strong northerly blow was prevailing at the time.

Martin had missed the steamer to Sturgeon Bay and hired two Menominee fishermen to take him across the Bay. None of them was ever seen again. According to an article in the DOOR COUNTY ADVOCATE, the boat was 28 feet long, 8 1/4 feet across the beam "and those who know the craft say she is a brand new boat and as staunch and seaworthy as any afloat on Green Bay." Local tug and steamers began searching the Bay. Rumors circulated that the fishermen had killed Martin for his money belt and dumped him over board and disappeared. Others said Martin had suffered from a "temporary mental aberration produced by worry and business cares, and that he was put ashore and is wandering about aimlessly." The beaches from Sturgeon Bay to Little Sturgeon were searched but no trace was found. Martin's relatives and friends offered $100 for information leading to the recovery of the body.

In late August of 1894, the tug *Mosher* with Captain Walker in command, began a systematic dragging operation looking for Martin, the fishermen and their boat. The captain was to receive $500 if he found them. Walker and his crew claimed to have seen the sailboat when she went down, having been three miles away at the time. They located a range from two mill stacks in Menominee and figured that the sailboat could not have been more than a mile from the government pier at the time.

In the spring of 1902, Captain Thomas Isabell, who was looking for the boiler from the *A.W. Lawrence* at the time, located an old pound net boat of large size with an exceptionally heavy mast. Isabell believed it was the vessel Martin had sailed in.

The following September, the bones of a man found washed up on Green Island were thought, by west shore papers, to be that of Charles Martin. This was considered a weak theory, because the two men with him were never found. The DOOR COUNTY ADVOCATE maintained, that because the skeleton seemed to be about ten years old, they might have been the remains of Hans Larson, a fisherman who disappeared in 1892. In addition to being a recognized business and civic leader, Martin wrote one of the early histories of Door County and was publisher of the STURGEON BAY EXPOSITOR. DOOR COUNTY ADVOCATE, July 28, September 1, 1894. DOOR COUNTY ADVOCATE, September 28, 1901. DOOR COUNTY ADVOCATE, May 3, 1902.

217) *L. May Guthrie*, #48476, Schooner, Stranded September 26, 1894.

The *Guthrie* was bound for Milwaukee with a load of bark when she was driven aground on Fisherman's Shoal in the early hours of that day. The waves were mountainous and were washing completely over the ship. The tug *Truscott* from Detroit Harbor, attempted to rescue Captain A.G. Brown and his four crewmen aboard the stricken vessel, but the waves were so overwhelming and the water around the wreck was too shallow. This was compounded by the fact that neither the tug nor the *Guthrie* had a small boat.

The rescue had to be postponed till the following day when the seas had lessened. Even then it took two tries before a small boat could be floated out to the schooner.

Detroit Harbor residents, Matt Foss, Henry Foss, and Thomas Johnson were assisted in the rescue by the *Truscott* and its owner, J.W. Cornell, Captain Peter Jordan, and crewmen, James L. Azone and Paul Z. Cornell.

The vessel was declared a total wreck and equipment was removed. The cargo of bark was salvaged.

The *Guthrie* was built in Conneaut, Ohio, in 1874. She measured 137.84 net tons with a length of 102 feet, 24 feet in breadth and seven feet in depth. DOOR COUNTY ADVOCATE, October 6, 13, November 17, 1894. List of Merchant Vessels of the U.S., 1888, p. 163.

218) *Maggie Johnson*, #90789, Schooner, Abandoned February, 1895.

The *Johnson* had been wintering at Kewaunee and her owner, Captain Frank Morris, had her stripped of all nautical paraphernalia and planned to pull her up on the beach and let the seas break her up. She was built in White Lake, Michigan, in 1875 and measured 27.33 gross tons. DOOR COUNTY ADVOCATE, February 23, 1895. List of Merchant Vessels of the U.S., 1884, p. 194.

219) *J.H. Johnson*, #76340, Steambarge, Stranded May 1, 1895.

The *Johnson* was bound for Manistique with a cargo of hay and bricks when she ran up on a rock the DOOR COUNTY ADVOCATE described as 40' by 22'..."It is only about four feet below the surface while all around it there is fully four times as much water." She then filled with water. The ADVOCATE stated that "The vessel ran ashore on a shoal in line with the Sister Island and Horseshoe Island about midway between Eagle Harbor and Sister Bay." Within three weeks, the steamer had broken up. The cargo of hay and the cabin washed ashore. The cabin remained intact and all the articles left inside stayed as they were when it ran aground. Nothing was left of the hull that could be seen. The engine and boiler were recovered that summer by the steam barge, *Imperial*, with Captain Charles Peok providing services as a diver.

The *Johnson* was valued at $3,000. She registered 52 gross tons and was built in St. Joseph, Michigan, in 1882. The hull measured 98.5 feet in length with a beam of 16.3 feet and a depth of four feet. DOOR COUNTY ADVOCATE, May 18, July 6, 1895. DOOR COUNTY ADVOCATE, January 11, 1896. List of Merchant Vessel of the U.S., 1888, p. 297.

220) *J. Evenson*, #76523, Tug, Foundered June 5, 1895.

The *Evenson* was attempting to take the steam barge, *I. W. Stephenson* in tow southeast of the Sturgeon Bay canal. The tug came around the barge to pass a tow line and as the *Evenson* passed in front of the steamer, her stern caught under the bow of the *Evenson*. Trapped by the thrust of the larger steamer, the tug swung around, careened, filled with water and sank. Martin Boswell*, ship's fireman, was alerted by the steward, Cyrus La Plant. Boswell tried to crawl out through the coal scuttle but was pushed back by the water pressure. Also on board were Captain John M. Laurie, engineer Ashley Cofrin and second mate Charles Risteau. All were sucked under by the undertow of the sinking tug and all popped back to the surface. Only Boswell was drowned. His body was recovered in mid-July and interred in the Ahnapee Public Cemetery.

The crew was picked up by the *Stephenson* but lost all their belongings. The *Stephenson* had been towing the barges, *Peshtigo* and *Alert* at the time. The *Evenson* was returning from Manitowoc and had stayed out in the lake to wait for a towing job.

Different news articles give conflicting descriptions of the location. The DOOR COUNTY ADVOCATE states that the vessel went down five miles north of Ahnapee off Stoney

Creek, four miles from shore in 15 fathoms of water, and a later story from the same newspaper changes the location to 80 feet of water off Foscoro, six miles north of Ahnapee. There was only 36 feet of water reported over her. The MENOMINEE DEMOCRAT and the KEWAUNEE ENTERPRISE agree on three miles off Stoney Creek in 102 to 132 feet of water. The MENOMINEE HERALD says ten fathoms.

Captain Alex Laurie had initially decided that raising the tug would be too expensive, however two years later made an effort only to decide once again that the project would wait till the following year. The *Evenson* was later dropped from the government listing.

The *John Evenson*, as she was commonly referred to, was owned by the Laurie brothers. She was valued at $4,500 but was insured for only $3,800 and that for fire, not for collision. The tug was built in Milwaukee in 1884 and registered 16.37 net tons. She measured 54.2 feet in length, 13.8 feet across the beam and 7.1 foot in depth. *Reported in some papers as "Martin Bershway." AHNAPEE RECORD, June 6, 1895. DOOR COUNTY ADVOCATE, June 8, 15, 1895. MENOMINEE DEMOCRAT, June 8, 15, 1895. MENOMINEE HERALD, June 7, 1895. KEWAUNEE ENTERPRISE, June 14, 1895. DOOR COUNTY ADVOCATE, January 11, 1896. DOOR COUNTY ADVOCATE, August 21, 28, 1897. List of Merchant Vessels of the U.S., 1888, p. 297.

221) *Mariner*, #16423, Schooner, Stranded July 10, 1895.

The *Mariner* was on her way from Menominee to Kewaunee with a load of lumber when she became water logged. Her cargo was transferred to the schooner *Lady Ellen* and the hulk cast ashore on Green Island. The *Mariner's* deck had to be pulled off to get the cargo out. When the lumber was removed the hull proved to be so rotten that she would not hold together. Only the rigging was thought to be of any value. The vessel was owned by Frank Morris of Kewaunee who replaced the *Mariner* with the steamer *M & M*.

The *Mariner* was built at Ohio City, Ohio, in 1854 and measured 30.64 gross tons. She measured 52 feet in length, 15 feet across the beam and 5 feet in depth. AHNAPEE RECORD, July 18, 1895. KEWAUNEE ENTERPRISE, July 19, 1895. DOOR COUNTY ADVOCATE, July 20, 1895. KEWAUNEE ENTERPRISE, August 2, 1895.

222) *Ira Chaffee*, #12131, Steambarge, Abandoned at an unknown time.

The *Chaffee* had burned in the Soo area in the early 1890s and was brought to Sturgeon Bay to have her engine and boiler removed. She was pushed up on the north end of Dunlap Reef and left to the elements. When a storm rolled in over the Bay in May of 1895, the DOOR COUNTY ADVOCATE illustrated the ferocity of the blow by pointing out that waves were making a "clean sweep" over the *Chaffee*. In November of 1902, the boiler was removed and taken to a quarry at the mouth of the Bay where it would furnish steam for a rock crushing outfit.

The *Ira Chaffee* was built in 1867 at Allegan, Michigan. She measured 193.62 gross tons, 127 feet in length, 25 feet in the beam, and 8 feet in depth. DOOR COUNTY ADVOCATE, August 4, 1894. DOOR COUNTY ADVOCATE, June 1, 1895. DOOR COUNTY ADVOCATE, November 22, 1902. List of Merchant Vessels of the U.S, 1884, p. 317.

223) *E.R. Williams*, #8987, Schooner, Foundered September 21, 1895.

The *Williams* was in tow with the barges, *Teutonia* and *Thomas Gawn*, behind the steam barge *Santa Maria* bound from Escanaba with iron ore. The entourage had come to anchor off St. Martin's Island to wait out a storm. Early the next morning the *Williams* sprang a leak and in five minutes had three feet of water in her hold. The ship's yawl was lowered and the crew of seven and the ship's dog no more than cleared the gunwale when the *Williams* broke in two and sank in twenty fathoms of water.

Crewmembers on board the *Santa Maria* could see the schooner's light until about 9 p.m. Shortly after that the tow line parted and the schooner disappeared in the darkness. The *Santa Maria* cruised around for some time looking for the missing schooner, but it was not until daylight that they discovered the *Williams'* masts sticking out of the water.

The crew of the *Williams* had to row through a roaring gale and threw cups of oil on the water to fight the big waves. This was credited with saving the yawl from being swamped. The crewmembers ultimately found safety at Big Summer Island. They were picked up the next day by the steam yacht *Osceola* and taken to Manistique.

The *Williams* was—and, for that matter, still is—loaded with 570 tons of iron ore consigned to Toledo. She was built at that port in 1873 and was valued at $2,000. The vessel measured 293.64 gross tons with a length of 137.2 feet, a beam of 26 feet and a depth of 11.6 feet. Door County Advocate, September 22, 1895. Kewaunee Enterprise, September 27, 1895. List of Merchant Vessels of the U.S., 1888, p. 97.

224) *Otter*, #19125, Schooner, Stranded October 9, 1895.

The *Otter* was driven ashore in a gale at Whitefish bay. She had taken on 130 cords of wood at Moshek's pier the day before and was pulled out in to the bay to weather the storm. At 8 a.m. the next morning she broke her anchor line and went ashore "nearly opposite the mill." The life-saving service brought their gear from Sturgeon Bay on horse drawn wagons and used a breeches buoy to rescue the eleven men on board. The crew lost everything except their clothing. When weather conditions permitted, the ship was stripped of all equipment and cargo. The vessel went to pieces shortly thereafter. Weeks later part of the stern washed on the beach. By the end of 1896, no trace of the vessel was visible anywhere near the shore.

The *Otter* was valued at $1,500 and was owned by a Mr. Ceaser of Chicago who also owned the cargo. William Kaufman was captain. She was built at Freeport, Ohio, in 1863 and measured 205 gross tons with a length of 105.4 feet in length, 25.9 feet across the beam, and 11.6 feet in depth. DOOR COUNTY ADVOCATE, October 12, 1895. DOOR COUNTY ADVOCATE, January 4, 18, 1896. List of Merchant Vessels of the U.S., 1888, p. 205.

225) *Venture*, #25849, Schooner, Stranded October 11, 1895.

The *Venture* had been driven ashore at Big Bay De Noquette and was scuttled to prevent her from pounding, however, nothing else is known of her disposition. She was built at Green Bay in 1869 and was owned by Captain Mitchell of De Pere. While a vessel of this age usually did not survive such difficult circumstances, the ship was not listed in the DOOR COUNTY ADVOCATE's annual list of shipping losses. The *Venture* measured 101 gross tons with a length of 101 feet, a 19 foot beam and a depth of 6 feet. DOOR COUNTY ADVOCATE, October 19, 1895. DOOR COUNTY ADVOCATE, January 11, 1896. List of Merchant Vessels of the U.S., 1888, p. 243.

226) *Mystic*, #17210, Schooner, Stranded October 15, 1895.

The *Mystic* was on her way to Little Bay De Noc to load Christmas trees when she ran hard aground on Pilot Island. The logbook of the Porte Des Morte lighthouse shows this entry: "S.W. moderate (winds) to fresh to gale at eve...A steamer nearly got on S. end of Pilot Island at 11 p.m. and a schooner did strand at that point at 12:20 midnight." The lighthouse staff helped get the ship's crew and their belongings ashore by line the next day, and over the next two weeks provided accommodations for the stranded sailors. The lighthouse staff also helped retrieve the ship's equipment and packed it off to Chicago on the schooner *Filer*. The sailors were provided passage on the steamer, *M&M.*

Captain Henry Schuenemann, who had chartered her for the Christmas tree trade, reported that the vessel was a total wreck. The *Mystic's* green hull and white bulwarks would be left to decorate the shoals of Pilot Island. Schuenemann said the stern of the ship was badly broken up and while her bow was in good condition, the ship was exposed to stormy weather from the east.

The *Mystic* was valued at $2,500 and hailed from Chicago. She was built in Milan, Ohio, in 1866 and measured 161.53 gross tons with a length of 112.5 feet, 25.7 feet across the beam and 8.4 feet in depth. DOOR COUNTY ADVOCATE, October 26, November 9, 1895. DOOR COUNTY ADVOCATE, January 11, 1896. Log Book of the Porte Des Morte Lighthouse on Pilot Island, October 15, 1895 - December 15, 1895. List of Merchant Vessels of the U.S., 1888, p. 197.

227) *Red, White and Blue*, #21301, Schooner, Stranded October 12, 1895.

The *Red, White and Blue* was in tow of the steamer *Otego*, bound for Green Bay with a load of coal from Toledo when both vessels "fetched up" on Whale Back Shoal. The *Otego* was able to work herself loose but her consort was hard aground. The tug *Charnley* went to the assistance of the schooner and found her three feet out of the water at the bow with sixteen feet of water below her stern. The vessel seemed to be in good condition and the tug returned to port for a steam pump. With some effort a pump was procured from Seoul Choix Bay and put to work. The water in the hold was brought down 18 inches until the pump broke. Another pump was sent up from Milwaukee. The steamer *M&M* was sent to Escanaba for still another pump but when she arrived back on the scene the *Red, White and Blue* had already started to break up. She was stripped of all useful equipment. Efforts were made to recover the coal, but the vessel had been sitting on the shoal so long, most of the cargo had been pilfered by fishing tugs. Only six tons were recovered from the original 800 tons of coal. The schooner was valued at $5,000. She was built in Madison Dock, Ohio, in 1863 and registered 447.34 gross tons. DOOR COUNTY ADVOCATE, October 19, 26, November 23, 1895. DOOR COUNTY ADVOCATE, January 11, 1896. List of Merchant Vessels of the U.S., 1884, p. 234.

228) *Mattie C. Bell*, #91420, Schooner, Stranded November 27, 1895.

The *Bell* went ashore on Summer Island with her escort, the steamer *James Sherriffs* in a snow storm. Both crews escaped to the island where they were rescued by the tug *Anabel*. The schooner rested on a bed of boulders which had penetrated her bottom. She was heading southeast in the bay, on the east side of the island and north of the east point with her starboard side to the island in about seven feet of water. There was nine feet of water on the port side.

The *Mattie C. Bell* was double decked and loaded with 900 tons of nut coal, of which 300 tons were between decks. Area fish tugs took her coal from between decks as well as the "outfit"...boiler fittings, pumps, rigging, and cabin fixtures. Efforts were made by the wrecking tug *Wright* to release her. The salvors heeled her over, pulled out the boulders, and using the main, mizzen and stay sails, wrapped her underside in a canvas jacket. She was raised, pumped out and put on stone abutments but the *Wright* could not move her from her resting place 200 feet from shore. The Steamer *Joseph L. Hurd* also assisted and only succeeded in losing her anchor and 20 fathoms of cable. After 72 days on the project she was abandoned. The *Bell* was stripped of both anchors, (2,200 lb. and 1,700 lb.) 120 fathoms of cable, her yawl, light spars, steering gear, windlass, etc. One hundred and fifty tons of coal was also clammed out of the hold.

The *Mattie Bell* was valued at $10,000 and measured 769.98 gross tons. She was a large schooner at 181 feet in length, with a beam of 35.4 feet and a depth of 11.5 feet. She was built in Saginaw, Michigan, in 1882. DOOR COUNTY ADVOCATE, November 30, December 14, 1895. DOOR COUNTY ADVOCATE, January 11, June 27, July 4, August 1, September 12, 1896. List of Merchant Vessels of the U.S., 1888, p. 190.

229) Railroad Cars, Lost over board January 10, 1896.

The *Ann Arbor Ferry #1* was an hour out of Kewaunee on her way to Frankfort, Michigan, when she was struck by huge waves. Seven railroad cars out of her compliment of 24 were washed overboard. One rail car washed ashore at Lily Bay six miles east of Sturgeon Bay. Weeks later, sacks of flour that had been loaded in the cars were washing ashore in the same spot. The loss was estimated at $50,000 and the cargo was uninsured. The remaining cars were found cast up on an island at the north end of Lake Michigan minus their running gear, in February of that year.

Later the KEWAUNEE ENTERPRISE reported:

"At Owosso, Michigan, a ton of butter was recently delivered to the Dudley Creamery on account of the Ann Arbor Railway Company. The butter had washed ashore from the cars lost by the ferry steamer No. 1 *in Lake Michigan. It was in excellent condition. The company settled with the Minnesota consignees for 10,000 pounds of butter at 23 cents a pound."* DOOR COUNTY ADVOCATE, January 18, February 1, 22, 1896. KEWAUNEE ENTERPRISE, March 6, 1896.

230) *Odin*, #18966, Schooner, Scrapped January 1896.

Captain Louis Olson decided that the vessel had become an old hulk. She was pulled up on shore and broken up for fire wood. No details were given as to where this took place. The *Odin* was built at Milwaukee in 1853 and measured 120.74 gross tons. Door County Advocate, January 4, 1896. List of Merchant Vessels of the U.S., 1884, p. 221.

231) *Emeline*, #7492, Schooner, Capsized August 8, 1896.

The *Emeline* had been bound for Kenosha with a load of tan bark from Charlevoix, Michigan. When off Baileys Harbor, she was struck by a squall and knocked over on her starboard side. Her deckload rolled off and she righted herself only to capsize to portside. The crew was able to save themselves by launching the yawl boat and rowing to Baileys Harbor. The tug *Sydney Smith* was sent out the next day and towed her into Baileys Harbor. An attempt was made to right her by pulling on the mast but this only broke the mast. The schooner *Nancy Dell* was used to right her but she rolled over again that night. The schooner was left in the mud off Anclam's Pier in 21 feet of water. Only her gunwales and spars showed above the surface.

The *Emeline* was commanded and owned by Captain A. Abrahamson who had saved the $1,500 to buy her by working aboard other vessels. The insurance brokers considered her a bad risk and the vessel was not covered. After the accident, Abrahamson sold her to the Brann brothers for $15 — enough to pay train fare back home to Chicago. The crew was left to fend for themselves.

By January of 1897, the wreck had broken in two. The forward section remained where it was, the stern section 600 feet north working its way ashore. It sat 400 feet west of the range light, in 19 feet of water.

In 1903, Captain Thomas Isabell retrieved the anchors from the wreck. The old schooner was subsequently dynamited as a menace to navigation.

The *Emeline* was built in Detroit in 1864 and measured 127 gross tons, with a length of 111 feet, a beam of 22 feet, and a depth of 7 feet. Door County Advocate, August 15, August 22, 1896. Door County Advocate, January 9, 1897. Door County Advocate, September 5, 1903. List of Merchant Vessels of the U.S., 1896, p. 56.

232) *Grace Williams*, #85882, Steamer, Foundered May 28, 1896.

The *Grace Williams* had recently been purchased by Joseph LeClaire, Joseph Harrington and Albert Mann of Two Rivers and was being towed to that port from Sutton's Bay, Michigan, when she and her tug encountered a gale. The *Williams* began to yaw causing her tow line to part. Shortly thereafter, she sank in 45 fathoms of water. The accident reportedly occurred midway between Manitou Island and the west shore.

The *Grace Williams* was built in Manitowoc in 1885 and measured 46 net tons. She had a length of 48 feet, a beam of 12 feet, and a depth of 5 feet. She was valued at $5,000 and was uninsured. Kewaunee Enterprise, June 5, 1896. List of Merchant Vessels of the U.S., 1896, 251.

233) *Fountain City*, #9680, Steam Barge, Foundered May 5, 1896.

Gutted by fire the vessel was pulled in to shallows of Sturgeon Bay and left in the boneyard. Her boiler was ruined and her owners were giving thought to turning her into a barge but that never came about. The *Fountain City* was at one time a proud passenger and packet steamer valued at $40,000. She was built in Cleveland, Ohio, in 1857 for B.F. Davidson and measured 630 gross tons with a length of 210, a beam of 30 feet, and a depth of 12 feet. Door County Advocate, May 16, 1896. List of Merchant Vessels of the U.S., 1888, p. 286. Beeson's Marine Directory, 1896, p. 47. Herman G. Runge Collection of the Milwaukee Public Library/Wisconsin Marine Historical

234) *Kate Hinchman*, #14036, Abandoned September 1896.

She was allowed to sink in the "marine cemetery" in Sturgeon Bay with her decks awash. The following month the *Hinchman* was temporarily taken out of retirement, pumped out and put to work hauling Christmas trees. She was later returned to the boneyard and laid there until the spring of 1903 when she was taken to the mouth of Sturgeon Bay where she was to be sunk for use as a dock for Thomas Smith. The *Hinchman* registered 236 gross tons and had a length of 116 feet, a beam of 26 feet, and a depth of 11 feet. DOOR COUNTY ADVOCATE, September 26, October 31, 1896. DOOR COUNTY ADVOCATE, May 2, 1903. List of Merchant Vessels of the U.S., 1888, p. 160.

235) *Australasia*, #106302, Steamer, Burned October 18, 1896.

The *Australasia* was bound from Cleveland for Manitowoc with 2200 tons of soft coal. She was off Baileys Harbor about 8 p.m. that evening when the ship was found to be on fire. Instead of making an effort to fight the fire, the crew, some of whom were about to sit down for dinner, lowered the jolly boat and abandoned the vessel.

Two hours later, the tug *Leathem* came upon the scene. A boarding party found the dinner and ate a quick meal before going out to inspect the fire. A line was made fast to the steamer and she was taken in tow towards the canal. With the the rudder left hard aport, the vessel did not tow well and the towline burned away eight times. Captain James Tufts, of the *Leathem*, realized that the ship was settling deeper in the water. Fearing she would founder before he could get her to port, Tufts rammed the *Australasia* into

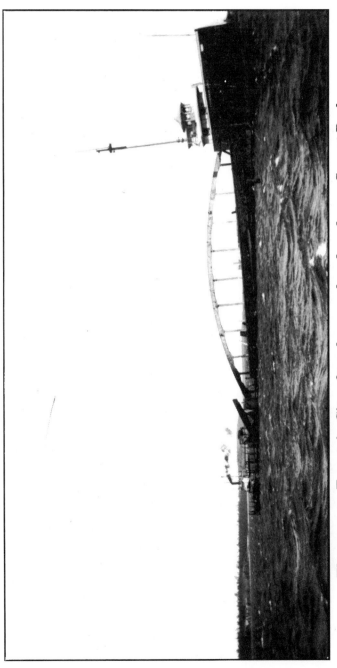

The steamer Fountain City after she was abandoned near Sunset Park.

Photo courtesy of the Wisconsin Maritime Museum, Manitowoc, Wisconsin

the beach south of Cave Point, then scuttled her by ramming the gunwale with the *Leathem*. The hulk was left in fifteen feet of water, ⅛th of a mile from shore, two miles from the north point of Whitefish Bay. She was laying on a northwest by west axis.

Meanwhile, the *Australasia's* master, Robert Pringle, and her crew of seventeen were able to reach Jacksonport in safety. However, by the time the *Leathem* arrived to pick them up, the sailors "had got about four sheets to the wind." A fist fight broke out on the tug during the trip back and again on the wharf in Sturgeon Bay. One sailor was badly beaten.

Captain C.H. Sinclair took pictures of the wreck for the C.A. McDonald Agency and salvage of the wreck was begun within the week. The smokestacks were recovered first, and later a diver was sent down to help retrieve the engine head, anchor, chains and other iron work. Most of the coal was also recovered.

By January, the hull started to break up. As it did so, what coal had not been salvaged washed ashore where it was collected by local farmers. One hundred and forty tons of coal, taken by farmers, was repossessed by the wrecking company with a Writ of Replevin*.

The following summer, salvors from the tug *Wright* succeeded in lifting the boilers and almost all of the equipment. Plans called for installing them in the *Joseph L. Hurd*. Plans were also in the making to retrieve the engines, fore and aft, the propeller and shaft. This called for dynamiting the hull. All salvage was completed by September of 1897.

The *Australasia* was wood hulled with two smoke stacks, three masts, and two decks. She was built at West Bay City, Michigan, in 1884 and measured 1539 net tons. She was 282 feet long, 37 feet across the beam and 21 feet in depth of hold. The vessel was valued at $85,000. *A Writ

The steamer Australasia.

Photo courtesy of the Great Lakes Marine Collection of the Milwaukee Public Library/Wisconsin Marine Historical Society

of Replevin is a legal order by which a person or business may take possession of goods from someone who has wrongfully taken them. Door County Advocate, October 24, 31, 1896. Door County Advocate, January 2, 16, August 28, September 25, 1897. List of Merchant Vessels of the U.S., 1896, p. 216.

236) *Allegheny*, #379, Steamer, and
237) *Transfer*, #59353, Barge, Stranded October 29, 1896.

The *Allegheny* with her consort barge, *Transfer*, was light and bound for Manistique from Chicago when they ran aground on the rocks on the east side of Big Summer Island. The two vessels were left abandoned in three to seven feet of water near the schooner, *Mattie Bell*. The ship's crew escaped safely to the island. Both escort and consort were owned by the Tonawanda Barge Line.

The *Allegheny* was burned for the iron in 1898. According to news reports, the job was done so well that nothing was left of her. She had been valued at $12,000 and was built at Jones Island, Milwaukee, in 1856. According to Beeson's Marine Directory for 1896 she measured 402 gross tons with a length of 167 feet, a 29 foot beam, and a 14 foot depth of hold.

The *Transfer* went to pieces on the rocks within eighteen months. She had been valued at $3,000 and rated at 360.98 gross tons with a length of 142.8 feet, a beam of 28.4 feet and a depth of 10.6 feet. The barge had been built as a schooner at Grand Haven, Michigan, in 1874. Door County Advocate, November 7, 1896. Door County Advocate, July 16, 1898. Beeson's Marine Directory, 1896. p. 78. List of Merchant Vessels of the U.S., 1896, p. 212. List of Merchant Vessels of the U.S., 1896, p. 190.

238) *Success*, #115376, Scow-Schooner, Stranded November 26, 1896.

The *Success* had come to Whitefish Bay for a load of wood. By the time she had arrived at the harbor a storm was blowing. She dropped anchor and rode out the gale for two days. After the weather cleared, the scow was brought to the pier to take on her cargo. She was no more than loaded when a second gale started blowing from the southeast. Once more she tried to ride out the storm at anchor. The vessel developed a leak and began to "make" water faster than the pumps could handle. Fearing that she would roll over, her owner and captain, Anton Olson, ordered a distress signal displayed. The anchor cables were cut allowing the storm to sweep the *Success* to shore. She hit shallow water a mile north of the Whitefish Bay pier. The crew was unable to reach shore and was saved in a daring rescue by Fred and Charles Raatz, Peter Peterson and Ed Thompson who were able to launch a fishing boat into the surf and bring the men to shore.

The cargo of wood was deemed salvageable but the scow was a total wreck. She was abandoned and by the end of the year had started to break up.

The *Success* was built in Manitowoc in 1875 and hailed from Milwaukee. She measured 151 gross tons with a length of 104 feet, a beam of 26 feet and a depth of 7 feet. DOOR COUNTY ADVOCATE, December 5, 1896. DOOR COUNTY ADVOCATE, January 2, 1897. List of Merchant Vessels of the U.S., 1896, p. 183.

239) *Nellie Johnson*, #130667, Schooner, Stranded Early December 1896.

The *Johnson* was bound for Manistique with a cargo of apples. As she was about to reach the harbor entrance in a storm, she struck the rocks leaving her in an exposed position. The *Johnson* was owned by John Johnson of St. James, Beaver Island and registered 41 tons. She was built in St. James only two years before. The schooner measured 51. 8 feet in length, 18 feet across the beam and 4 feet in depth. DOOR COUNTY ADVOCATE, December 12, 1896. List of Merchant Vessels of the U.S., 1895, p. 152.

240) *Irene*, #100573, Tug, Burned May 15, 1897.

The *Irene* burned at her dock in Menominee where she was owned by the Menominee River Shingle Company. She was built in Marinette in 1894 and was valued at $2,000. There was no insurance.

The *Irene* registered 10.07 gross tons with a length of 46 feet, a beam of 12.5 feet and a depth of 4.8 feet. DOOR COUNTY ADVOCATE, May 15, 1897. List of Merchant Vessels of the U.S., 1896, p. 255.

241) *Alfred Mosher*, #1395, Tug, Burned May 16, 1897.

The *Mosher* had been chartered by Captain Peter Peterson of Menominee for raft towing. The crewmembers were all Sturgeon Bay men and had come to that port to visit their families. Captain Anderson and engineer Henry Dumann left the tug in charge of the fireman while they went to their homes. Fire started from unknown causes early in the morning and went undetected until 3 a.m. By the time the fire crews were able to respond, the pilot house was gone and the hold was ablaze from stem to stern. The tug *Nelson* moved her from the old mill slip to a point east of the slip and poured water on her until she filled and sank. The *Mosher's* engine and boiler were thought to be salvageable, but it was unlikely that anything would be done with the hull.

The abandoned hull settled into the soft bottom until it could barely be seen. The boiler was left to sit until the summer of 1912 when it was salvaged by Captain Thomas Isabell.

In 1933 the Weber Dredging Company was dredging at the Peterson Boat Works when it dragged up part of the stern of the *Mosher*. The machinery was still in the hull and was removed. The remaining hull was left to sink back into the mud.

The *Mosher* was owned by John Walker, Henry Dumann and William Helmholtz of Sturgeon Bay and was valued at

$3,500 but insured for only $2,500. She was built at Chicago in 1863 and measured 37.34 gross tons with a length of 70.8 feet, a beam of 15 feet, and a depth of 7.4 feet. DOOR COUNTY ADVOCATE, May 20, 1897. DOOR COUNTY ADVOCATE, January 30, 1908. DOOR COUNTY ADVOCATE, August 1, 1912. DOOR COUNTY ADVOCATE, May 5, 1933. List of Merchant Vessels of the U.S., 1896, p.212.

242) *Frank W. Gifford*, #9752, Schooner, Foundered October 21, 1897.

The *Gifford* was twenty-five miles off Ahnapee when she sprang a leak. She was loaded with iron ore. The crew of eight crowded into the lifeboat and drifted around through the dark of night. Their use of oil to calm the waves around them was thought to be the only factor that saved them from swamping. They were subsequently picked up by the schooner, *City of Sheboygan*.

A week later Captain Cox of the steamer *R.A. Seymour* reported passing through a large quantity of wreckage in mid-lake. At the time the Seymour was on a course from Frankfort to Two Rivers Point, about thirty miles off the point when it encountered a large number of planks, timbers and other debris. Cox reported seeing an unbroken section of a deck house, painted white. It was generally agreed that this was from the *Gifford*.

The *Gifford* was built in Cleveland in 1868 and was a large schooner at 397.8 gross tons. She measured 160 feet in length with a beam of 31.2 feet and a depth of 11.2 feet. KEWAUNEE ENTERPRISE, October 29, November 12, 1897. List of Merchant Vessels of the U.S., 1896, p. 71

243) *Nahant*, #18766, Steamer, Burned November 30, 1897.

The *Nahant* was at her pier in Escanaba when she caught fire. By the time the fire was discovered, it had made such headway that the crew had a difficult time getting out. The fire started in the cabin of Jacob Blesner who had gone to bed intoxicated. He and another crewman perished in the flames. Almost nothing was left of the victims. Remains of the vessel lay off shore near what is now the Coast Guard station. The *Nahant's* rudder is now on display at the Delta County Historical Society's museum down the shore from where the wreck lays.

The steamer was valued at $28,000 and was built in Detroit in 1873. She measured 1,204.18 gross tons with a length of 213.3 feet, a beam of 35 feet, and a depth of 16.2 feet. DOOR COUNTY ADVOCATE, December 4, 11, 1897. List of Merchant Vessels of the U.S., 1896, p. 278.

244) *Agnes Arnold*, #2781, Tug, Burned May 30, 1898.

The *Arnold* was destroyed by fire at Chambers Island. She was owned by Captain James Clow and was valued at $3,500, $2,500 of which was covered by insurance.

The tug was built at Buffalo, New York, in 1864 and measured 30.41 gross tons. She had a length of 68.4 feet, a beam of 13 feet, and a depth of 5.4 feet. DOOR COUNTY ADVOCATE, June 4, 1898. List of Merchant Vessels of the U.S., 1896, p. 211.

245) *Keystone*, #14452, Steamer, Burned September 12, 1898.

The *Keystone* was bound from Lake Erie with a cargo of coal for Manitowoc when she stranded on Big Summer Island in a heavy northwest gale. After she hit the rocks she caught fire and burned to the water line. The crew saved themselves. The ship and cargo were a total loss. It was ironic if not fortunate that she burned. Her insurance did not cover her loss of stranding or foundering. She was however, fully covered by Gibbs and Joys of Milwaukee for loss by fire. The cargo of coal was also covered.

The *Keystone* was valued at $17,000. The coal was valued at $3,000. She was built in Buffalo, New York, in 1880

The steamer Nahant wintering in Detroit Harbor.

Photo courtesy of the Great Lakes Marine Collection of the Milwaukee Public Library/Wisconsin Marine Historical Society

and measured 722.54 gross tons. The steamer was 163.9 feet in length, 34.4 feet across the beam, and 11.3 feet in depth. DOOR COUNTY ADVOCATE, September 24, December 31, 1898. List of Merchant Vessels of the U.S., 1895, p. 267.

246) *Active*, #105081, Schooner, Stranded September 29, 1898.

The *Active* was bound for Ford River with forty tons of hay from Sister Bay. Fighting a strong south wind, heavy seas, and a hazy atmosphere, Captain F. Hogenson mistook a lighted house for the harbor light. He realized his mistake and came about trying to find deep water but hit a shoal instead. The *Active* struck so hard that she was raised two feet all around. She was left sitting perfectly upright on the shoal a mile due south of the Ford River pier. Two tugs attempted to pull her off but could not budge her. Thirty tons of hay was salvaged but the vessel was stripped and abandoned. She was valued at $300.

The *Active* was built in 1869 at Sheboygan, and registered 50.72 gross tons. She measured 68 feet in length, 17 feet in the beam and 5 feet in depth. DOOR COUNTY ADVOCATE, October 8, December 31, 1898. List of Merchant Vessels of the U.S., 1888, p. 54.

247) *Alide J. Rodgers*, #1552, Schooner, Stranded October 16, 1898.

The *Rodgers* ran on a reef near the lighthouse at Sturgeon Bay and punctured her bottom. Captain Frank Couslin and his crew escaped to the lighthouse. The wind pushed her off the reef and she went to pieces and sank. It is not known if she was at Sherwood Point, Dunlap Reef or the canal. She was later reported at Mission Point.

The *Rodgers* measured 340 gross tons, with a length of 137.5 feet, a beam of 26 feet, and a depth of 12.5 feet. She was built in Madison, Ohio, in 1862. DOOR COUNTY ADVOCATE,

October 22, 1898. DOOR COUNTY ADVOCATE, January 7, 1899. List of Merchant Vessels of the U.S., 1896, p. 9.

248) *Annie Dall*, #106182, Schooner, Stranded, October 18, 1898.

The loss of the *Annie Dall* was one of a number of events that made for a bad time for the Leathem & Smith Towing and Wrecking Company.

The *Dall* had been loaded with wood and was riding out a southeasterly gale when her anchor cable broke leaving her to drift ashore at Jacksonport. Her rudder was gone, her stern twisted and with holes punched in her bottom, the schooner filled with water. The tugs, *Nelson* and *Wright*, with the schooner, *Harry Johnson*, were later sent to pump out the *Dall* and take her in tow to Sturgeon Bay. A steam pump was placed aboard and the hull was pumped. Efforts were then made to pull the hulk off the rocks. Twice the tow line broke. On the third try, the tow line wrapped itself around the tug's propeller and a diver had to be sent down to cut away the hawser. On the fourth try, the tug, *Nelson*, was finally able to free the stranded schooner.

The *Dall's* owner and Captain, Tom Christenson, was on board the schooner and with an assistant, kept the steam pump working for the anticipated trip to Sturgeon Bay. Christenson asked for more coal for the pump, there being only enough for a half hour's steam. He was told there was only enough for the tug. The *Wright* started for the canal with the *Dall* in tow, bucking a south gale. The two vessels had only gone a mile when it was realized that the trip was an impossible one, particularly with the *Dall* again full of water. An attempt was made to beach the schooner again, but in coming about, she careened over, dumping the steam pump overboard. The *Wright* rescued the two men aboard and abandoned the *Dall* which washed ashore south of the piers at Jacksonport. The *Wright*, with the *Harry Johnson* in tow, headed north to look for a safe anchorage. (See *Harry Johnson*, #249 following.)

Leathem & Smith reportedly spent $8,000 trying to save the *Annie Dall* which was valued at $1,500 and her cargo of wood valued at $150. There was no insurance on either. The steam pump was recovered the following March. The following February, Tom Christenson filed suit against Leathem & Smith Towing & Wrecking Company for $1,500 for the loss of the *Dall*. The case was dropped when Christenson's witnesses failed to show.

The *Annie Dall* had been purchased by Christenson and his two sons just two years before for $1,200. She was built in Chicago in 1883 and registered 149.53 gross tons. The vessel measured 110.9 feet in length, 24.6 feet across the beam, and 7.7 feet in depth. DOOR COUNTY ADVOCATE, October 22, 29, 1898. DOOR COUNTY ADVOCATE, January 7, March 11, 18, September 9, 1899. KEWAUNEE ENTERPRISE, February 17, 1899. List of Merchant Vessels of the U.S., 1896, p. 15.

249) *Harry Johnson*, Unrigged Barge, Stranded October 18, 1898.

Having abandoned the *Annie Dall* at Jacksonport, the tug *Wright* was too low on coal to fight her way through a southern gale to Sturgeon Bay. The tug, with the *Johnson* in tow, ran before the storm in hopes of finding refuge on the other side of the Door Peninsula. When abreast of Spider Island, the *Johnson* broke loose with two Jacksonport men aboard. The *Wright* sought the safety of Hedgehog Harbor. The next morning the tug, with the assistance of the Plum Island lifesavers, found the *Johnson* washed ashore and broken up in Rock Island passage. The barge was valued at $2,000 and was uninsured. No vessel by the name of *Harry Johnson* is listed in the government list. However this barge may be the *Henry W. Johnson*, #11617, a schooner of 104.76 gross tons, built in New

York, New York, in 1865. Door County Advocate, October 29, 1898. Door County Advocate, January 7, 1899. List of Merchant Vessels of the U.S., 1884, p. 151.

250) *C. Harrison*, #4569, Schooner, Stranded October 31, 1898.

The *Harrison* had been loading wood at Whitefish Bay when a storm started brewing. The schooner tried to set sail into the storm but was thrown back into the shallows where she quickly broke up. She was loaded with 36 cords of wood.

The *Harrison* was an old vessel, having been built in Milwaukee in 1854. Her last owner bought her for $50. She measured 137. 24 gross tons with a length of 93.9 feet, a beam of 23.9 feet, and a depth of 8.1 feet. Door County Advocate, November 5, 12, 1898. List of Merchant Vessels of the U.S., 1896, p. 26.

251) *M. Capron*, #90772, Schooner, Stranded, October 31, 1898.

The *Capron* had taken on a load of wood at Brann's pier, in Baileys Harbor and was attempting to set sail when a storm came up. She started dragging her anchor towards the schooner *Vermot*, also anchored in Baileys Harbor. She just missed striking the *Vermot* but was headed for the beach so a line was secured to the *Vermot*. Both vessels then started drifting toward the beach and the *Vermot's* crew cut the *Capron* free. She hit the shore becoming a total wreck. The crew was rescued. The vessel was valued at $1,000 was owned by Captain A.J. Anderson who also owned the cargo of wood. The wood was salvaged.

The *M.Capron* was built in Conneaut, Ohio, in 1875 and measured 169.66 gross tons. She measured 116.4 feet in length, 22.5 feet across the beam, and 8.9 feet in depth. Door County Advocate, November 5, 1898. Door County Advocate,

252) *Joys*, #76537, Steamer, Burned December 24, 1898.

The *Joys* burned at her moorings at the west end of the canal. The steamer had been bound from Milwaukee to Menominee to pick up cargo and stopped at the Sturgeon Bay ship canal to wait for the weather to settle. She caught fire late that night and the captain and crew of thirteen escaped with just their lives and the clothes on their backs. Some jumped to the ice in their bare feet and night shirts. Nothing was saved. When she caught fire, the *Joys* started drifting down the canal endangering area buildings. She was towed back to her moorings by her crew and the life-saving crew. There she burned to the waterline and sank.

The *Joys* was purchased by Leathem & Smith for the engine and boiler. The following summer, the steamer was raised and the steel from her frames was taken out as well as the propeller, shaft, and shoe. The burned out hulk was a menace to navigation and was shoved in the sand on Dunlap Reef. She ended up as a breakwater for the Pankratz Lumber Company on the north side of the dock. A 1907 article reported that the *Joys*, wrecked and burned, was deposited on the flats above the island mill, 1,000 feet north of the edging dock on a line with the outer end of the wharf and the Leathem & Smith quarry in Sturgeon Bay. Several years later, the Chicago yacht *Corona* ran on the wreck and was so firmly grounded that the efforts of three other yachts and the life saving crew were needed to free her. The DOOR COUNTY ADVOCATE noted, "These sunken hulks are a serious menace to the navigation of small boats in this bay and it is a wonder no serious accidents have occurred."

The steamer was owned by Captain Connelly and Mrs. Christiana Sheriff and was valued at $15,000. She was built in Milwaukee in 1884, and measured 268 gross tons with a length of 131 feet, a beam of 28.2 foot beam, and a 9.9 depth of hold. DOOR COUNTY ADVOCATE, December 24, 1898. DOOR COUNTY ADVOCATE, January 21, May 6, 13, 1899. DOOR COUNTY ADVOCATE, June 20, 1907. DOOR COUNTY ADVOCATE, July 14, 1910. List of Merchant Vessels of the U.S., 1896, p. 263.

253) *O.M. Nelson*, #155066, Schooner, Stranded June 4, 1899.

The *O.M. Nelson* was attempting to maneuver through a dense fog with a southwest gale prevailing when she ran up on the southwest reef off Pilot Island. She was bound north with a load of lumber when she hit. Her captain and part owner, Peter Hanson, had two crewmen in the cross-trees watching for obstacles, but discovered their position too late. Lighthouse keeper Martin Knudsen of the Porte Des Morte lighthouse wrote in his logbook, "Sunday, a dense fog has prevailed here nearly all day...at 12:10 noon the schooner *O.M. Nelson*, Captain Peter Hanson of Detroit Harbor was seen on S.W. reef off Pilot Island (after oiling the engine) I (keeper) at once sounded 4 blasts to call the life savers, I blew 4 blasts 3 times with a short interval, Capt. I Olsen responded 1 hour and 20 minutes after with the sailboat, could not board the schnr., went home and came back with the surf boat 2:50 p.m. took off the crew and returned to the station." The crew of five men and one woman stayed on as guests of the lighthouse crew while they stripped the schooner of all salvageables. The next day the wrecking tug, *Monarch*, tried unsuccessfully to pull the schooner off.

Several days after the *Nelson* went aground, the tug *Else*, schooner *Ma Donna* and a barge arrived to remove the rigging and running gear and her cargo of lumber. The abandoned hull aroused the interest of the captain of the *Ann Arbor Car Ferry No. 3* who was certain that if he could get a tow line on the *Nelson* he could pull it free. He did. It

The steamer Joys

Photo courtesy of the Great Lakes Marine Collection of the Milwaukee Public Library/Wisconsin Marine Historical Society

snapped. The ferry came back twice to inspect the schooner, but when the autumn storms came, the *Nelson* was still hard aground on Pilot Island. A December gale did what no steamer could do — moving the schooner, completely turning it around. In mid-January, Knudsen reported that the schooner's starboard side washed away. Three weeks later he added that the vessel had gone to pieces. That notwithstanding, the lighthouse crew was able to salvage the capstan.

In addition to Captain Hanson, the *O.M. Nelson's* owners included the Milwaukee Yard Company, John Malloch and a "Mr. Halverson." She was built in 1882 at Sutton's Bay, Michigan, and registered 167 gross tons. The *Nelson*, which was named for a Sturgeon Bay businessman, measured 107.7 feet in length, 25.3 feet across the beam and 8.4 feet in depth. Logbook of the Porte Des Morte Lighthouse on Pilot Island, June 4, 1899 - April 24, 1900. DOOR COUNTY ADVOCATE, June 10, July 1, 1899. List of Merchant Vessels of the U.S., 1896, p. 153.

254) *Pilot*, #150270, Tug, Burned July 29, 1899.

The *Pilot* was on her way from her home port, Cedar River, to Menominee to pick up a raft of logs. About midnight, she was eight miles north of that city when "the forward hatch blew off and the flames blew forth." Captain J.B. Rood ordered the pumps manned. Rood severly burned his hands holding onto the whistle cord trying to signal for help from Menominee. The fire gained to such a degree that he ordered the vessel abandoned. Captain and crew lowered the small boat and reached shore safely. All personal belongings and papers were lost. The tug burned to the waterline and sank in forty feet of water. The cause of the fire was described as "spontaneous combustion."

Newspaper accounts give conflicting information on the location. The MENOMINEE HERALD says eight miles north of Menominee and three miles out in the Bay. The

MARINETTE STAR maintains it was six miles north of Menominee and two miles out in the Bay.

A month before she was destroyed, the *Pilot* was reported to be haunted by the ghost of John Hill, a former engineer who had died suddenly in his cabin a few days before. A news story stated the captain and crew refused to sleep on·board the vessel at night adding, "...the occupants declare his ghost lingers there, walking with phantom tread and beckoning in a weird way to his old associates."

The tug was owned by the Spalding Lumber Company and was valued at $6,000. She measured 30.83 gross tons with a length of 55 feet, a 16.6 foot beam and a 7.9 foot depth in the hold. She was built in Milwaukee in 1882.

DOOR COUNTY ADVOCATE, August 5, 1899. MARINETTE STAR, July 31, 1899. MENOMINEE HERALD, July 31, 1899. List of Merchant Vessels of the U.S., 1896, p. 285.

255) *Stone City*, #116689, Fishing Tug, Stranded October 12, 1899.

This fish boat was attempting to find its way through a dense fog to Big Cedar when it ran on the rocks near Cedar River, Michigan. She later pounded to pieces and wreckage of the tug washed ashore several days later. She was loaded with salted fish, most of which were lost. The tug was owned by Strickenback and Shilling of Green Bay and valued at $6,000 for vessel and cargo.

Not satisfied with the accuracy of news stories describing the loss, the tug's captain was quick to write a letter to the DOOR COUNTY ADVOCATE with his own story of the event.

Marine Editor of The Advocate: Seeing so many false reports in the different papers as to the loss of the fishing tug Stone City, *I will try through the* ADVOCATE *to correct them. Will say the* Stone City *went on Little Cedar shoal on Oct. 12, 1899 at 6 p.m. in thick fog. We were not swept from our moorings at all. We were on our way to Big Cedar. There was not an ounce of fisherman's supplies on board, and only 76 packages of salt fish on board, 42 of which were lost, balance were saved. None of the crew were ashore as reported in the Green Bay Gazette. J.D. Livermore, Captain* Stone City.

The *Stone City* was built in Lockport, Illinois, in 1895 and registered 42 gross tons. She measured 55 feet in length, 13.3 feet across the beam. DOOR COUNTY ADVOCATE, October 21, 28, November 4, 1899. GREEN BAY GAZETTE, October 25, 1899. List of Merchant Vessels of the U.S., 1896, p. 178.

256) *Badger*, #3156, Scow, Foundered October 24, 1899.

The *Badger* was on her way to Sturgeon Bay with a load of hemlock ties when she waterlogged off Cedar River. For twelve hours, Captain Aldrich and the crew pumped to keep the vessel afloat. They were finally rescued by fishermen. The scow's stern was later torn to pieces and she sank. The ties floated to shore.

The *Badger* was owned by Captain P.W. Kirtland of Green Bay and was valued at $1,100. She was built at Fort Howard, in 1881 and registered 65.4 gross tons and had a length of 80 feet, a beam of 20.6 feet and a depth of 4.4 feet. GREEN BAY GAZETTE, October 25, 1899. DOOR COUNTY ADVOCATE, October 28, 1899. List of Merchant Vessels of the U.S., 1896, p. 20.

257) *Emmanuel*, #136121, Schooner, Scrapped December of 1899.

The *Emmanuel's* owner, K.S. Thompson, ran the vessel ashore at Fish Creek to pull her apart for the iron. She was completely dismantled. Thompson had built her at Fish Creek only nine years before but was dissatisfied with the way she handled. The craft was a poor sailer and he was unable to make her pay in the coastwise trade. A small news article stated, "...it was simply impossible to get anywhere unless the vessel had a fair wind, in other words, the vessel was built on lines equal to a dry goods box, and to ratch to windward was simply out of the question." Her shallow draft suggests the boat was a scow, a flat bottomed vessel with a pram bow. Many scow captains were quite proud of their vessels for their ability to handle shallow water, and, if they were built and handled well, sail close to windward.

The *Emmanuel* measured 23.13 gross tons with a length of 65 feet, a beam of 13.8 feet, and a depth of 4.3 feet. Door County Advocate, December 9, 1899. List of Merchant Vessels of the U.S., 1896, p. 58.

258) *Sardinia*, #22583, Schooner, Stranded June 29, 1900.

The *Sardinia* had pulled in at Voight's Pier to take on a load of wood. The big anchor had been dropped 65 fathoms out. About midnight, the schooner started pounding against the pier and her captain, Max Pfile, ordered the vessel winched out into the inlet. A storm was blowing out of the west and blew waves almost as high as the wood piles on the pier. Her anchors dragged and she soon found bottom. The hull was punctured by rocks and she settled in shallow water.

The next day, the lifesavers arrived from Plum Island and helped Captain Pfile attempt to refloat the vessel but were unsuccessful. The rigging was sold to pay the crew which included Pfile's two brothers, Reinhard and Otto, as well as Albert Richter of Washington Island.

A Door County Advocate correspondent reported that by the end of August, the *Sardinia* had been driven high and dry on to the beach. She was still intact and not much damage had been done to her that could be seen.

In 1874, the *Sardinia* had been cut in two when she was run down by the steamer, *Nebraska*. Her owner at that time, S. Goodenow of Chicago had her rebuilt and lengthened during that winter. On April 28, 1875, she was relaunched and returned to service with a whole new appearance.

The *Sardinia* was owned by Captain Pfile and his brother, Ernest, and was valued at $800. She was not insured. The vessel was built in Penetanguishene, Ontario, in 1856 and measured 142 net tons. She had a length of 105 feet, a beam of 24 feet and a depth of 8 feet. Door County Advocate, July 14, September 1, 1900. Chicago Tribune, April 28, 1875. List of Merchant Vessels of the U.S., 1896, p. 177.

259) *City of Stiles,* #125925, Freighter, Burned August 2, 1901

The *City of Stiles* was small package freighter of 100 foot length used in the Gladstone — Green Bay trade. She was anchored in the Fox River, in De Pere, off shore from the "driving park" (or what is now the Brown County fairgrounds). There she had taken on a load of 31,000 bricks from the Roffers Brick factory. Early that morning, about 3 a.m., the vessel caught fire. The crew made an effort to launch the ship's yawl but in the excitement the boat capsized. Wheelsman Frank Burns was severely burned about the head and face. The ship's cook Mrs. Sophie Archie jumped overboard in panic. She and the rest of the crew were rescued. The *Stiles* burned to the waterline and was left where she was settling in the soft mud of the river bank pending her fate. Plans were initially made to salvage the steamer but a late report in the Green Bay Advocate stated,

"Those who have seen her say that there are large holes in her which extend far below the waterline and that only the bottom of the boat is whole. The brick which were on board were so heavy that they have spread her badly as the upper works which acted as a brace have all burned away. Even if the insurance covers the loss it will be cheaper it is

thought to build an entirely new boat to take her place next season."

Nothing more was ever reported on the *City of Stiles* and she was dropped from the government list the next year. A large obstruction is left in the approximate area where she would have been moored. The *Stiles* may have been in whole or in part salvaged, and that obstruction could be a natural shoal, or perhaps it is a part of the ship or its cargo.

The steamer had burned in Green Bay some years before and had sat on the bottom for sometime until 1900 when her owners, Maloney and Roulette raised her and had the vessel rebuilt. Green Bay Advocate, August 2, 9, 1901. Green Bay Gazette, August 2, 7, 1901. Green Bay Gazette, (Semi-weekly), August 7, 1901. De Pere News, August 7, 1901. List of Merchant.Vessels of the U.S., 1892, p. 283. List of Merchant Vessels of the U.S., 1892, p. 283. List of Merchant Vessels of the U.S., 1901.

260) Unnamed Scows, Abandoned August 14, 1900.

Three consort scows were under escort by the tug *Sport*, bound from Ludington to Escanaba. One scow had been carrying fuel for the tug. But for that, the consorts were empty. About ten miles southeast of the Sturgeon Bay canal, all three scows water logged creating such a drag for the tug that she used up her fuel. Captain J.T. Crawford ordered the scows cut free. They were considered old and unsound and no effort was made to locate them. It was thought they would go to pieces when they went ashore. Door County Advocate, August 18, 1900.

261) *Farrand H. Williams*, #120474, Scow-Schooner, Stranded September 11, 1900.

The *Williams* washed ashore at Horseshoe Bay and went to pieces. She was owned by C.D. Peterson of Detroit Harbor. The scow measured 95 gross tons.

The *Williams* was built in Manitowoc in 1882 by Farrand

184

P. Williams for his own use and measured 88.8 feet in length, 22.8 feet at the beam and 6.6 feet in depth. KEWAUNEE ENTERPRISE, September 28, 1900. List of Merchant Vessels of the U.S., 1895, p. 66.

262) *Boaz*, #2791, Schooner, Stranded November 9, 1900.

The *Boaz* was bound from Pierpont to Racine with a cargo of elm lumber, when she began to leak. Attempting to find refuge in North Bay, she hit the north point and swung free. The schooner was kept off the beach by her anchors, but her crew of four feared she would capsize. They crawled into the yawl tied off the stern and spent the night in a drenching rain.

The following morning, the steam barge, *Two Myrtles*, was summoned for assistance. The crew was rescued, the anchor cables were cut and the hull was pushed up on the beach. Captain Larsen of the *Boaz* thought the schooner was unsalvageable.

A week or so later, a claim of $200 for sailors' wages was to have been put on the *Boaz* by Deputy U.S. Marshall E.H. Glantz. Glantz, discovering that the vessel was over thirty years old and was under water, decided to cancel the attachment. The vessel was left to the mercy of Lake Michigan. Three years later, Captain Thomas Isabell, a local salvor, retrieved the spars from the wreck.

The *Boaz* was valued at less than $500 and was owned by Charles S. Burnham of Milwaukee. She was uninsured. The schooner registered 127.22 gross tons with a length of 114 feet and 22 feet across the beam. She was built in 1869. KEWAUNEE ENTERPRISE, November 16, 1900. DOOR COUNTY ADVOCATE, November 17, 24, December 1, 1900. DOOR COUNTY ADVOCATE, September 5, 1901. List of Merchant Vessels of the U.S., 1896, p. 25.

263) *William Finch*, #80696, Schooner, Stranded November 14, 1900.

The *Finch* had been brought to Egg Harbor by Captain W.P. Kirtland to salvage the cargo of the schooner *Norma* which had gone ashore at that harbor. When a northwest gale started blowing, the vessel pounded and started taking on water. When the pumps gave out, Kirtland was forced to cut the anchor and allow the vessel to go ashore in hopes of saving himself and a crewman. Signals of distress were sounded and villagers came down and rescued the two after the schooner grounded. The *Finch* beached herself, not far from the *Norma*, on a rocky bottom and soon pounded herself to pieces in the waves. This was the third vessel Kirtland had lost that year. In addition to the *Norma* and the *Finch*, the *Badger* had also been lost. Everything that was saved from the *Norma* was also lost.

The *Finch* was valued at $400 and was built in South Haven, Michigan in 1878. She registered 49.49 gross tons and measured 68 feet in length, 17.3 feet at the beam and 5.2 feet in depth. KEWAUNEE ENTERPRISE, November 16, 1900. DOOR COUNTY ADVOCATE, November 17, 1900. List of Merchant Vessels of the U.S., 1896, p. 201.

264) *Pankratz Barge No. 2*, Foundered November 20, 1900.

Laden with 150 cords of stone, the *Pankratz Barge No. 2* was in tow of the tug, *Duncan City* when she sank in the canal. She was being towed out to the lake when she was passed by a tug and suddenly veered to port, slamming into the north side of the canal. She punctured her bow on a row of fender pilings and sank squarely across the canal. This occurred about 5:00 p.m. Canal superintendent Adam Dier gave George Pankratz, owner of the barge and the lumber company, until noon of the next day to remove the barge or the government would do it. Pankratz needed a dredge to pull off the stone and the only ones available were government owned and could not be hired out.

Pankratz decided to let the government do it. Two dredges pulled the stone off and put it on lighters. A diver was sent down and the hull inspected. The vessel was found to be solid and intact and nothing keeping her on the bottom except the hole.

It was thought that once she was free of stone the barge would float. However, not even two dredges pulling at once could pull her off the bottom. Two tugs were tied to the stern and one to the bow pulling in opposite directions to straighten her out. Still the barge didn't move. Once more a diver inspected her and found that she was wrenched amidship and the bow and stern caught in the revetments of the canal and stuck deep in the mud. It was decided that she'd be blown up. Dynamite was placed in the hold and triggered electrically. Great pieces of her deck and gunwales were torn out and some blown higher than the lighthouse. Dredges also worked at pulling the wreck apart. Tugs pulled the debris out in the lake and dumped it. Loss on the scow was total and she was uninsured.

The vessel was valued at $7,500. She had been built by Riebolt and Walter for the lumber company and launched the previous spring. The stone was put in dump scows and deposited in the lake. There were 145 cords being shipped by Graff & Nebel and was valued at $400. DOOR COUNTY ADVOCATE, November 24, December 1, 1900

265) *Mary Mills*, #90493, Steam Barge, Burned December 12, 1900.

The *Mills* was destroyed by fire at Nettie Mac Eacham's pier at the head of the bay where she had gone to take on a cargo of hay. The fire was discovered about 3 a.m. and owing to the fact that the pier was in such an out-of-the-way place, no fire fighting equipment could be found. Those crewmembers who were sleeping in the forward section escaped with their clothes but little else. Those who were in the aft barely escaped with their bed clothes. Everything on board the vessel was destroyed including the ship's papers and compass. Chief engineer David Machia lost his tools and a new suit of clothes. John Cornelius, the steward, lost a watch and a bicycle. The cargo of hay was also lost. Other members of the crew were; mate, James Coffey; second engineer, James Oakley; wheelsman, Ben Johnson; firemen, George Johnson and Willis Lockhart.

James Oakley purchased the boiler and engine which were lifted out in June of 1902. The stern was later dynamited and the shaft and propeller taken out.

The *Mary Mills* was co-owned by her captain, John Bolton, and the Hilty Lumber Company of Milwaukee. She was valued at $7,000 and was insured for $4,500. The barge was built in 1872 at Vicksburg, Michigan, and registered 119.2 net tons. She measured 117.9 feet in length, 24.2 feet at the beam, and 8.6 feet in depth. DOOR COUNTY ADVOCATE, December 15, 1900. DOOR COUNTY ADVOCATE, June 7, 1902. List of Merchant Vessels of the U.S., 1896, p. 272.

266) Unnamed Scow, Abandoned prior to 1901.

In May of 1901, the tug *Waupoose* ran onto a sunken scow in Green Bay. The tug was later raised. No identity was given for the scow although it may have been the steamer Otego. That vessel burned and sank at the west end of the Mason Street bridge in October of 1895. Extensive plans were made in September of 1901 to raise the vessel. DOOR COUNTY ADVOCATE, May 25, 1901. GREEN BAY GAZETTE, August 7, 1901.

267) *Dollie M.*, #157373, Schooner, Stranded May 31, 1901.

The *Dollie M.* was abandoned at Schumacher's Point after she had been blown ashore there in high winds. When the water receded, she was so far ashore that it would be impossible to float her without going to a large expense. The schooner was extremely old and her owners decided that she was not worth the trouble and expense. She was stripped of her canvas and everything removable and was left to rot where she lay. (Schumacher's Point is located on the east side of the Bay of Green Bay.)

In spite of her description as "ancient," the *Dollie M.* was built in 1893 at Escanaba. She registered 38 gross tons and measured 80 feet in length, 19.9 feet at the beam and 5.7 feet in depth. KEWAUNEE ENTERPRISE, June 14, 1901. List of Merchant Vessels of the U.S., 1895, p. 46.

268) *Little Gregory*, #15806, Scow-Schooner, Stranded in Mid-May of 1901.

The *Little Gregory* went ashore at Two Creeks, Wisconsin, during a fierce storm. Her bottom was pounded out and she became a total wreck. The *Little Gregory* was built at Sheboygan in 1870 and registered 52.35 gross tons. She measured 81 feet long, 17 feet across the beam and 5 feet in depth. KEWAUNEE ENTERPRISE, May 31, 1901. List of Merchant Vessels of the U.S., 1895, p. 122.

269) *Sir Luke*, #116530, Tug, Stranded Early July of 1901.

The *Sir Luke* was a side-wheel steam tug used exclusively for towing logs for the Van Winkle & Montague Lumber Company of Van's Harbor, Michigan. She was involved in her trade when she was caught in a storm off the north shore of the Bay of Green Bay. Officers and crew were forced to abandon the vessel in the small boat and made the safety of shore. The tug went to pieces and was abandoned as a total loss. Only a small portion of the machinery could be salvaged.

The story of the wreck was reported to the KEWAUNEE ENTERPRISE by Captain James Bridger who had been sent to out to find another tug for the lumber company.

The *Sir Luke* was built in Van's Harbor in 1892 and registered 44.39 gross tons. She had a length of 79 feet, a beam of 19.9 feet, and a depth of 4.7 feet. KEWAUNEE ENTERPRISE, July 19, 1901. DOOR COUNTY ADVOCATE, July 20, 1901. ESCANABA IRON PORT, July 27, 1901. List of Merchant Vessels of the U.S., 1896, p. 296.

270) *Cleveland*, #4376, Steamer, Abandoned July 1901.

This old steamer settled to the bottom in Reynold's slip in Sturgeon Bay. In November of that year she was raised and taken to the Leathem & Smith wharf. After an inspection, it was decided that she would be taken to the Graef and Nebel quarry on the east side of the bay, filled with stone and sunk for a dock. She was sunk there next to the *J.S. Williams* in June of 1902.

The *Cleveland* was built in Cleveland in 1860 and measured 286 gross tons. She had a length of 135 feet, a 25.9 foot beam, and a 11.6 foot depth of hold. DOOR COUNTY ADVOCATE, November 23, 1901. DOOR COUNTY ADVOCATE, June 7, 1902. List of Merchant Vessels of the U.S., 1896, p. 227.

271) Christine Michelson, # 5531, Schooner, Stranded October 30, 1901.

The *Michelson* was bound from Escanaba for Milwaukee with 200,000 feet of lumber when she stranded fifteen miles south of Escanaba. Most of the lumber was saved. She was owned by her Captain, Sam Martin, who had also lost the scows, *Laurina* and *Silverlake* in the previous nine years.

The *Michelson* was built at White Lake, Michigan, in 1867. She measured 137.46 gross tons and had a length of 102.3, a beam of 25.1 feet, and a depth of 7.9 feet. DOOR COUNTY ADVOCATE, November 16, 1901. List of the Merchant Vessels of the U.S., 1896, p. 26.

272) Unnamed Scow, Foundered November 3, 1901.

The scow was carrying a dredge and was in tow of the tug *Temple Emory* when she snapped her tow line and sank off Cedar River. She was brought to the surface and taken in to the harbor where she sank again. Escanaba Iron Port, November 9, 1901.

273) *Emily Taylor*, #136386, Schooner, Stranded November 9, 1901.

The *Emily Taylor* was bound from Arthur Bay for Green Bay with a load of wood when she stranded at Seizar's Bay, twenty miles north of Menominee. Captain Charles Stone, his wife, and two children and two crew men hung on to the hulk through the night expecting it to break apart at any minute. The vessel was discovered the following morning by fishermen who were able to launch a boat into the storm and rescue the six souls aboard. The storm sent waves crashing completely over the wreck all night and by the time of their rescue, the crew of the *Taylor* was nearly dead from exposure.The fishermen took them home and cared for them.

The *Emily Taylor* was built in Ahnapee in 1893 and measured 55.52 gross tons. She had a length of 71 feet, a beam of 20 feet and a 4.9 depth of hold. Door County Advocate, November 16, 1901. List of Merchant Vessels of the U.S., 1896, p. 56.

274) *Peoria*, #19668, Schooner, Stranded November 10, 1901.

The *Peoria* was blown ashore on Baileys Harbors lighthouse reef when she was one of fifty some vessels to be wrecked in the "Big Blow" of October 16, 1880. The schooner was abandoned as a total loss and was later relieved of her equipment by George Bennet and Lincoln Erskine of Baileys Harbor. In mid-may of 1881, however, the *Peoria* was successfully salvaged and returned to service.

Twenty years later, November 10, 1901, the *Peoria* was bound for Chicago from East Jordan, Michigan, when she was caught in the grasp of a southern gale. The old schooner was blown down the length of Lake Michigan before she was finally able to pull into Baileys Harbor to weather out the storm. Owner and master, Captain M.J. Bonner, ordered one and later a second "mud hook" dropped to hold her in place. Neither anchor held and she started dragging towards lighthouse reef. She struck at almost the very spot where she had been wrecked twenty years before. Bonner signaled for the lifesaving crew who responded immediately. The captain and his crew of five were rescued and taken to the lifesaving station where they were cared for.

The vessel was laden with 140,000 feet of hardwood lumber owned by the East Jordan Lumber Company and consigned to the Maxwell Brothers of Chicago. Most of the cargo was saved, much of it having been picked up on the beach.

The *Peoria* was built in Black River, Ohio, in 1854 and registered 158 net tons. She measured 112.1 feet in length, with a beam of 24.3 feet, and a depth of 8.8 feet. DOOR COUNTY ADVOCATE, November 16, 1901. List of Merchant Vessels of the U.S., 1896, p. 159.

275) *Pride*, #19770, Schooner, Stranded November 22, 1901.

The *Pride* was in Washington Harbor, Washington Island, where she had taken on board several cords of wood and a large cargo of potatoes (700 bushels according to the DOOR COUNTY ADVOCATE, 1,000 according to the Kewaunee Enterprise.) She tried to tack across the harbor but missed stays and drifted ashore where she pounded and filled with water. She hit shore near the dock belonging to

Matthew Foss. The *Pride* was owned by Captain C. Klingenberg of Sturgeon Bay who was in command of the vessel when she was wrecked. The cargo of potatoes was valued at $500. One hundred bushels were saved.

The *Pride* was built in 1849 at Sandusky, Ohio, and measured 83 gross tons. There were actually two vessels by this name, approximately the same size, sailing this area at the same time. KEWAUNEE ENTERPRISE, November 29, 1901. DOOR COUNTY ADVOCATE, November 29, 1901. List of Merchant Vessels of the U.S., 1896, p. 161.

276) *Rambler*, #110613, Scow-Schooner, Stranded May 8, 1902.

The *Rambler* broke away from her moorings at Red River and went ashore where she broke up. She was valued at $300 and was owned and captained by Louis Ligot who replaced her with the "hooker" *Minnie*. The *Rambler* was built in Milwaukee in 1883 and registered 29.16 gross tons with a length of 60 feet, a beam of 16.7 feet and a depth of 3.4 feet. DOOR COUNTY ADVOCATE, May 24, 1902. List of Merchant Vessels of the U.S., 1895, p. 167.

277) *J.S. Williams*, #20224, Barge, Abandoned Mid-May, 1902.

The *Williams* was one of many old vessels left abandoned in the various mud flats around Sturgeon Bay. The firm of Graef and Nebel had her raised and taken to the mouth of the bay where she was sunk in front of their quarry for use as a pier. (Her final resting place was described by one source as "McCracken's Cove.") It was said to be cheaper than sinking cribs and disposed of some of the old wrecks. Plans were made to do the same with the old steamer, *Cleveland.* Remains of the *Williams* were later destroyed by fire.

The *Williams* was built as the lumber schooner, *Phoenix,*

in 1868. When her career as a working schooner came to an end, the vessel was converted to a tow barge and given her new name. As a schooner she registered 206.25 gross tons. Door County Advocate, May 24, 1902. Herman G. Runge Collection of the Milwaukee Public Library/Wisconsin Marine Historical Society. List of Merchant Vessels of the U.S., 1884, p. 228.

278) *Thomas C. Wilson*, #25479, Schooner, Stranded Mid-November, 1902.

Having capsized off Egg Harbor, the *Wilson* was towed to that port in a waterlogged condition. She was righted and an effort was made by the tug, *Sylvia*, to tow her to the shipyard, but a sudden burst of bad weather made the attempt impractical. That night, strong westerly winds built up a heavy sea in the harbor. The *Wilson* broke her mooring lines and went on the beach. There was apparently considerable damage done to her bottom by rocks and boulders. Captain John Devine intended to tow her off and make repairs there at Egg Harbor, but could not find help in time. Before she could be pulled off and pumped out, the schooner fell victim to further westerly winds. The following August, she was torn apart and the timbers and planks used for firewood.

The *Thomas C. Wilson* registered 30.87 gross tons with a length of 58.5 feet, a beam of 15.4 feet and a depth of 5 feet. She was built in Black River, Ohio, in 1868. Her shallow depth suggests that she might have been a scow, although neither newspaper stories nor the government list describe her as such. Door County Advocate, November 29, December 27, 1902. Door County Advocate, August 22, 1903. List of Merchant Vessels of the U.S., 1895, p. 191.

279) *Bay State*, #2141, Schooner, Abandoned April of 1903.

The *Bay State* was removed from the "boneyard" below

The schooner J.S. Williams under tow.
Photo courtesy of the Great Lakes Marine Collection
of the Milwaukee Public Library/Wisconsin Marine Historical Society

the Leathem & Smith dock and taken to the mouth of the
Bay, by the tug *John Leathem*, where she was sunk for use
as a dock for Thomas Smith. Also removed were the
schooners *Kate Hinchman* and *Emerald*.

The *Bay State* was built in 1855 at Buffalo, New York,
and registered 249.38 gross tons. Door County Advocate, May 2,
1903. List of Merchant Vessels of the U.S., 1884, p. 80.

280) Unknown Schooner, Stranded May of 1903.

Captain James Larson of the schooner *Three Sisters*
reported to the Marinette customs office that an unidentified schooner was left high and dry on Squaw Island, Bay

De Noque. She was thought to have been beached by ice and abandoned. DOOR COUNTY ADVOCATE, May 23, 1903.

281) Unknown Yacht, Abandoned August 10, 1903.

This unidentified yacht floated ashore in front of the property belonging to John Nelson in Ellison Bay. The vessel was a total wreck and was empty except for a duck hunting coat. An envelope, found inside, was addressed to Kelso Parkinson, Grace Port, Door County. DOOR COUNTY ADVOCATE, August 15, 1903.

282) Unknown, Sunk September 2, 1903.

The scow was accidentally rammed by the tug *Two Myrtles* in the harbor at Green Bay. As the scow was sinking, she was pushed into shallow water by the tug. DOOR COUNTY ADVOCATE, September 5, 1903.

283) *La Petite*, #15100, Schooner, Stranded September 7, 1903.

The *La Petite*, in command of Captain William Glockner, left Torch Lake, near Grand Traverse Bay bound for Milwaukee with a load of slabs. Twenty-four hours into the voyage, they hit a southeast gale. Battered by heavy seas, the vessel began to leak and become unmanageable. Glockner tried to reach Manitowoc but the vessel would not handle well enough to make that port. The weather swept away the deckload of shingles, and carried the helpless vessel down the lake till she passed Ahnapee (now Algoma). Finding water of an appropriate depth, she came to anchor and a signal of distress was hoisted. The lifesavers, at the canal, sighted the distress signal, hired a tug and went to the aid of the stricken schooner. The tug *Sydney Smith* was able to take the vessel in tow and the crew was taken off. While under tow, the *La Petite* fell victim to a high wave and rolled over. The lifesavers who had been left on the schooner to man the pumps were taken off, the tow line was taken in and the vessel cast adrift. She ultimately went ashore seven miles south of the canal at Clay Banks.

Captain Glockner visited the wreck several days later and found that it had broken up in the heavy seas. The masts were broken off and the stern was pulled off and beached some distance from the rest of the hull. Captain Thomas Isabell, with the schooner *German*, salvaged what he could of the wreck.

The crew consisted of mate, Anton Anderson; cook, Ole D. Dohl; and seamen William Anderson and John Arntsen, all of Milwaukee. Captain Glockner shared ownership of the craft with Theodore Plathner, also of Milwaukee.

The *La Petite* was valued at $2,000 and her cargo was valued at $275. There was no insurance. The schooner measured 172 tons with a length of 119 feet, a beam of 24 feet and a depth of hold of 8 feet. She was built at Huron, Ohio, in 1866. Door County Advocate, September 12, 1903. List of Merchant Vessels of the U.S., 1895, p. 115.

284) *R. Kanters*, #125223, Schooner, Stranded September 7, 1903.

The *Kanters* was caught in the teeth of a heavy southeast gale and was thrown ashore seven miles south of Manistique, Michigan. She was, at last report, left lying on a rocky exposed bottom and was thought to be seriously damaged. The *Kanters* was built in 1873 in Manitowoc and registered 164 gross tons. She measured 112.6 feet in length, 25.6 feet across the beam, and 8.4 feet in depth. Door County Advocate, September 12, 1903. List of Merchant Vessels of the U.S., 1895, p. 166.

285) *Dawn*, #157211, Schooner, Stranded September 19, 1903.

The *Dawn* was bound from Milwaukee to Portage Bay, Michigan, when she was caught in a southeast gale. She sought out the safety of Kewaunee harbor and while attempting to enter that port she struck the south pier and drifted ashore. Captain R.T. Kierwan was master and owner of the vessel. She was not insured.

The *Dawn* registered 26 gross tons and measured 60.5 feet in length with a beam of 14.1 feet and a depth of 3.7 feet. She was built in Milwaukee in 1888. DOOR COUNTY ADVOCATE, September 26, 1903. List of Merchant Vessels of the U.S., 1896, p. 40.

286) *H.W. Sage*, #95414, Barge, Foundered October 3, 1903.

The *Sage* was in tow of the steamer, *Samoa*, and bound for a Lake Erie port with a cargo of iron ore from Escanaba. When it was learned that the vessel was making water, the crew transferred to the *Samoa*. They were no more than taken aboard the steamer, when the *Sage* lurched and sank. The crew was safely landed at Port Huron.

The vessel was built in 1875 at Bangor, Michigan. She registered 848 gross tons and measured 202 feet in length, with a beam of 36 feet, and a depth of 13 feet. The barge was owned by John Kelderhouse of Buffalo. DOOR COUNTY ADVOCATE, October 10, 1903. List of Merchant Vessels of the U.S., 1884, p. 145.

287) *Erie L. Hackley*, #135615, Steamer, Foundered October 3, 1903.

Five months before she foundered, the *Erie L. Hackley* had been brought from Charlevoix, Michigan, to become the flag ship, actually the only ship, for the newly founded Fish Creek Transportation Co. The new line had been founded by her captain, Joe Vorous, E.T. Thorp, Orin Rowen and Henry Robertoy to run a standard route from

Marinette to Egg Harbor, Fish Creek, Ephraim, Sister Bay and Ellison Bay.

It was on the Marinette-Egg Harbor leg of the journey that the *Hackley* encountered, east of Green Island, what was later described as a tornado. The steamer's cabin was swept off and the vessel careened and sank. Eleven of the 19 people on board were lost with the wreck, making the wreck of the *Erie L. Hackley* the worst maritime disaster in northeastern Wisconsin history. The DOOR COUNTY ADVOCATE covered the catastrophe with the first special edition in the newspaper's 42 year history. Survivors were left clinging to the cabin and other wreckage. Victims of the *Hackley* disaster included two of her three owners, Robertoy, and Captain Vorous who had felt some foreboding about the trip and refused to take his sister along. Others lost with the steamer were Carl Pelkey, Hugh Miller, Lawrence and Edna Barringer, George LeClair, Nels Nelson, and Edna and Ethel Vincent

The tugboats *Pilgrim* and *Leona R.* started searching for the wreck by dragging a chain, strung between them, around the bottom of the bay. The bodies of eight victims had not been accounted for and searchers hoped that by finding the hull, they could find the missing passengers. By mid-December the hull was thought to be located but it was decided that no diver would be sent down due to the impracticality of sending a diver to such great depth.

In 1931, the *Hackley* was again thought to have been located, this time by Captain Frank Drew. The vessel was located by diver Frank Hoffman in early June of 1980. Hoffman had already located and raised the schooner, *Alvin Clark*, and hoped to add the *Hackley* to his display. The Hoffman expedition worked through the summer and into the fall, gathering artifacts and preparing the *Hackley* for raising. The group did not pump the hull free of silt as they had done with the *Clark*. Nylon slings were pulled underneath the hull to cradle it for the lift to the surface. When tension was taken on the cables, one sling cut through the hull, slicing off part of the stern.

Skeletal remains were recovered from the wreck site by the expedition and for years were kept in a museum drawer due to a "catch-22" situation involving money and the law. The remains, by law, had to be buried in a legal grave which would have cost up to $1,000. No one wanted to pay for the interment. A reburial at sea was considered "polluting." By law the remains were the responsibility of living relatives, but none could be found. A burial site was finally arranged for by the charity of a Sturgeon Bay mortuary.

The *Hackley* had more than her share of bad luck in the fall of 1903. A week before she was lost, a voyage had to be canceled when heavy winds lowered the water in her slip at Detroit Harbor leaving her grounded. Two weeks before that, her boiler gave out as she was leaving Menominee harbor and the steamer had to be towed back to port for repairs. The week before that, the vessel was leaving Menominee when she picked up a log in her propeller, damaging that shaft coupling.

In December of 1903 a government court of inquiry was convened. After hearing testimony of witnesses, fishermen, caulkers, machinists, boiler makers, etc., George Uhler, inspector general of steam vessels, concluded that the "tornado" that sank the *Hackley* would have wrecked any vessel of her class. A sarcastic letter published in the DOOR COUNTY ADVOCATE accused the government of "whitewashing" the true story.

The *Erie L. Hackley* was built in 1882 at Muskegon, Michigan. She registered 91 gross tons with a length of 79 feet, a beam of 17.4 feet, and a depth of 5.2 feet. DOOR COUNTY ADVOCATE, May 1, 9, September 5, 12, 26, October 5, 10, 24, November 7, 1903. KEWAUNEE ENTERPRISE, December 25, 1903. DOOR COUNTY ADVOCATE, February 6, 1931. GREEN BAY PRESS-GAZETTE, June 5,

1980. GREEN BAY PRESS-GAZETTE, February 7, 1986. List of Merchant Vessels of the U.S., 1903, p. 227.

288) Pile Driver, Foundered prior to 1903.

The pile driver was on a scow in tow of the tug, *Temple Emory*, bound from Menominee to Escanaba, when the entourage was overwhelmed by a storm. The scow capsized and everything sank.

In December of 1903, the Menominee River Shingle Company, owners of the driver, took out a suit in Milwaukee against the Mann Brothers, owners of the tug. DOOR COUNTY ADVOCATE, December 12, 1903.

289) *Ann Arbor #4*, Small Craft, Foundered January, 1903

The January 29, 1903 issue of the KEWAUNEE ENTERPRISE reported, "A small craft, dubbed the *Ann Arbor #4* and in the service of the Ann Arbor line at Manistique, was recently blown out into the lake and is lost. Reports, first of the week, said that it was one of the car ferries but the rumor was false."

290) *Leo*, #14803, Schooner, Abandoned 1904.

The *Leo* was left to settle in the mud below the bridge in Sturgeon Bay. Her decks were covered. The previous August, the tug *Brooks* had brought the vessel from Algoma where she had been sitting on the bottom of the river. For a time the schooner had been used as a boarding house for fishermen at Washington Island.

The *Leo* was left to sit for fifteen years until 1919 when the Leathem Smith yard, in front of which she was abandoned, grew tired of the obstacle. The wreck was dynamited by diver Pearl Purdy.

The *Leo* was built in 1861 in Sheboygan and measured 94.43 gross tons. DOOR COUNTY ADVOCATE, December 6, 1902. DOOR COUNTY ADVOCATE, August 8, 1903. DOOR COUNTY ADVOCATE, May 7, 1904.

DOOR COUNTY ADVOCATE, May 23, 1919. List of Merchant Vessels of the U.S., 1884, p. 182.

291) *Ebeneezer*, #136136, Schooner, Abandoned in 1905.

In February of 1905, the DOOR COUNTY ADVOCATE reported that Captain F. Hoganson could not get his schooner, the *Ebeneezer*, off the beach at Ephraim. Hoganson sold what portions of the ship as he could and abandoned her. She had gone on the beach near the Evergreen hotel some time before. The hotel was also the property of Captain Hoganson. The vessel was dropped from the government list for 1904. The *Ebeneezer* was built in Ephraim in 1890 and boasted three masts. She registered 39.29 gross tons with a length of 57 feet, a beam of 15.5 feet, and a depth of 5.5 feet. DOOR COUNTY ADVOCATE, September 26, 1896. DOOR COUNTY ADVOCATE, February 18, 1905. List of Merchant Vessels of the U.S., 1895, p. 49. List of Merchant Vessels of the U.S., 1903, p. 45.

292) *Vlasta*, Tug, Abandoned Early Spring of 1905.

The *Vlasta* was left to decay a short distance up the Kewaunee River. Her engine and boiler were removed.

The tug was built in Manitowoc and brought up to Kewaunee where she became the first steam vessel to navigate the Kewaunee River. She was originally mastered by Captain Reed who used her for an excursion boat among other things. Later John Borgman bought her and installed a larger engine and marine boiler. For a while she was in the stone trade and was used in building the harbor piers. No steamer by the name of *"Vlasta"* or any version of it could be found in the List of Merchant Vessels of the U.S. KEWAUNEE ENTERPRISE, March 17, 1905.

293) *George Presley*, #86038, Steamer, Burned July 26, 1905.

The *Presley* was passing through Death's Door Passage on her way to pick up iron ore at Escanaba, when she caught fire. Fire broke out about 11 a.m. and was soon out of control. The Plum Island lifesaving crew rescued the crew and most of their valuables and they were landed safely at Escanaba by the tug, *Lilly E.* The hull was grounded on a rocky beach but was later towed to Sturgeon Bay where she was left in the "boneyard."

The wreck was stripped of all fixtures, furniture, etc. by Captain Thomas Isabell. Isabell later purchased the hulk with intentions of removing the portable machinery, chains, anchors and any other salvageable equipment.

The *George Presley* was owned by the Mona Transportation Co. of Cleveland, valued at $95,000 and insured for $70,000. She was built in 1889 and measured 1,936.24 gross tons with a length of 265 feet, a beam of 41 feet, and a depth of 20 feet. DOOR COUNTY ADVOCATE, July 29, September 9, 1905. DOOR COUNTY ADVOCATE, May 18, 1906. List of Merchant Vessels of the U.S., 1895, p. 249.

294) *Julia*, Schooner, Stranded September 2, 1905.

The *Julia* was blown ashore near Ford River in the big storm of 1905. She had been loaded at Escanaba with posts for delivery at the Wolverine Lumber Co. at Menominee. Attempts were made to salvage her but she was declared a total loss and abandoned. The schooner was valued at $300 and was under the command of Captain Bjorklund. She hailed from Marinette.

There were two schooners by this name sailing in the Lake Michigan area. Number 76732 was built at Fort Howard in 1888. It measured 47.11 gross tons with a length of 71 feet, a beam of 19 feet, and a depth of 4 feet.

Number 76140 was built at Bay City, Michigan, in 1880. It measured 36.65 gross tons with a length of 57.6 feet, a beam of 18 feet, and a depth of 5 feet. DOOR COUNTY ADVOCATE,

The steamer George Presley.

Photo courtesy of the Great Lakes Marine Collection of the Milwaukee Public Library/Wisconsin Marine Historical Society

295) *Iver Lawson*, #12436, Schooner, Stranded September 2, 1905.

The *Iver Lawson*, like the schooner, *Julia*, was a victim of the big storm of 1905. The *Lawson* had come from St. Joseph, Michigan to take on a load of lumber at Masonville, Michigan. Shortly after the schooner passed into Green Bay, she was struck by a north wind of hurricane force. With her sails shredded, the *Lawson* was swept down the bay until she grounded on the south shore of Horseshoe Bay. Captain Henry Larson and his crew of four waited out the storm in the vessel. When the blow subsided, they found their vessel far up on the beach at a point two miles south of Horseshoe Bay. With an off shore breeze, visitors to the wreck could walk all the way around the hull without getting their feet wet.

Captain David Ramage intended to release the *Lawson* from the beach. The following summer, plans were made for raising the hull on jackscrews, and building launching ways underneath the vessel so she could be slid 75 feet to water deep enough to float her. Ramage had a tug off shore to pull the *Lawson* down the ways but the vessel would not budge.

Because of the failed effort, Ramage brought suit against the salvor, Dell Cleveland who in turn brought suit against Ramage. The case was ultimately decided in favor of Cleveland for the full amount.

By the summer of 1908 the *Iver Lawson* was still waiting to be floated. Ramage decided to continue the salvage effort on his own. In July of that year, an attempt was made by Captain Thomas Isabell to pull the hull into deep water. The crew was chased off the site by a storm and returned to find the *Lawson* pushed off the ramp and a hole punched in her bottom. Everyone thought the vessel would be abandoned except Isabell who thought with some good weather he could release her. The schooner was ultimately dismantled.

The *Iver Lawson* was built in Chicago in 1869 and was valued at $1,800 but was not insured. She registered 149.43 gross tons with a length of 116 feet, a beam of 25.5 feet, and a depth of 8 feet. DOOR COUNTY ADVOCATE, October 28, 1905. DOOR COUNTY ADVOCATE, August 2, 1906. DOOR COUNTY ADVOCATE, February 7, 1907. DOOR COUNTY ADVOCATE, July 9, 16, 1908. List of Merchant Vessels of the U.S., 1895, p. 96.

296) *Senator*, #22917, Schooner, Stranded September 27, 1905.

The carferry, *Ann Arbor No. 3* reported the *Senator* ashore ten miles south of Point au Barque. She was stripped and abandoned. Her spars were gone and she was "making heavy weather in the gale." There was no sign of the crew. The schooner was owned by the Chandler brothers of Detroit. According to the MANISTIQUE EVENING she was loaded with timber. The DOOR COUNTY ADVOCATE reported she had left Cleveland, September 15, loaded with 600 tons of soft coal for Leathem & Smith at Sturgeon Bay.

The *Senator* was built at Clayton, New York, in 1863. She measured 332.38 tons with a length of 136.8 feet, a beam of 26 feet and a depth of 12 feet. MANISTIQUE EVENING, September 27, reprinted by the DOOR COUNTY ADVOCATE, September 30, 1905. List of Merchant Vessels of the U.S., 1895, p.182.

297) *Elizabeth*, #135939, Scow-Schooner, Sunk October 19, 1905.

The List of Merchant Vessels of the United States for 1907 reported the *Elizabeth* lost after she collided with the pier at Menominee. The two people aboard were saved.

The scow measured 25 gross tons with a length of 51

The Iver Lawson laying upon what is probably the remains of her launch ramp.

Photo courtesy of the Great Lakes Marine Collection
of the Milwaukee Public Library/Wisconsin Marine Historical Society

feet, a beam of 15.4 feet and a depth of 4 feet. She was built at Sturgeon Bay in 1887. List of Merchant Vessels of the U. S., 1905, p.47. List of Merchant Vessels of the U. S., 1907, p. 375.

298) *Foam*, #120575, Scow-Schooner, Stranded October 26, 1905.

The *Foam* was a victim of the Big Storm of 1905. She was blown ashore near the A.B. Stevenson wharf and in the gale was washed over the abandoned schooner, *Charley Smith*, already sunk there.

The *Foam* registered 42.9 gross tons with a length of 81.4 feet, a beam of 18.6 feet, and a depth of 4.6 feet. She was built at Menekaunee, Wisconsin in 1882. DOOR COUNTY ADVOCATE, October 28, 1905. List of Merchant Vessels of the U.S., 1895, p. 69.

299) *Charley J. Smith*, #125749, Schooner, Abandoned October 28, 1905.

The schooner was reported abandoned at the A.B. Stevenson wharf at the head of Little Sturgeon Bay where it was reportedly going to pieces.

While the *Smith* was commonly referred to as the *Charles Smith*, the List of Merchant Vessels listed her as *Charley*. (Apparently they were on good terms.) She was built at South Haven, Michigan in 1879 and carried a crew of two. The *Smith* registered 42 gross tons and measured 60 feet in length, 16.8 feet across the beam and a 4.9 foot depth in the hold. DOOR COUNTY ADVOCATE, September 28, November 11, 1905. List of Merchant Vessels of the U.S., 1904, p. 30.

300) R.J. Hackett, #21934, Steamer, Burned November 12, 1905.

The *Hackett* was on her way from Cleveland with a load of coal. She was in the Cedar River area when fire was discovered, and, with the flames out of control, she was run aground on Whale Back Shoal. The crew of thirteen men escaped in the lifeboats and were later picked up by the fishtug, *Stewart Edward*, which took them to Marinette.

The steamer was owned by her captain, H.C. McCallum. She was built by Peck and Masters in Cleveland in 1869 and was valued at $16,000

The *Hackett* was the first Great Lakes ship built to carry bulk cargoes. She was the first to feature the classic profile of a Great Lakes ore boat with the engine room astern, the pilot house at the bow, and a long expanse of hatches in between. She measured 211 feet in length, 32.5 feet at the beam, 19.2 feet in depth and registered 1,129 tons. Door County Advocate, November 18, 1905. List of Merchant Vessels of the U.S., 1895, p. 291. Beasley, Norman. Freighters of Fortune, The Story of the Great Lakes. New York : Harper & Brothers. 1930. pp. 183, 227.

301) *Nellie and Annie*, #18748, Scow-Schooner, Stranded November 21, 1906.

The *Nellie and Annie* had been lying on the bottom at Sawyer Harbor but was washed up on the beach in a storm November 21, 1906.

The scow registered 37.05 gross tons with a length of 67.3 feet, 17.6 foot beam, and a 4.4 foot depth. She was built in Chicago in 1872. Door County Advocate, November 29, 1906. List of Merchant Vessels of the U.S., 1895, p. 158.

302) *Liberty*, Steam Barge, Scuttled December, 1906.

The *Liberty* was one of several hulks left abandoned on the bottom of the Kewaunee Harbor. The contract for her removal was given to Major J.V. Judson who, according to the Door County Advocate, intended to fix her up and put her into commission.

The Kewaunee Enterprise also reported that the *Liberty* was under consideration for possible resurrection. The newspaper also stated that the steamer, currently laying in the north basin of the harbor, was to be hauled up on the beach near the aluminum sign company. Judson had given the contract for removing her to the tug, *James E. Brooks*, with wrecking master Charles Metzner in charge.

In spite of all good intentions to recommission the *Liberty*, she was taken out in the Lake and scuttled off Kewaunee in December. The steamer was described as measuring 70 gross tons.

There were a number of vessels by this name operating in the Kewaunee area, none of which were close to 70 tons.

A likely possibility is #141011. This stern wheeled steam barge had been built in Fort Howard in 1889 for Freeman and Kellogg of Green Bay. Shortly after she was launched she was partly destroyed by fire while moored at her pier. A spark from a passing steamer was thought to have started the blaze which destroyed all of her upper works. The steamer, valued at $8,000, was deemed unsalvageable and was pushed on to the river bank where she sat abandoned for over a year. In September of 1890 she was hauled off, given a new life and returned to service. The *Liberty* (#141011), measured 143.55 gross tons with a length of 96.8 feet, a beam of 18.3 feet, and a depth of 5.5 feet. DOOR COUNTY ADVOCATE, August 17, November 9, 1889. DOOR COUNTY ADVOCATE, September 6, 1890. KEWAUNEE ENTERPRISE, October 26, 1906. DOOR COUNTY ADVOCATE, November 1, December 27, 1906. List of Merchant Vessels of the U.S., 1888, p. 288. List of Merchant Vessels of the U.S.,1902, p. 266.

303) *Katoosch*, Sloop, Scuttled December, 1906.

The *Katoosch* had been left lying near the north arm of the Kewaunee harbor near the government pier. Government contractor, Major J.V. Judson, of the Army Corps of Engineers, had her towed out into the lake and scuttled. DOOR COUNTY ADVOCATE, December 27, 1906.

304) *James N. Brooks*, #75718, Tug, Scuttled December, 1906.

The KEWAUNEE ENTERPRISE reported the *Brooks* as one of the old wrecks in Kewaunee harbor scheduled for removal. Her boiler and twelve horsepower steam engine were still aboard and were later removed in preparation for her disposal. Like the other wrecks, the tug was towed out into the lake in December and sent to the bottom.

According to the ENTERPRISE, the *Brooks* was one of the first, if not THE first tugs to engage in fishing on Lake Michigan. She had been used in the fishing trade for almost thirty years until she was brought to Kewaunee in 1905 and allowed to sink.

The *James N. Brooks* was built in Milwaukee in 1872 but was registered at Grand Haven, Michigan. She had measured 10 gross tons with a length of 41.1 feet, a beam of 11.5 feet, and a depth of 4.8 feet. Kewaunee Enterprise, October 26, 1906. Door County Advocate, November 1, December 12, 1906. List of Merchant Vessels of the U.S., 1895, p. 262.

305) *Exchange*, #8796, Schooner, Scuttled December 1906.

The *Exchange* was one of the wrecks left to sink in the north basin of the Kewaunee harbor. In October of 1906, Major J.V. Judson, of the Army Corps of Engineers, gave orders for her removal to Lake Michigan, where she would be scuttled. The *Exchange*, in her earlier days, had been a well known west shore trader.

The *Exchange* was built in 1871 at Sheboygan, Wisconsin, and registered 27 gross tons. She measured 52 feet in length, 15 feet across the beam, and 5 feet in depth. Kewaunee Enterprise, October 26, 1906. Door County Advocate, November 1, December 27, 1906. List of Merchant Vessels of the U.S., 1896, p. 62.

306) *Edith H. Koyen*, #13647, Scow-Schooner, Scuttled December of 1906.

The *Koyen* was one of a number of vessels condemned to the bottom of the lake by the Army Corps of Engineers. Compared to other vessels sentenced to destruction, the schooner was relatively young, having been built in 1890. She came to grief when, under the command of Captain Chris Braunsdord, she started taking on water while moored at the Clay Banks pier. She was brought to Kewaunee harbor and allowed to settle on the bottom. Major J.V. Judson gave the contract for her removal to the

Aluminum Sign Company and in December she was towed out into the lake off Kewaunee and sunk.

The *Koyen* was built at Washington Harbor and measured 38 gross tons with a length of 55.6 feet, a beam of 17 feet, and a depth of 5.5 feet. KEWAUNEE ENTERPRISE, October 26, 1906. DOOR COUNTY ADVOCATE, November 1, December 27, 1906. List of Merchant Vessels of the U.S., 1895, p. 50.

307) *John M. Nicol*, #76786, Steamer, Stranded December 13, 1906.

The *Nicol* had left St. Ignace, Michigan, Thursday morning bound for Gladstone, Michigan. Even as she left, the steamer was taking on water. Several hours after she left port she encountered a gale with fifty mile per hour winds. Water poured into her hold until her captain, J.M. Saunders, could barely control her and ordered her beached on Summer Island. Saunders told a newspaper reporter that when the storm struck, heavy winds made for mountainous waves, adding, "every crash was followed by ripping and breaking of the hull...I never thought she would last through the night."

After the *Nicol* was beached, her stern was ripped away by the waves and the forward section of the hull threatened to break apart at any moment. The crew saved nothing but the clothes they wore. The nineteen sailors suffered from exposure and several endured frozen hands and feet. Two attempts were made to launch a lifeboat resulting in the near drowning of two crewmen. A third attempt was successful and the little craft headed to shore with a lifeline. When it approached shore, the line fouled and had to be cut.

The captain and crew had nearly given up when the wreck was sighted by three fishermen from Fairport. The threesome made their way to the wreck in a small gas launch and rescued captain and crew. The sailors were taken to Garden, Michigan, from where they made their way to Escanaba. The wrecking tug, *Favorite*, was sent to salvage what it could of the wreck.

In later weeks, efforts began to recover the 2,500 tons of barbed wire valued at $60,000. During the salvage program, one diver, Pearl Purdy, was nearly killed. Purdy was diving in the hold retrieving spools of wire when he fell. Trying to retrace his steps he accidentally walked around the ladder twice, cutting off his air supply and tangling his safety line. His tender, Frank Isabel, ordered his men to pull the entangled diver to the surface. Purdy came up feet first. Isabel then jumped into the icy water and cut Purdy's hose and safety line releasing him from the ladder. Both Isabel and Purdy recovered in a short time.

By early March the cargo of wire had been salvaged. Isabel did not think any attempt would be made to salvage the hull. "Land pirates" had boarded the vessel and taken anything of value. Even the the windows in the pilot house and the cabin were pried off.

The *John M. Nicol* was a wooden package freighter, built in West Bay City, Michigan, 1889. She measured 2126 gross tons with a length of 263 feet, a beam of 41.6 feet and a depth in the hold of 15.7 feet. Door County Advocate, December 20, 1906. Manistique Pioneer-Tribune, December 21, 1906. Door County Advocate, January 3, February 28, March 7, 1907. List of Merchant Vessels of the U.S., 1895, p. 265.

308) *Mishicott*, #91439, Scow-Schooner, Capsized April 4, 1907.

The *Mishicott* had been at the Pankratz Lumber Mill in Sturgeon Bay where she filled with water, capsized and sank. In July of that same year, Captain Thomas Isabel succeeded in raising the schooner and it was run up on the mud on the east side of the shipyard (presumably Leathem -Smith) in Sturgeon Bay.

Years later, in 1912, she was reported rotting in the mud and going to pieces with her spars falling over.

The *Mishicott* was built in 1882 at Manitowoc. She registered 73.49 gross tons with length of 79.2 feet, a beam of 21.5 feet and a depth of 6.1 feet. DOOR COUNTY ADVOCATE, April 4, July 25, 1907. DOOR COUNTY ADVOCATE, April 18, 1912. List of Merchant Vessels of the U.S., 1896, p. 145.

309) *Sea Flower*, #116782, Sloop Yacht, Stranded January 14, 1907.

The List of Merchant Vessels for 1907 lists the *Sea Flower* as having been lost at Green Bay where she stranded. She was built in 1896 at Marinette and registered 7 gross tons with a length of 30.5 feet, a beam of 11.3 feet and a depth of 3.2 feet. List of Merchant Vessels of the U.S., 1904, p. 157. List of Merchant Vessels of the U.S., 1907, p. 377.

310) *S.B. Paige*, #116335, Schooner, Stranded September 10, 1907.

The *Paige* was bound from Fish Creek to Sturgeon Bay with 30 cords of shingle bolts. Having fought heavy weather, Captain Alfred Graham ordered the anchor dropped when they reached the mouth of the bay. The schooner labored against the strong northwest winds until the anchor let go. She was swept before the wind before she stranded on the "middle ground" in Sturgeon Bay and settled in six feet of water.

The lifesaving service arrived on the scene the following morning and attempted to pump out the hull. The effort was futile and Graham and his assistant were taken off the vessel. The *Paige* had been built in 1863 and was deemed unworthy of the expense to salvage her. The following March the ADVOCATE reported the the old ship was still on the shoal and "will leave her bones on the spot." The news article stated that she was in bad shape even before the ice

The steamer John M. Nicol.

Photo courtesy of the Wisconsin Maritime Museum, Manitowoc, Wisconsin

inside raised the decks and bulged the sides. The cargo of shingle bolts was salvaged within the month.

In the autumn of 1906, the *S.B. Paige* had been blown on the beach at Sturgeon Bay in the bight of the Leathem Smith pier. She was left to sit for nine months before her owner, Nels Nelson, pulled her off with great difficulty. After she found the shallows of the "middle ground," Nelson stripped her of her spars, rigging and anything else of value.

The old hulk affected the currents flowing around the shoal creating a sand bar. In 1908, George Pittenger, a summer cottage owner on the Bay shore, asked the Federal government for permission to dynamite the wreck. The sand bar had grown to such proportions that Pittenger and his neighbors feared they would not be able to pull their "motor power boats" up to the docks. Indeed, the following year, a news article warned,

" The wrecks of the schooner S.B. Paige *and the steamer Joys, which are submerged at a point below the island mill property—one abreast of Pittenger's dock and the other just below the Pankratz breakwater—are a dangerous menace to small motor boats and should be destroyed or marked so as to give this class of craft warning. Some day a boat will run onto one of them with a load of passengers and there will be a disaster of more or less magnitude."*

The *S.B. Paige* was built in Oshkosh in 1863 and for 30 of her 45 years had carried lime, brick, and other building materials. She was rigged like a Maine fishing schooner...

"with two tall tapering masts, short bowsprit, (no jibboom), a very large jib and two large fore and aft sails, a short main top mast, hemp standing rigging and jib hanks made of wood. She was built by a Mr. Fowler, a Maine shipbuilder, and was launched on a Friday, disproving the old curse about Friday launchings."

The *Paige* registered 47.49 gross tons with a length of

79.0 feet, a beam of 20 feet and a depth of 4.5 feet. Door County Advocate, November 22, 1906. Door County Advocate, March 5, 26, June 27, September 12, October 3, 1907. Door County Advocate, March 5, 1908. Door County Advocate, April 30, June 25, 1908. Door County Advocate, June 10, 1909. List of Merchant Vessels of the U.S., 1895, p. 174.

311) *Romuldus*, #111159, Schooner, Abandoned August of 1907.

The Door County Advocate, August 15, 1907 included a small item stating that the *Romuldus* was left sunk in the mud near Baileys Harbor. No other information was available on her ultimate disposition. According to the List of Merchant Vessels of the U.S., 1907 (page 127), she was built in 1897 at Muskegon, Michigan, and registered 15 gross tons. She measured 42 feet in length, 11.4 feet across the beam and 4.2 feet in depth.

312) *Cecilia Hill*, #127154, STEAMER, BURNED April 7, 1906.

The *Hill* caught fire and burned in the harbor at Fish Creek. The burned hulk was towed out to Horseshoe Island where she was shoved up on the beach pending her fate. Thomas Isabel had her taken to Sturgeon Bay, there to be left beside the burned steamer, *George Presley*, where she would be stripped of anything useful.

The *Cecilia Hill* was built at Fish Creek in 1896 and registered 44 gross tons with a crew of seven. She measured 93 feet in length with a beam of 19.5 feet and a depth of 7.5 feet. Door County Advocate, September 17, October 3, 1907. List of Merchant Vessels of the U.S., 1903, p. 208. List of Merchant Vessels of the U.S., 1907, p. 378.

313) *Anspatch*, #106402, Fish Tug, Foundered February 19, 1908.

The *Anspatch* reached the harbor entrance at Sturgeon

217

Bay in a blizzard. A gale wind blew her from her course. As she was blown by the pier a line was thrown to onlookers. They were unable to catch it and she was carried away. The tug was blown up against a shelf of ice, puncturing the hull, and just as this occurred, a wave hit the vessel wiping away the cabin. Crewmen Jacobson and Bellinghouser were lost. The *Anspaich* was owned by the Smith Fishing company and was valued at $5,000. She measured 15 gross tons with a length of 45.3 feet, a beam of 12.3 feet and a depth of 5.3 feet. She was built in Detroit in 1879. DOOR COUNTY ADVOCATE, February 27, 1908. List of Merchant Vessel of the U.S., 1907, p.166.

314) *Rob Roy*, #21795, Schooner, Stranded April 27, 1908.

The *Rob Roy* was destroyed in a northeaster while on her way from Menominee to Masonport, Michigan. She was only a couple miles from her destination when the storm hit. Both anchors were dropped but the cables parted and she drifted ashore and broke up. Her captain and crew reached shore safely. She was owned and sailed by Captain Emanuel Halgren who stripped her of what little usables she had aboard and abandoned her.

The *Rob Roy* was built at Perry, Ohio, in 1868 and measured 98 feet in length with a beam of 22 feet, and a depth of 6 feet. She registered 97 gross tons. DOOR COUNTY ADVOCATE, April 30, 1908. List of Merchant Vessels of the U.S., 1907, p. 126.

315) *Kate Williams*, #14040, Tug, Abandoned in early August of 1908.

In September of 1907, the *Williams* sank in the harbor at Jackson Harbor, Washington Island, and later washed up on a reef in the harbor. Attempts were made later that year to salvage her, but the effort was abandoned in November.

Thomas Smith bought the wreck for $1,200. The summer of 1908 brought renewed efforts to rescue the tug, but during the salvage effort, she was washed up on the rocks. With her frames and sides broken in, she was deemed unworthy of recovery. Smith decided to salvage the boiler and machinery and abandon the rest.

Problems abounded for the *Williams*, her captain, her various owners and her salvors. The wreck was originally sold when her captain, John Hayes had her libeled for $400 for wages. He was the first of ten libelants and before he could get his money the Federal Marshal's office had to pay their expenses of $1,400. When salvage of the tug's machinery began, Smith's crew found themselves fighting the weather continuously. Work was scheduled, canceled, and rescheduled as the winds came and went. After much effort the boiler was finally removed. Something slipped and it was dropped into the lake. The "kettle" was later recovered. Ultimately, pilings were sunk to protect the operation from the relentless west winds. When it came time to recover the tug's shaft and wheel, the decision was made to dynamite the stern. Before anything could be done, diver Pearl Purdy blew off part of his hand when he attempted to pick up a blasting cap with a knife.

In 1876 during her early career, the *Kate Williams* was the subject of something of an international scandal. The DETROIT FREE PRESS reported, and the CHICAGO TRIBUNE reprinted:

"It is not often that lawyers get a chance to steal a steamboat any more than other people. Probably that may not be what ails the tug Kate Williams. *Monday night she was still taking a rest where she had been for many months chained beneath the shadow of the Dominion flag at Windsor. Why she was there does not belong in this chapter. Monday morning at 9 o'clock the tug* Winslow *pulled up to one of the American docks with the* Kate Williams *in tow. The officer and lawyer (accidentally on board) report*

finding the wandering Kate *tied loose in American waters, down the river and brought her hither and were disposed to retain possession of her. The sequel is not yet. Meanwhile she lies at Clark's 'boneyard.'"*

No explanation was ever given for the *Williams'* having been seized by Canadian authorities. It may have something to do with that fact that at this time Canadian port officials were seizing American vessels for towing and salvaging wrecks in Canadian waters and vice versa.

The *Kate Williams* registered 164 gross tons with a length of 112.6 feet, a beam of 20.9 feet and a depth of 9.8 feet. She was an old vessel having been built at Cleveland, Ohio, in 1862. CHICAGO TRIBUNE, September 22, 1876. DOOR COUNTY ADVOCATE, October 3, 24, 1907. KEWAUNEE ENTERPRISE, May 29, 1908. DOOR COUNTY ADVOCATE, July 23, August 6, 27, September 10, 1908. List of Merchant Vessels of the U.S., 1907, p. 238.

316) *S.C. Baldwin*, #23957, Stone Barge, Capsized August 27, 1908. (Author's note: While this vessel was not wrecked in the geographical area covered by this book, parts of it did float here...and it makes a good story.)

The *S.C. Baldwin*, with the barge, *Great Lakes*, had been in tow of the tug *Torrent*, bound from Sturgeon Bay with a load of stone for Manitowoc. A heavy sea swept over the lake all evening of the 26th, and in coping with the weather, the *Baldwin* sprung a leak. She parted her line and went adrift in the darkness about five miles north of Twin Rivers Point light. The vessel began to labor in the waves and suddenly flipped over and sank taking down with her two of her three crewmen. The *Torrent* spent some time looking for the missing men before she headed for Two Rivers to alert the lifesaving crew. The following afternoon the steamer, *Caroline*, discovered the sole survivor, Captain George Heins, shortly after leaving Kewaunee.

The tug Kate Williams

Photo courtesy of the Great Lakes Marine Collection of the Milwaukee Public Library/Wisconsin Marine Historical Society

Heins told authorities that the cargo of stone shifted in the wind and the craft developed an increasing list. Heins and another sailor, Jacob Wiltgen, were able to put on life jackets. After the barge sank, the sailors were able to stay together until late morning when they were separated in the wind. Wiltgen's body was found several miles north of Kewaunee two days later. Heins was able to pull himself up onto some floating wreckage.

According to a report made to Major J.V. Hudson of the Corps of Engineers, the *Baldwin* was lying in sixty feet of water, two and a half miles southeast by south from Twin Rivers Point light. Because of her depth, the *Baldwin* was not considered a menace to navigation. No plans had been made as yet to salvage the wreck which was valued at $1,500.

In April of 1913, wreckage, identified as being from the *Baldwin*, was found ashore a mile south of the store in Carlton, Wisconsin. It was said to be part of the wreckage on which George Heins had saved himself five years before.

The *S.C. Baldwin* was built in Detroit in 1871 as a steamer and was used for years in the ore trade between Escanaba and Chicago. She was later purchased by Sturgeon Bay interests and converted into a stone carrier. The *Baldwin*, like her consort and escort, was the property of the Green Stone Company. She measured 412.54 tons, with a length of 160 feet, a beam of 30 feet, and a depth of 11 feet. KEWAUNEE ENTERPRISE, August 28, September 4, 11, 1908. DOOR COUNTY ADVOCATE, April 17, 1913. List of Merchant Vessels of the U.S., 1895, p. 295.

317) *Seaman*, #23466, Schooner, Stranded November 15, 1908.

The *Seaman* stranded on the outer shoal of Pilot Island and, with her cargo of 3,000 bushels of potatoes, became a total loss. She was under the command of Captain Gunder Hansen. He and his crew of four were rescued by the Plum Island life saving crew. Built in Cleveland in 1848, the *Seaman* was one of the oldest vessels then serving on the lakes. She was owned by M.O. Parker of Milwaukee and measured 181 gross tons. The Seaman was 120 feet in length with a beam of 25.6 feet and a depth of 8.7 feet. DOOR COUNTY ADVOCATE, November 26, 1908. <u>List of Merchant Vessels of the U.S.</u>, 1907, p. 134.

The schooner Berwyn
Photo courtesy of the Great Lakes Marine Collection
of the Milwaukee Public Library/Wisconsin Marine Historical Society

318) *Berwyn*, #21585, Schooner, Stranded November 23, 1908.

The *Berwyn* was in tow of the steam barge, *Walter Vail*, bound for cargo at Nahma when both vessels stranded on the south end of Plum Island in a dense fog. The *Vail* was able to free herself. Both vessels were under the charge of Captain Robert Evans who ordered the steamer to pull her consort off the rocks. Several attempts were made with the tow line parting each time.

The tug, *Duncan City*, was sent for, however, the wind shifted to the southeast and drove the wreck on a rock ledge and pounded her side off. She was then abandoned. Captain Fred Richter was left in charge of the ship's outfit which was to be stripped and forwarded to Chicago.

The *Berwyn* was built as the *R.C. Crawford* in Algomac, Michigan, in 1866. She was owned by J.P. Bates of Chicago and was uninsured. The schooner measured 269 gross tons with a length of 132 feet, a beam of 29.2 feet and a depth of 10 feet. She carried a crew of six. DOOR COUNTY ADVOCATE, November 26, December 3, 1908. KEWAUNEE ENTERPRISE, December 4, 1908. List of Merchant Vessels of the U.S., 1907, p. 18.

319) *Mary L.*, #92661, Schooner, Abandoned December 5, 1908.

The *Mary L.* was punctured by ice at the head of the bay. Captain Chris Braunsdorf and his two sons were rescued by the launch, *Ariadne*, which took the leaking schooner to the life saving station to be pumped out before running her into the muck. She was left in the shallows on the west side of Sturgeon Bay halfway between the city and the south end of the canal.

The schooner was left to sit for over a year and in July of 1910, was destroyed by fire. The blaze was thought to have been set accidentally by local boys using the vessel as a club house. Braunsdorf figured on rebuilding the craft although those who examined it thought it would be expensive and difficult. The List of Merchant Vessels of the U.S., for 1911 describes her as having burned at Sturgeon Bay and dropped from the registry.

The *Mary L.* was built in 1895 and was owned by Braunsdorf. She registered 30 tons and measured 62 feet in length, 17 feet across the beam and a depth of 4.7 feet. Door County Advocate, December 24, 1908. Door County Advocate, July 14, August 4, August 25, 1910. List of Merchant Vessels of the U.S., 1907, p. 102. List of Merchant Vessels of the U.S., 1911, p. 411.

320) *Madonna*, #90717, Schooner, Burned January of 1909.

Captain Ole Christianson of Washington Island was finished with his old schooner. He cut out the cabin and hauled it ashore for use as a shop. The remains of the vessel were set afire, destroying everything above the ice.

The *Madonna* was built at Milwaukee in 1871. In her working days she had required a crew of four and registered 76 gross tons. She measured 79.8 feet in length, 24.4 feet in the beam and 6.2 feet in depth. Door County Advocate, February 7, 1909. List of Merchant Vessels of the U.S., 1907, p. 96.

321) *Lily Amoit*, #15899, Schooner, Exploded June 6, 1909.

The *Lily Amoit* had stopped off at the pier in Ellison Bay on her way home to Washington Island. The schooner was loaded with general freight including 100 lbs. of dynamite and 25 barrels of gasoline. (The Green Bay Gazette reported 500 lbs. of dynamite and 34 barrels of gasoline.) While the vessel was tied up, her owner, John C. Jessen, discovered a leak and, in an effort to pinpoint it, lit a match. The hold quickly became engulfed in flames and attempts to extinguish it proved futile. The lines were cut and the burning vessel was allowed to drift away from the pier. Two hours later, when the *Amoit* had drifted to the west side of Ellison Bay, she exploded shooting her masts up in the air and tossing up an ignited barrel of gas which blew up. The blast shook buildings for a radius of five miles and was reportedly heard as far away as Washington Island, fifteen miles away.

The *Lily Amoit* belonged to John and Abraham Jessen. Neither the vessel or its cargo, which was valued at $300, were insured. Interestingly enough, the craft was missing from Federal listings for 1907 and 1909. She registered 25 gross tons with a length of 47.4 feet, a beam of 12.4 feet, and a depth of 4.7 feet. She was built in Cheboygan, Michigan, in 1873. Green Bay Gazette, June 7, 1909. Door County Advocate, June 10, 1909. List of Merchant Vessels of the U.S., 1904, p.104.

322) *German*, #39249, Schooner-Barge, Abandoned 1909.

The *German* had seen duty in the Sturgeon Bay area most recently as a salvage barge under the ownership of Captain Thomas Isabel. She was finally abandoned in the boneyard south of the shipyard in Sturgeon Bay and was dropped from the government list sometime after 1908. Her spars and rigging were taken off and she was left to go to pieces.

The *German* was built in 1868 at Black River, Ohio. She registered 77.88 gross tons and measured 80.8 feet in length, 20.7 feet at the beam and 5.9 feet in depth. Door County Advocate, July 7, 1910. List of Merchant Vessels of the U.S., 1895, p. 77.

323) *Defiance*, #202375, Schooner, Stranded Late fall of 1909.

The *Defiance* dragged her anchors and ran aground at Ford River. She was later declared a total loss. The schooner was owned by Captain James Larson of Menekaune. The *Defiance* was a relatively new vessel having been built at Marinette in 1905. She registered 111 gross tons and measured 90.6 feet in length, 24.4 feet across the beam and 7 feet in depth. Door County Advocate, December 30, 1909. <u>List of Merchant Vessels of the U.S.</u>, 1907, p. 34.

324) *Forward*, #120614, Schooner, Foundered May 30, 1910.

The <u>List of Merchant Vessels of the U.S.</u>, 1910, page 405, listed this little craft as having foundered at Kewaunee Bay, Kewaunee, Wisconsin, without loss of life. The vessel was registered to carry a crew of three, but only had two on board at the time. She claimed 36 gross tons and was built in 1884. The *Forward* measured 67.6 feet in length, 18.5 feet in the beam and 4.2 feet in depth. <u>List of Merchant Vessels of the U.S.</u>, 1909, p. 47.

325) *Trude Wiehe*, #106368, Steamer, Burned July 21, 1910.

The *Wiehe* had several barges in tow when she ran on a reef at Portage Bay, "twelve miles from Barque Point." The tug, *Gifford*, from Manistique went to her assistance but after breaking several tow lines, gave up. The tug took the *Wiehe's* entourage of barges, leaving the steamer on the rocks. About an hour after the *Gifford* left, fire was discovered in the engine room of the *Wiehe*. The crew of fourteen, was unable to extinguish the blaze and was forced to abandon ship in the vessel's yawl. They rowed to Van's Harbor.

The steamer belonged to the Edward Hines Lumber Co. and was valued at $15,000. She was built as the *A. Folsom* in West Bay City, Michigan, in 1885 and registered 768 gross tons. The *Wiehe* measured 187 feet in length and 33 feet across the beam. Door County Advocate, July 28, 1910. <u>List of Merchant Vessels of the U.S.</u>, 1896, p. 302.

326) *Challenge*, #4349, Schooner, Stranded Early September, 1910.

The *Challenge* had been bound for Port Washington but unable to reach that port, turned back for Sheboygan. She caught herself in pound nets and started taking on water leaving her captain no other choice but to run her aground. The vessel was finally beached twelve miles south of Sturgeon Bay. The ship's "outfit was stripped off and taken to shore." Ship's company included Captain O'Brian of Chicago, his wife, their son, Edward, and Charles and William Wolf of Milwaukee. The party walked to a summer resort several miles down the beach.

The *Challenge* was built in Manitowoc in 1852 and registered 87 gross tons. She measured 87.5 feet in length, 22.7 feet at the beam and 7.2 feet in depth. Door County Advocate, September 15, 1910. List of Merchant Vessels of the U.S., 1907, p. 25.

Part 4:
Vessels lost after 1911

327) *Ottawa*, #19408, Schooner, Stranded April 13, 1911.

The *Ottawa* was bound from Manistique with a load of lumber for Chicago when she was overcome by a southeaster of cyclone force. The vessel was blown ashore on Stoney Creek reef off shore from the Chris Braunsdorf farm, six miles south of Sturgeon Bay. Braunsdorf spotted the schooner about 5 a.m. when it seemed to be all right. About 10 a.m., Braunsdorf's daughter found lumber washing ashore. The lifesaving service was sent for but by the time they arrived, the schooner's wrecked yawl boat washed ashore followed by the bodies of the ill-fated crew. Fearing the breaking up of the ship, the captain and four crewmen had apparently launched the yawl but were washed out and drowned. There were no survivors. Killed were Captain Claus Weborg, mate Peter Buset, and seamen Frank (?), Carl Nyquist, and Victor Nordene. With the exception of Buset, who was from Norway (Michigan?), all were from Marinette.

The Roper Lumber Company, co-owners of the vessel with Captain Weborg, ordered her stripped. Attempts were made to pump out the craft but the hull was too badly damaged below the water line. Salvors also tore her to pieces. Captain Thomas Isabel was given the job of salvaging the remaining lumber and to accomplish this, had to dynamite holes in the deck.

The *Ottawa* was valued at $2,000. Her cargo of lumber, which was saved, was valued at $3,000. She was built in Grand Haven, Michigan, in 1874. The *Ottawa* measured 125 feet in length and 25 feet at the beam. DOOR COUNTY ADVOCATE, April 20, May 4, 1911. List of Merchant Vessels of the U.S., 1911,

328) *Vencedor*, #161773, Sailing Yacht, Stranded July 23, 1911.

The *Vencedor* was partaking in the Chicago-to-Mackinac yacht race—a race she had won in the past—when she was caught in a heavy squall and driven ashore on Fisherman Island. The vessel had dropped her anchors but had dragged until she went on the rocks and pounded to pieces. The crew was rescued by the lifesaving service.

The *Vencedor* was built in 1896, registered 18 gross tons and measured 49.5 feet in length, 12.3 feet across the beam and 4.9 feet in depth. DOOR COUNTY ADVOCATE, July 27, 1911. List of Merchant Vessels of the U.S., 1911, p. 171.

329) *Elva*, #7300, Schooner, Stranded July 24, 1911.

The List of Merchant Vessels of the U.S., 1912 in her listing of vessel losses, mentions the *Elva* as having stranded at Sturgeon Bay. Four people were on board at the time.

The *Elva* carried a crew of two and was built in Port Huron, Michigan in 1862. She registered 69 gross tons and measured 86.9 feet in length, 19 feet at the beam and 6 feet in depth. List of Merchant Vessels of the U.S., 1910, p. 35. List of Merchant Vessels of the U.S., 1912, p. 417.

330) *Inishka*, Yacht, Burned October 22, 1911.

The *Inishka* burned at an unstated location. She was the property of R.B. Power and was a cup winner several times and was the flagship of the Green Bay Yacht Club. DOOR COUNTY ADVOCATE, October 26, 1911.

331) *Sanilac*, #23108, Steamer, Sunk December of 1911.

The *Sanilac* settled in eight feet of water alongside the dock north of the shipyard in Sturgeon Bay. Nothing is stated for her ultimate fate, however the steamer was 44 years old...ancient for a wooden vessel on the lakes, and it is unlikely that she would have been repaired and returned to service.

The *Sanilac* was built at Algomac, Michigan, in 1867 and registered 310 gross tons. The 1911 <u>List of Merchant Vessels of the United States</u> described her as an "inland freighter" of 161.5 feet in length, 27.5 feet at the beam, and 10.1 feet in depth. DOOR COUNTY ADVOCATE, December 28, 1911. <u>List of Merchant Vessels of the U.S.</u>, 1911, p. 295.

The steamer Sydney C. McClouth
Photo courtesy of the Great Lakes Marine Collection
of the Milwaukee Public Library/Wisconsin Marine Historical Society

332) *Sydney C. McClouth*, #110438, Steamer, Burned June 27, 1912.

The *McClouth* had just delivered a load of cement to the Hurlbut dock in Green Bay. Having left that port in the afternoon, she was twenty miles out when fire was discovered near the stern. The old wooden steamer was quickly engulfed in flames. Unable to control the fire, Captain

W.W. Shorkey and his crew of fifteen escaped in the lifeboats and rowed to Pensaukee. With the exception of the engineer, who burned his hands, there were no injuries. Later that year the burned hulk was purchased for $300 by Captain Thomas Isabel who intended to strip the hull of any junk iron left on the wreck.

The *McClouth* was owned by Sydney C. McClouth of Marine City, Michigan, but was built as the *Rochester* in 1880 and was considered one of the oldest packet steamers around. Most recently she had been used for the cement trade.

The *Sydney C. McClouth* is often confused with the steamer, *Sidney O. Neff* which was abandoned some miles to the north, off Menominee harbor. It is easier to remember, the *Neff* is north, the *McClouth* is south.

The *Sydney C. McClouth* registered 2,220 gross tons with a length of 266.9 feet, a beam of 40 feet and a depth of 16 feet. GREEN BAY GAZETTE, June 28, 1912. DOOR COUNTY ADVOCATE, July 4, October 31, 1912. List of Merchant Vessels of the U.S., 1911, p. 296.

The Spatula prior to her launching in West De Pere.
Photo courtesy of the De Pere Historical Society

333) *Spatula*, Gas Launch, Burned August 12, 1912.

The *Spatula* caught fire and burned to the water line while laying at the dock in Fish Creek. The fire was thought to have started with an explosion of gasoline fumes. The yacht had been in good condition and had been used only two seasons. It was valued at $2,000. The *Spatula* was owned by Jules Cauwenberg, commodore of the Green Bay Yacht Club. Cauwenberg and his wife, A.C. Tilton and his wife and children were on board the yacht at the time. Cauwenberg burned his hand while escaping. Everyone else escaped without injury. GREEN BAY ADVOCATE, August 13, 1912. DOOR COUNTY ADVOCATE, August 15, 1912.

334) *D.F. Rose*, #35149, Steamer, Dismantled September, 1912.

The *Rose* had laid in the mud in the boneyard in Sturgeon Bay for two or three years and had become a worthless wreck. Her stack, spar and house had fallen in and the hull had broken in two. By late fall of that year, the iron, machinery and 76 horsepower engine were being removed with a clam shell shovel. The rest of the hull was left to rot where it lay. The steamer measured 258.82 tons with a length of 140.1 feet, a beam 26.3 feet, and a depth of 10.9 feet. She was built at Marine City, Michigan in 1868. DOOR COUNTY ADVOCATE, April 18, September 5, 1912. List of Merchant Vessels of the U.S., 1895, p. 235.

335) *Joses*, #13015, Schooner, Stranded October 11, 1912.

The *Joses* was bound for Van's Harbor to pick up a cargo of lumber when she was caught by a heavy southeast wind and blown ashore at Point Detour, near Fairport, Michigan.

The schooner had been declared a total loss. Nonetheless, later that month efforts were made to release her. The hull had been jacked up and put on ways and was awaiting a tug to pull her off. No mention is made of her ultimate disposition.

The *Joses* was built in 1866 and was valued at $4,000. She was captained by Ole Olsen and was owned by Olsen and Thomas Finn of Marinette. The schooner registered 120 gross tons and measured 100 feet in length, and 24 feet at the beam. DOOR COUNTY ADVOCATE, October 17, 31, 1912. List of Merchant Vessels of the U.S., 1911, p. 61.

336) *Minnie Warren*, #91275, Fish Tug, Dismantled November of 1912.

The *Warren* had sunk at her slip at the Pankratz Mill in Sturgeon Bay in October of 1912. The following month, she was raised but during a storm she broke away from her mooring, drifted across to the shipyard where she struck the corner of one of the dry dock "boxes" and sank. The water had been deep enough that her presence was not a problem to the yard owners and business went on as usual over her. The following August, the steamer *City of New Baltimore* towed her out from underneath the boxes. The yard removed her machinery, shaft and wheel. The equipment found a new home in the *Isabella C.*, a new fish tug built for Captain Pat Casey of Fayette. The *Warren's* hull was then towed out and abandoned in the boneyard north of the Pankratz Mill site.

The *Minnie Warren* was owned by the Baker Brothers. She was built at Buffalo in 1869 and registered 19 gross tons with a length of 47 feet, a beam of 12.4 feet and a depth of 5.4 feet. DOOR COUNTY ADVOCATE, October 17, November 21, 1912. DOOR COUNTY ADVOCATE, August 14, October 16, 23, 1913. List of Merchant Vessels of the U.S., 1911, p. 250.

337) *Rufus P. Ranney*, #110486, Inland Freighter, Abandoned November 1912.

The *Ranney* was brought in from Manitowoc where she had been sitting for some time. The tug, *Smith*, deposited her in the maritime "graveyard" next to the *Empire State*.

The schooner Joses in Milwaukee harbor.

Photo courtesy of the Great Lakes Marine Collection of the Milwaukee Public Library/Wisconsin Marine Historical Society

With her stack broken over and her upper works dilapidated, she was in bad shape.

The *Rufus P. Ranney* was built at Cleveland in 1881 and had had a crew of fifteen. She registered 1,627 gross tons. The freighter measured 247.6 feet in length, a beam of 36.3 feet and a depth of 20.3 feet. Door County Advocate, November 21, 1912. List of Merchant Vessels of the U.S., 1911, p. 292.

338) *Hustler*, #96219, Gasoline Schooner, Burned November 8, 1912.

The *Hustler* was on her way from Peshtigo to Menominee when an explosion below deck blew out the deck and one side of the cabin. The schooner was seven and a half miles away, on a bearing of 185° from Menominee when the explosion occurred. Captain Orin Angwall and his brother, Forest, were the only ones on board. The two men fought the ensuing blaze for two hours. Finally, with the foremast gone, two feet of water in the hold, and a heavy wind and sea blowing in from the northwest, the Angwalls abandoned the schooner in their yawl boat. They lost their oars while abandoning ship and were forced to float about the Bay before being rescued by Captain Ed. Stevenson in a fishing tug.

The *Hustler* measured 13 gross tons with a length of 44 feet, a beam of 11.3 feet and a depth of 4.2 feet. She was built in Detroit in 1893. Door County Advocate, November 14, 1912. List of Merchant Vessels of the U.S., 1911, p. 79.

339) *Three Sisters*, #145884, Schooner, Stranded November 24, 1912.

The *Three Sisters* had set sail from Chaudoir's Dock with a load of hay for Cedar River. She sailed into the teeth of a "norther" with wind, rain and snow and ran before the storm, before coming to anchor off Red River. The schooner rode out the storm most of Saturday but that night

The schooner Hustler
Photo courtesy of the Great Lakes Marine Collection
of the Milwaukee Public Library/Wisconsin Marine Historical Society

her cable chains broke and she was swept into the shallows only three hundred feet from shore. The wreck stranded at a point 1.5 miles south of Chaudoir's Dock in a position perpendicular to shore. Heavy seas broke clear over her to such an extent that at times she was completely hidden. Despite this, the three men on board lasted through the night. They were: Phillip Klumb, 34, master and owner; a sailor, Andrew Hanson, 32; and Soren Torgeson, 50 (who was originally identified as engineer and sailor, Neil Tillman).

By Sunday morning, November 24th, the three had apparently given up hope. Klumb tied on a life jacket and jumped overboard. People watching from shore dragged him on to the beach where he died a short time later.

Edward Delfosse, a resident of the area, launched a small boat in an attempt to rescue the two remaining sailors. He successfully rowed to the wreck where he found Hanson dead and Torgeson semi-conscious from the cold. Torgeson had a death grip on the railing, but Delfosse physically dragged him into the rowboat and started for shore only to be capsized by the breakers. Onlookers waded out and pulled the two ashore. Torgeson was carried to a nearby saloon where efforts were made to revive him with "spirits." The attempt was fruitless and he died a short time later.

In the weeks following the disaster, Louis Johnson, brother-in-law of Captain Klumb, stripped the vessel of everything that could be taken off, including sails, gas engine, etc. The hull was permitted to go to pieces where it lay.

In May of 1915, Edward Delfosse, George DeBaker, and Rev. W.C. Melchoir were each awarded the Carnegie Bronze Medal for their courage in attempting to rescue the crew of the *Three Sisters*.

The *Three Sisters* was built at Fish Creek in 1901 by Captain James Larson. She measured 69 feet in length, 19 feet across the beam and 7.2 feet in depth. DOOR COUNTY ADVOCATE, November 28, December 5, 1912. DOOR COUNTY ADVOCATE, May 6, 1915. List of Merchant Vessels of the U.S., 1911, p. 167.

340) *Iris*, #12096, Schooner-Barge, Stranded in March of 1913.

The *Iris* was listed among the lost in the List of Merchant Vessels of the U.S., for 1913 after she stranded at Jackson Harbor, Wisconsin. Three people were on board at the time. All were saved. She was stripped of her outfit and left to rot. The vessel now rests about fifteen yards, northeast of the boat launch in Jackson Harbor where she tends to be a hazard to passing boats. At low water periods, wreckage projects above the surface. In spite of that the vessel still sports her deadeyes and chainplates, items normally taken off by salvors, old and new. The *Iris* was a local schooner plying the fishing and cord wood trade on the Bay of Green Bay. She was a small vessel registering 62.18 gross tons with a length of 74 feet, a beam of 19.2 feet, and a depth of 6.6 feet. The *Iris* carried a normal crew of three and was built in Port Huron, Michigan in 1866. James Cornell, personal interview, August 18, 1996. List of Merchant Vessels of the U.S., 1895, p. 95. List of Merchant Vessels of the U.S., 1912, p. 49. List of Merchant Vessels of the U.S., 1913, p. 422. SCUBA dive with Barbara Malcolm, October 26, 1996

341) *Leir Grant*, #15874, Barge, Stranded July 11, 1913.

The *Grant* was blown ashore near Little Cedar River in a heavy southeaster. Having been anchored 500 feet off shore while loading cedar posts, she dragged her anchor in to shore. She was owned by Captain William Anderson.

The *Leir Grant* was built in 1872 and registered 204 gross tons. List of Merchant Vessels of the U.S., 1914, p. 431.

342) *Grace*, #208971, Gas Screw, Stranded August 22, 1913.

The *Grace* stranded at North Bay. No lives were lost. She registered 7 gross tons and was built in 1901. List of Merchant Vessels of the U.S., 1914, p. 429.

343) *Pewaukee*, #150233, Barge, Abandoned October, 1913.

The *Pewaukee* had been left in the mud at the end of Liberty Street. She was later pumped out, pulled off and taken to the stone quarry at the head of Sturgeon Bay where she was filled with stone and sunk for a breakwater. Two pumps had to be used to raise her. In marking her approaching fate, the DOOR COUNTY ADVOCATE observed, "Some of the old wrecks that lay in the mud between the Leathem & Smith property and the shipyard were cut up during the past winter for firewood by beachcombers. Pity the hulks could not be towed out in the lake and sunk."

The *Pewaukee* was built as the British bark, *Two Friends*, in 1873. In 1881 she was converted to a steamer. In 1905, she was stripped of her engines and converted into a stone barge. She originally registered 310.26 gross tons with a length of 135.5 feet, a beam of 26.4 feet, and a depth of 10.8 feet. DOOR COUNTY ADVOCATE, April 24, October 30, 1913. List of Merchant Vessels of the U.S., 1884, p. 227. List of Merchant Vessels of the U.S., 1895, p. 288.

344) *Joseph L. Hurd*, #46576, Stone Barge, Stranded September 20, 1913.

The *Hurd* had been moored at the quarry pier. A high northwest wind caused the water to rise, putting a heavy strain on the vessel's mooring lines until they snapped. The barge washed ashore next to the pier. When the water level went down, the load of stone on the ship's stern caused her to wrench herself. Attempts were made to pump her out, but the pump would not work. The lifesaving crew arrived on the scene but left when it was obvious they could do nothing. She was finally abandoned by her owners, the Leathem and Smith Company.

The steamer *Joseph L. Hurd* was built in 1869 and named for a Detroit businessman. In 1877, the schooner *Magellan* was sunk with all hands near Manitowoc by what local mariners identified as a collision. Not long after, the *Hurd* came into Manitowoc harbor with her bow badly damaged. According to Captain Edward Carus who was present on the pier at the time, the *Hurd* was about to tie up at the dock when a lynch mob gathered to hang Captain Thomas Lloyd and his crew. The *Hurd* quickly pulled

The steamer Joseph L. Hurd

Photo courtesy of the Great Lakes Marine Collection of the Milwaukee Public Library/Wisconsin Marine Historical Society

away from the dock and left the harbor. Accusations of her sinking the *Magellan* were never proven. Years later, in 1895, the *Hurd* was involved in a collision with the steel steamer, *Cayuga*, at Skillagalle Point. The *Cayuga* went to the bottom with a loss of $250,000. The *Hurd* is also credited with ramming Chicago's Clark Street bridge.

In August of 1906, the *Hurd* was steaming through a storm with a load of cedar poles for Chicago when she sprang a leak. Captain McCaffery ordered the hand pumps and steam pump into action but nothing could keep up with the rising water. The water level finally reached the engine room where it snuffed out the boiler fires. High waves and strong winds broke away the ship's cargo of cedar poles. McCaffery, his wife, their daughter and nine crew members abandoned the sinking steamer in the ship's yawl. Poking their way through cedar logs and tossed about by the waves, they had only rowed ten yards away from the *Hurd* when she sank by the stern and settled in the water to deck level. For six hours, they rowed and bailed until they were picked up by the steamer, *Mohawk*. McCaffery prevailed upon the *Mohawk's* captain to look for the waterlogged vessel. She was found not far from where she was abandoned and taken in tow to Chicago. Shortly thereafter, the *Hurd* was taken to Sturgeon Bay where her equipment was removed and she was cut down to a stone barge. As a barge, the *Joseph L. Hurd* measured '459 gross tons and carried a crew of two. Edward Carus Marine Notes, Wisconsin Maritime Museum, Manitowoc Wisconsin. DOOR COUNTY ADVOCATE, August 16, 1906. DOOR COUNTY ADVOCATE, September 25, October 16, 1913. DOOR COUNTY ADVOCATE, January 21, 1915. List of Merchant Vessels of the U.S., 1911, p. 357.

345) *C.C. Hand*, #110860, Steamer, Burned October 6, 1913.

The *C.C. Hand* was bound from Cleveland for Chicago

with 2,400 tons of soft coal. About 7 p.m. that evening she was trying to find her way through a dense fog when she ran aground twice on Big Summer Island. She was able to pull herself off and drop anchor. After coming to anchor, the crew went below for their evening meal but the mess room filled with smoke. The crew fought the fire with hand extinguishers and later steam extinguishers but were unsuccessful. Flames overwhelmed the vessel so quickly that the portside lifeboat was burned before the crew could get to it. The heat was so intense that Captain Hackett had to stop some crew members from jumping overboard. The crew of eighteen managed to launch the starboard lifeboat. The boat was sent to shore with a small group of seamen, returned to the burning steamer for more and made for shore again. The captain left his ship with the last group to head for shore. They had pulled away from the burning vessel just as her load shifted. She up ended and settled in thirty feet of water leaving only her blackened bow showing above the surface. The crew made a shelter on the island.

Captain Pat Casey of Fairport had seen the flames of the burning steamer and set out in his fishing launch to investigate. As he neared the island he saw the campfire of the stranded sailors and within an hour had them evacuated to Fairport. They were later taken to Escanaba

The *C.C. Hand* was built as the steamer *R.E. Schuck* in 1890. She was owned by Captain Francis Hackett of Detroit who had spent $18,000 of his own money purchasing her from the receivers of the Gilchrist Transportation Co. and bringing her up to his standards. Hackett was making his first voyage as captain and sole master and was answering a hurried call for coal in Chicago–so hurried that he did not have time to arrange for insurance for the vessel. The captain thought he would have time for that in Chicago.

The steamer C.C. Hand

Photo courtesy of the Great Lakes Marine Collection of the Milwaukee Public Library/Wisconsin Marine Historical Society

The cargo of coal was purchased by Captain Thomas Smith who used a clam shovel to pull it out of the hold. When Smith and his salvage crew arrived on the sight to retrieve the coal, the *Hand* was still burning. In May of 1920, the boilers were recovered from the wreck by the tug *Smith* and the lighter, *Advance*, for removal to Sturgeon Bay. The *Hand* boasted 2,122 gross tons and measured 266 feet in length with a beam of 41 feet. ESCANABA MORNING PRESS, October 8, 1913. DOOR COUNTY ADVOCATE, October 9, 16, 23, 1913. DOOR COUNTY ADVOCATE, May 20, 1920. List of Merchant Vessels of the U.S., 1911, p. 144.

346) *Harvey Ransom*, #95912, Schooner, Foundered November 1, 1913.

The List of Merchant Vessels of the U.S. describes the *Ransom* as a 28 ton vessel that foundered in the Bay of Green Bay. Four people were aboard, all saved. According to Our Heritage, A Local History of the Garden Peninsula, the *Ransom* was on her way to Fayette harbor when she was overtaken by the "Big Blow of 1913." The vessel was pulled into the lee of Burnt Bluff and was safe until a wave dropped her on top of a pound net stake, ripping her open.

The *Harvey Ransom* was owned by Dan Seavey and was built in 1887 at South Haven, Michigan. She measured 59 feet in length, with a beam of 16.4, and a depth of 5.3 feet. Garden Peninsula Historical Society, Our Heritage, Garden Peninsula Delta County, Michigan 1840 - 1980, Garden, Michigan, p. 173. List of Merchant Vessels of the U.S., 1909, p. 56. List of Merchant Vessels of the U.S., 1914, p. 427.

347) *Louisiana*, #140882, Steamer, Burned November 8, 1913.

The *Louisiana* had delivered a cargo of coal to Milwaukee and was bound for Escanaba to take on a cargo of iron ore when she sailed into the grip of the "Big Blow of 1913." The steamer pulled into the comparative safety of Washington Harbor. Even there the storm was too much for her and she was blown ashore. The next morning fire was discovered in the hold. Attempts to fight the blaze were unsuccessful and the crew of seventeen abandoned the vessel in the ship's jolly boat.

The ship's boilers were salvaged from the wreck by the tug *Smith* in 1920.

The *Louisiana* was built in Marine City in 1887, was owned by Frank Osborne and captained by Fred McDonald. She measured 267 feet in length, 40 feet across the beam and registered 1,929 gross tons. DOOR COUNTY ADVOCATE, November 13, 1913. DOOR COUNTY ADVOCATE, May 14, 1920. List of Merchant Vessels of the U.S., 1911, p. 235.

348) *Plymouth*, #19621, Barge, Foundered November 8, 1913.

The *Plymouth* with a Federal Marshall on board was in tow of the tug, *James H. Martin*, bound from Menominee to Search Bay, Michigan, for a load of cedar posts. They were in the vicinity of Death's Door when they were hit with the full force of what would later be called the "Big Blow of 1913." The captain of the tug, Louis Setunsky, was ill-prepared for the endeavor and in piloting the entourage through the straits and coming north, steamed too close to the shoals allowing the tug to pound on the bottom. The tug's engineer and owner, Donald L. McKinnon, had once or twice, come up from the engine room to check on the tug's condition to find the barge passing her. The tug by this time, was leaking and, with the barge in tow, was unable to make headway through the storm. McKinnon decided that if they were going to survive they would have to leave the *Plymouth* at anchor in the lee of Gull Island and run for the safety of Big Summer Island where they could find protection from the hurricane force northwest winds.*

The next day the *Martin* returned to Gull Island, but the *Plymouth* had disappeared. It was concluded that she had broken loose from her anchorage and foundered with all hands somewhere in the middle of the lake. This was born out when bodies of the crewmen were washed ashore in the Pentwater, Michigan area. Also washed up was a bottle with a note inside from Christ Keenan, Deputy Federal Marshall and custodian of the barge. The note read:

"Dear wife and children: We were left up here in Lake Michigan by McKinnon, captain of the tug James H. Martin *at anchor. He went away and never said good bye or anything to us. Lost one man last night. We have been out in the storm 40 hours. Good bye dear ones, I might see you in heaven. Pray for me. Christ K. I felt so bad I had another man write for me. Huebel owes $35.00 so you can get it. Good Bye forever."*

Lost with the *Plymouth* were: Keenan; Axel Larson, acting master of the barge; James Sabota; Henry Kossak; Peter Johnson and Clifford Duchaine, all of the Marinette-Menominee area.

Feelings ran very high against Setunsky and McKinnon in the region and it was thought that a federal investigation would be forthcoming. Captain Setunsky maintained that he was not forewarned of the poor seaworthiness of the tug, only discovering it in the storm. Furthermore, leaving the *Plymouth* at Gull Island was the only way to save the tug.

Federal inspectors ordered the tug to be put up on blocks at Sturgeon Bay. Before this could be done, the *James H. Martin* sank at her dock in Menominee.

D.L. McKinnon, in a lengthy letter to the DOOR COUNTY ADVOCATE, wrote that he was perfectly correct in leaving the barge behind. The engineer stated that the *Plymouth* was evidently dry and sound and, anchored a mile in the lee of Gull Island, did not pitch or roll. McKinnon cited the *Martin's* crew for being inexperienced and Setunsky for being incompetent and noted the tug's steaming too close to the shoals and pounding on the bottom.

The *Plymouth* had gone through a general overhaul the previous season and a recalking several months before her loss and had been considered to be in excellent shape. The *Martin* had gone through a recalking in preparation for this trip.

The *James H. Martin* was raised from the river bottom and, upon inspection by federal authorities, was found to have her seacocks open. The boat's officers denied any knowledge of the tug having been scuttled. The tug was found unseaworthy and was condemned.

McKinnon and Setunsky were brought to trial for violation of navigation laws in the incident. The pilot's license of Donald McKinnon was revoked for having hired Setunsky in spite of the fact that Setunsky's license did not cover the vessel involved. McKinnon was also found at fault for not notifying the government of the poor condition of the tug's boiler. Captain Louis Setunsky's license was revoked for having taken a position for which he was unqualified, the tug being larger than those specified on his ticket. The voyage would also have involved navigation into Lake Huron. Setunsky was only licensed to navigate northern Lake Michigan.

At the time of the accident, the C.J. Hubel company, owners of the barge, were suing the owners of the tug, McKinnon and Scott Transportation and Company, which explains the presence of a Federal Marshall on the barge. Troubles between the two companies landed McKinnon's partner, Captain William Scott, in jail.

The barge, *Plymouth*, was built as a schooner in 1854. She registered 776 gross tons and had a length of 213 feet in length, 35 feet across the beam and a depth of 13.6 feet.

*Some time before the *Plymouth* was cut loose, her cook, Margaret Olive, was transferred to the *James H. Martin*. When she was swept overboard, McKinnon dove in after her. They were married the following summer.

DOOR COUNTY ADVOCATE, July 10, July 24, November 20, 27, December 4, December 11, 1913. MENOMINEE HERALD, November 12, 17, 1913. DOOR COUNTY ADVOCATE, January 29, July 2, 1914. List of Merchant Vessels of the U.S., 1912, p. 355.

349) *Emma Bloecker*, #136095, Tug, Foundered April 1914.

The *Bloecker* was sunk by the action of the ice near the south dock of the shipyard where she had been kept for the winter. Her machinery had been removed the previous fall. She was built as a steam propeller at Grand Haven, Michigan, in 1889 and carried a crew of five.

The *Bloecker* measured 56.2 feet in length, 13.9 feet across the beam, 4.7 feet in depth and registered 31 gross tons. DOOR COUNTY ADVOCATE, April 16, 1914. List of Merchant Vessels of the U.S., 1911, p. 176.

350) *James H. Martin*, #75114, Tug, Abandoned in April 1914.

The *Martin* was one of several vessels wintering near the south dock of the shipyard in Sturgeon Bay. It was thought that ice opened up her seams. She settled in twelve feet of water with her decks submerged.

The *James H. Martin* was the tug used to tow the barge *Plymouth* which was lost with all hands the previous fall. In the ensuing federal investigation, the *Martin* was declared unseaworthy and condemned.

The *Martin* was built in Cleveland in 1869 and registered 54 gross tons. She measured 72 feet in length, 15 feet in the beam, 8 feet in depth and carried a crew of 4.

For all of the news coverage the *Martin* received in the *Plymouth* incident, she was, afterward, given little notice anywhere else except the government list. She was dropped from the listing after 1914. DOOR COUNTY ADVOCATE, December 13, 1913. DOOR COUNTY ADVOCATE, April 16, 1914. List of Merchant Vessels of the U.S., 1911, p. 215.

351) *Oneida*, #18920, Schooner, Sunk April 1914.

The *Oneida* had been taken out of commission the previous fall and had been left by her dock south of the shipyard, by the end of the canal. With spring's arrival the moving ice pulled out the oakum allowing the vessel to sink. The bow rested on the shore, while the stern was in about twelve feet of water. The following year, the *Oneida* broke in two.

The schooner was owned by James R. Andrews of Escanaba and was built in Ashtabula, Ohio in 1857. She registered 201 gross tons with a length of 134 feet and a beam of 24 feet. DOOR COUNTY ADVOCATE, April 16, 1914. DOOR COUNTY ADVOCATE, December 2, 1915. List of Merchant Vessels of the U.S., 1911, p. 87.

352) Lydia E. Raesser, #10206, Schooner, Dismantled May of 1914.

The *Lydia Raesser* was built as the *Gypsy* at Cleveland in 1847 measuring 106 feet in length and 23 feet at the beam. Having outlived her usefulness, she was stripped of all useable equipment and left at her dock in Menominee. She was owned by Pete Peterson of Menominee. DOOR COUNTY ADVOCATE, May 21, 1914. DOOR COUNTY ADVOCATE, January 21, 1915. List of Merchant Vessels of the U.S., 1895, p. 128.

353) *Resumption*, #110384, Schooner, Stranded November 7, 1914.

The *Resumption* was blown ashore on Plum Island in a

The Lydia Roesser years after she was abandoned in Menominee Harbor.

Phot courtesy of the Wisconsin Maritime Museum, Manitowoc, Wisconsin

heavy gale. She was in ballast (sailing without cargo) and bound from Chicago to Wells, Michigan. Sailing along with a strong southwesterly gale, the schooner was off Plum Island when she attempted to come about and lost her momentum. Before she could drop anchor she went up on the island. The next day, the tug *Torrent* pulled on the schooner and moved her eight feet but she settled in the sandy bottom. Despite a united effort by the tugs, *Torrent* and *Wawa*, and the steamers, *I.W. Stephenson*, *Herman Hettler* and the revenue cutter, *Tuscarora*, the *Resumption* did not budge. The following summer, another effort was made to release the *Resumption*. That attempt also failed. The schooner was owned by the I.W. Stephenson Company and was used for hauling lumber and carried a crew of six.

The *Resumption* was built in 1879 and was launched at the time of the resumption of specie payment, hence the name. The vessel's figurehead was decorated with facsimiles of gold dollars. The schooner measured 143.4 in length, and 29 feet across the beam. DOOR COUNTY ADVOCATE, November 20, 1884. DOOR COUNTY ADVOCATE, November 12, 1914. DOOR COUNTY ADVOCATE, June 24, 1915. List of Merchant Vessels of the U.S., 1911, p. 94.

354) *Myron Butman*, #91758, Barge, Stranded November 19, 1914.

The *Butman* was blown ashore at Sturgeon Bay in a heavy gale. The Bay was low at the time and her owners thought that as soon as the water level returned to normal she could be floated free. By mid-December she still had not been released from her resting spot (she was sitting in the inlet of the west approach to the bridge) and she had frozen in place. It was decided that she could be recovered in spring. However nothing more was reported on her condition and the vessel was eliminated from the Federal list after 1916.

The *Butman* was built as a schooner at Gibraltar,

The schooner Resumption.

Picture courtesy of the Wisconsin Maritime Museum, Manitowoc, Wisconsin

253

Michigan, and registered 424.22 gross tons. She measured 164.3 feet in length, 31.2 feet across the beam and 10.2 feet in depth. Door County Advocate, November 26, 1914. Door County Advocate, December 17, 1914. List of Merchant Vessels of the U.S., 1895, p. 150.

The tug Torrent bringing a tow into Detroit Harbor.
Photo courtesy of the Great Lakes Marine Collection
of the Milwaukee Public Library/Wisconsin Marine Historical Society

355) *Torrent*, #24786, Tug, Abandoned March of 1915.

The *Torrent* was condemned after an inspection by her owners, Adolph and Otto Green of the Green Stone and Quarry Co. Most of the equipment had already been removed for installation in a new vessel. After all equipment was removed, the tug was to be abandoned, probably by scuttling out in Lake Michigan.

Built in Cleveland in 1869, the *Torrent* registered 203 gross tons and carried a crew of eight. She was used primarily for towing. She measured 115 feet in length, 21.2 feet at the beam and 12.3 feet in depth. Door County Advocate, March 18, May 6, 1915. List of Merchant Vessels of the U.S., 1911, p. 305.

356) *Holland*, #125906, Steam Barge, Burned in Spring of 1915.

The *Holland* was tied up at the Pankratz dock in Sturgeon Bay when she was partially damaged by fire. It was decided that, with her machinery and boiler removed, she might be kept for use as a carrier. Instead, her equipment was taken out and broken up. She was raised to be towed to the Leathem & Smith yard where she was to be filled with stone and sunk.

The *Holland*, according to one account, was an iron hulled sidewheel steamer. The List of Merchant Vessels of the U. S. lists her with the wooden hulls. She was built as a passenger steamer at Wyandotte, Michigan, in 1881 and registered 1,148 gross tons with a crew of 31. She measured 230 feet in length, with a beam of 33.8 feet, and a depth of 12.3 feet. DOOR COUNTY ADVOCATE, September 9, October 7, 1915. DOOR COUNTY ADVOCATE, May 2, 1919. List of Merchant Vessels of the U.S., 1911, p. 205.

357) *R.P. Mason*, #21877, Schooner, Burned May 30, 1915.

The *R. P. Mason*, like the pier, home and saw mill that burned with it, were owned by Dan Seavey in Gouley's Bay. Seavey had contracted with Robert Brody of Fairport, Michigan, to cut lumber and with Brody's sons, James and Robert, Jr. and Lucius Mercier spent all of that day disassembling and loading the engines and saws on board the *Mason*. That night Seavey went to bed while the others opted to continue working. Fire broke out in the Seavey mill and spread to the residence, pier and finally to the *R.P. Mason*. James Brody went to the aid of Seavey and was lost in the fire. Seavey threw himself through a window but lost consciousness. He suffered severe burns but was taken to a hospital in Escanaba where he recovered. While young Brody was looking for Seavey, Lucius Mercier was attempting to save his boat, and when asked if he needed help, replied that he was okay. His body was later found on the bottom of the bay. The *Mason* drifted away from the pier before it burned to the waterline and sank. As of 1975, parts of the hull were still visible.

Dan Seavey is still a local legend in the north end of the Bay of Green Bay. He was a big man, known far and wide for his love of brawling, his boundless energy and for some exploits that have been described as "piracy" or a big misunderstanding, depending upon who tells the story. He was also known for his love of children, most of whom are now in their seventies and eighties and have fond memories of him.

The *R.P. Mason* had foundered near Fayette, sometime before and Seavey with his usual industriousness, raised the vessel, repaired and restored it to service—his service.

The *R.P. Mason* was built in 1867 at Ferrysburg, Michigan. She measured 155.23 gross tons with a length of 115 feet, a beam of 24.6 feet and a depth of 7.9 feet. Garden Peninsula Historical Society, Our Heritage, Garden Peninsula Delta County, Michigan 1840 - 1980, Garden, Michigan, p. 173. ESCANABA MORNING PRESS, June 2, 1915. List of Merchant Vessels of the U.S., 1895, p. 166.

358) *Peter Coates*, #150368, Tug, Sank June 17, 1915.

The *Coates* sank at her dock on the west side of Sturgeon Bay. She was raised and shoved in the mud where, a month later, she filled with water and rolled over on her side.

The *Coates* was built at Grand Haven, Michigan in 1886, registered 32 gross tons and carried a crew of 2. She had been, most recently, used for fishing. The tug had a length of 61.5 feet, a beam of 15.2 feet, and a depth of 6.8 feet. DOOR COUNTY ADVOCATE, June 17, July 15, 1915. List of Merchant Vessels of the U.S., 1911, p. 269.

359) *Pup*, #150668, Fish Tug, Foundered July 19, 1915.

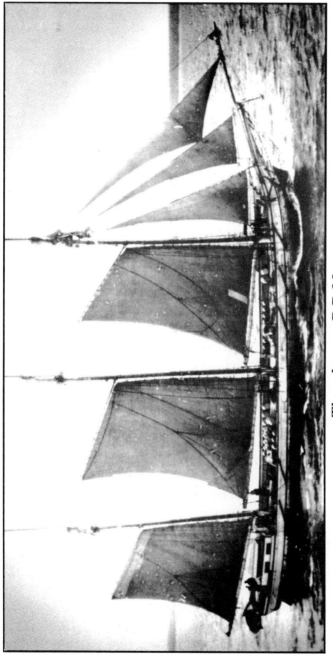

The schooner R.P. Mason.

Photo courtesy of the Great Lakes Marine Collection of the Milwaukee Public Library/Wisconsin Marine Historical Society

After the *Pup* was damaged by fire, her owner, Mr. Peterson, used her as a small barge. He was on his way from Washington Harbor to West Harbor (on the southwest corner of Washington Island) towing the *Pup* with the gas screw, *Challenger*, when the old tug sprung a leak. The crew continually pumped her out, but ultimately the vessel filled and sank. All of her machinery had been removed and the tug went down taking only twenty bags of cement with her. Neither vessel nor cargo were of much value.

The *Pup* was built in Saugatuck, Michigan, in 1894 and registered 13 gross tons. As a working fishtug, she was licensed for three crewmen. She measured 45 feet in length, 11.8 feet across the beam and 4.6 feet in depth. DOOR COUNTY ADVOCATE, July 22, 1915. List of Merchant Vessels of the U.S., 1911, p. 273.

360) *Starlight*, #116780, Gas Schooner, Burned November 12, 1915.

The *Starlight* was bound for Marinette from Sister Bay with a load of potatoes, grain, apples and hay. The vessel was only ten miles from Menominee when fire was discovered in the cargo of hay. The schooner came about for Chambers Island and was only a few miles from that island when strong northwest winds whipped the flames into an inferno driving the crew from the vessel. The three crewmen were able to launch the yawl boat and row towards shore. When only several hundred yards from shore, the boat capsized and the men had to swim for it. They ultimately reached a lighthouse on the Michigan shore in safety.

The *Starlight* was captained by Sam Christiansen and owned by Captain Olsen and C.E. Larsen of Marinette. She was 60 feet in length, 15 feet at the beam. The *Starlight* was built at South Haven, Michigan, in 1897, and was valued at $1,500 for which there was no insurance. DOOR COUNTY

ADVOCATE, November 18, 1915. <u>List of Merchant Vessels of the U.S.</u>, 1914, p. 300.

361) *Glen Cuyler*, #10338, Schooner, Condemned July of 1917.

The *Cuyler* was built at Pultneyville, New York, in 1858 and reached an age of uselessness. She was owned by P.F. Goodlet of Marinette. Nothing was stated of what was done with the condemned hull. The *Cuyler* measured 49.05 gross tons with a length of 72. 5 feet, a beam of 16.2 feet and a depth of 5.5 feet. DOOR COUNTY ADVOCATE, July 19, 1917. <u>List of Merchant Vessels of the U.S.</u>, 1895, p. 78.

The schooner Glen Cuyler
Photo courtesy of the Great Lakes Marine Collection
of the Milwaukee Public Library/Wisconsin Marine Historical Society

362) *City of Glasgow*, #126729, Barge, Stranded October 6, 1917.

The *City of Glasgow* with her fellow consort, the *Adriatic*, were in tow of the tug, *John Hunsader*, bound light from Milwaukee, when the towing hawser snapped.

The entourage was just beginning its turn into the canal when the line parted and both barges were able to drop anchor. With a heavy south wind blowing, the vessels dragged their anchors until they went aground four miles north of the canal at Lily Bay. The crew of the *Glasgow*, Charles Wilman and Tom Torstenson were rescued with great difficulty.

The *Adriatic* was released within two weeks, but the *City of Glasgow* had been driven so far from deep water that no one had a line long enough to reach the stranded barge. The owners, who wanted the job done cheap, were not about to buy a new line that was worth more than the barge. The *Hunsader* was able to reach the barge once but started pounding on the bottom. Salvors decided to work on the salvaging of the barge only at times of high water. The vessel's gas engine and steam pump were removed but the *Hunsader* fell into busy schedule and when there was time to continue work on recovering the *Glasgow* it was not worth the effort.

The *City of Glasgow*, as a barge, was a mere shadow of what she was as a steamer. Her bad luck started in late 1907 when, on her way into Green Bay, she stranded on Peshtigo Reef. She was finally able to reach the port of Green Bay, but upon leaving the harbor she caught fire. The blaze quickly gained on the crew and control of the vessel was lost. The *Glasgow* swung across the channel between Long Tail Point and Grassy Island where she burned to the waterline and sank. Major J.V. Hudson of the Army Corps of Engineers was asked to remove the wreck and it was thought that he would dynamite it. It was later decided that the vessel could be raised and salvaged but the *Glasgow* had to be removed before the opening of the Straits of Mackinac in the coming spring. The Leathem and Smith Company was given the task of raising the steamer with William Binks as wrecking master. Binks found the

The steamer City of Glasglow early in her career.

Photo courtesy of the Great Lakes Marine Collection of the Milwaukee Public Library/Wisconsin Marine Historical Society

hulk laying in ten feet of water, burned to the waterline all the way around except at the stern where the hull was burned down six feet below the waterline. After the vessel was raised, she was taken to Sturgeon Bay where two thirty ton boilers, anchors, chains and the steam steering apparatus were salvaged. The engine was removed in pieces. The burned hulk was left to sit on the bottom at the end of Liberty Street in Sturgeon Bay for most of the following year. She was later hauled out, cut in two and rebuilt with a new stern for her new career as a stone barge. The old stern, still in the Leathem & Smith yard, was burned for the iron and bolts. Fate was not kind to the *City of Glasgow* and in 1916 she settled on the bottom at her berth near the Leathem & Smith yard. She was raised once again and returned to service. Her grounding at Lily Bay made the final chapter in her life.

The *City of Glasgow* was built in 1891 at West Bay City, Michigan, and originally registered 2,400 gross tons with a length of 297 feet and a beam of 41 feet. She was owned by the Hutchinson company of Cleveland until her destruction by fire. Door County Advocate, December 17, 1907. Door County Advocate, May 28, June 4, August 13, December 3, 1908. Door County Advocate, December 23, 1909. Door County Advocate, September 22, 1910. Door County Advocate, March 14, 1912. Door County Advocate, August 17, 1916. Door County Advocate, October 11, 25, November 15, 1917. List of Merchant Vessels of the U.S., 1907, p. 183.

363) *Eddie*, #136294, Schooner, Abandoned April of 1918.

The *Eddie* was a small schooner of 30.34 gross tons which was towed to the Leathem & Smith quarry where she was allowed to sink. The *Eddie* was built in 1892 at Mount Clemens, Michigan, and measured 59.5 feet in length, 17.6 feet across the beam, and 3.6 feet in depth. Door County Advocate, April 25, 1918. List of Merchant Vessels of the U.S., 1895, p. 50.

The scow-schooner Augustus.

Photo courtesy of the Great Lakes Marine Collection
of the Milwaukee Public Library/Wisconsin Marine Historical Society

364) *Augustus*, #29961, Scow-Schooner, Burned November 24, 1918.

The *Augustus* was destroyed by fire which was thought to have started in the ship's cook stove. The scow was moored at the Red River dock at the time and was loaded with 58 tons of hay which was to have been delivered at Marinette the following day. No one was aboard the craft at the time. The vessel was valued at $800 and her cargo was valued at $1,700. A nearby warehouse also sustained $500 in damage.

The *Augustus* was jointly owned by her master, Captain George Cota, and Captain Charles E. Larsen and was built at Spoonville, Michigan, in 1885. She measured 74.4 feet in length, 18.8 feet at the beam, 6.6 feet in depth and registered 54 gross tons. Door County Advocate, November 29, 1918. List

365) *Libby Nau*, #14808, Schooner, Abandoned May of 1919.

The *Libby Nau* was raised from the old Island Mill dock slip and towed to the Leathem & Smith shipyard. There she would be filled and sunk on the south side across the end of the old steamer, *Holland,* for use as a dock. In September of 1922, a fire that destroyed the Door County Produce Company's warehouse, spread to the *Nau* and burned whatever was left down to the waterline.

The *Libby Nau* was built at Green Bay in 1867 and registered 231.54 gross tons. She measured 129 feet in length, 26 feet across the beam and 10 feet in depth. DOOR COUNTY ADVOCATE, May 2, 1919. DOOR COUNTY ADVOCATE, September 8, 1922. List of Merchant Vessels of the U.S., 1895, p. 120.

366) *Mike Dohearty*, #162498, Scow, Wrecked Early June of 1919.

The *Dohearty* was chartered from the Leathem & Smith Company to take on a load of ties at Cedar River for the Crawford Cedar Company. After she was loaded, she sank and one side of the hull gave way. It was not considered salvageable.

The *Dohearty* was licensed for one crewman and was registered as an "unrigged barge." She measured 726 gross tons and was built in Sturgeon Bay in 1899. DOOR COUNTY ADVOCATE, June 6, 1919. List of Merchant Vessels of the U.S., 1914, p. 375.

367) *Frank O'Connor*, #126899, Steamer, Burned October 2, 1919.

The *Frank O'Connor* was bound for Milwaukee with 3,000 tons of hard coal from Buffalo. She was abreast of Cana Island when fire was discovered. The Baileys Harbor Coast Guard arrived on the scene and rescued Captain

William Hayes and his 21 crewmen. The *O'Connor* continued to burn and drifted northward as she did so. She finally burned to the waterline and sank off Parker's Reef just off North Bay. Some suspicions were voiced about the fire, but an investigation by the U.S. Steamboat Inspection Bureau exonerated Captain Hayes of all wrong doing.

In August of 1920, entrepreneur Clarence Labeau of the Labeau Wrecking Company of Toledo, bought the wreck for $1,100. The 3,000 tons of coal was valued at $50,000, but the wreck had not been found up to that time. The vessel was thought to be sitting in 70 feet of water two miles off North Bay. Labeau figured that during the World War, airplanes were used successfully to locate submarines and he hired the Green Bay Aero Club's plane to locate the wreck from the air. The effort proved to be unsuccessful due to poor weather conditions.

The *O'Connor* was left undiscovered for two years until June of 1922 when Charles Innis of North Bay and Chester Smith of Milwaukee located the wreck by dragging a 1,000 foot hawser between two gas launches. The two said the wreck was located at a reachable depth but declined to state the location until a settlement could be made with the owners. Previous searchers were looking closer to Spider Island. Once a settlement was made, the Milwaukee Wrecking and Salvage Company moved a tug and a lighter over the wreck site and began pumping the coal out with a centrifugal pump. The salvors claimed that the sides of the vessel had burned down so far that most of the cargo was lost to the lake. Of the original cargo of 3,000 tons of coal, only 700 tons were reclaimed. The coal that was salvaged, was loaded on the barge, *Liberty* and taken to De Pere and sold.

Years later, in 1935, Innis convinced Chicago diver Frank Blair that the remaining coal could be recovered with the use of a suction dredge, a heavy duty underwater vacuum

The steamer Frank O'Connor.

Photo courtesy of the Great Lakes Marine Collection of the Milwaukee Public Library/Wisconsin Marine Historical Society

cleaner. Blair made several dives on the wreck and found that the sides of the vessel had split open when she hit bottom making the cargo readily accessible.

Once the cargo was recovered the location of the *O'Connor* was forgotten. Area SCUBA divers renewed the effort to relocate the wreck. Lynn Fredickson, a local SeaGrant official located the *O'Connor* in the late 1970's, but lost the location and the search continued. A number of years later the wreck was found again, this time by Chicago diver Sam Mareci. The *Frank O'Connor* continues to be a popular dive site.

The *Frank O'Connor* was built as the *City of Naples* in 1892, at West Bay City, Michigan. She registered 2,109.37 gross tons with a length of 301 feet, a beam of 42.5 feet and a depth of 20.1 feet. DOOR COUNTY ADVOCATE, October 3, 1919. DOOR COUNTY ADVOCATE, March 5, August 27, 1920. DOOR COUNTY ADVOCATE, June 20, August 24, September 21, 1922. DOOR COUNTY ADVOCATE, October 18, 1935. List of Merchant Vessels of the U.S., 1895, p. 230.

368) Unnamed Fish Tug, Stranded December 25, 1919.

This little vessel went ashore at the lime kilns near Little Sturgeon. The owner, Marinette fisherman Andrew Christianson, and his two small boys were out lifting nets when the engine failed. They drifted ashore early Christmas morning and the boat went to pieces. The craft was valued at $500. Christianson was able to salvage the engine. DOOR COUNTY ADVOCATE, January 3, 1919.

369) Coller, Fish Tug, Stranded January 19, 1921.

The *Coller* broke away from her moorings behind the dock at Jacksonport and washed ashore where she became a total wreck. The only thing salvageable was the engine. The owners, Charles Heald and Bert LeClair, gave up fishing. DOOR COUNTY ADVOCATE, January 28, 1921.

370) *Advance*, #105102, Barge, Stranded October 19, 1921.

The *Advance* was blown ashore near the north point of Sand Bay where she was being used to lighter coal off the steamer, *Frank Billings*. The *Billings* had run aground on a shoal in the middle of Sand Bay and the *Advance* was tied to her bow for the rescue operation. When a storm came up, the salvage operation's tug boat was forced to abandon the steamer and barge. The *Advance* was found to be leaking and fearing she might founder, Captain Pearl Purdy ordered her cut loose. She was allowed to drift in the heavy northwest winds towards shore a mile away. Burdened with two derricks on board, the barge rolled in the waves until her decks went under. The Coast Guard was standing by and with "expert seamanship on the part of Captain Christensen" the Coast Guard rescue boat nosed up to the drifting barge and took off the stranded crew moments before the *Advance* hit the rocks. The next day the *Frank Billings* was released with little damage.

The *Advance* did not fare so well. The bottom of the lighter was badly damaged and she was abandoned by her owners, the Leathem D. Smith Dock Company. It was thought that another strong northwest wind would break her up. Captain Martin Petersen came in with a small scow and his gasoline freighter, the *Favorite,* to take off the derricks, wrecking pumps, and other salvageable equipment.

The *Advance* was built in 1871 and was 141 feet long and 38 feet at the beam. She had been a lumber barge in tow of the tug *Boscobel* for the Peshtigo Lumber Company. When the lumber trade between Menominee and Chicago dwindled, the barge was purchased by the Leathem D. Smith Company and made into a stone barge. Later, her owners equipped her with derricks and made her into a lighter for their wrecking operations. It was her fiftieth year in commission. DOOR COUNTY ADVOCATE, October 21, 28, 1921.

371) *W.H. Meyer*, #81637, Tug, Abandoned in August of 1922.

The *Meyer* was removed to the boneyard north of the shipyard in Sturgeon Bay. She was built in Benton Harbor, Michigan, in 1898 and was designed for towing. She registered 94 gross tons with a length of 89 feet, a beam of 24 feet and a depth of 11.2 feet. Door County Advocate, August 10, 1922. List of Merchant Vessels of the U.S., 1919, p. 175.

372) *Vermillion*, #76695, Steamer, Abandoned August of 1922.

In 1917, the *Vermillion* had burned to the waterline and sank at her slip at the Leathem and Smith shipyard. She sat there for two years until the yard owners decided to raise her and make her into a stone barge. They later reconsidered and intended to build her into a drydock. She was found to be too small for their plans and in the interim, she sank again. She was ultimately raised and removed to the Smith quarry where she was sunk as a breakwater.

The *Vermillion* was built as the *J.C. Gilchrist* at Trenton, Michigan in 1887. She came off the ways as a steam propeller, measuring 252 feet in length, 42 feet across the beam and 20.4 feet in depth. As a working freighter, she carried a crew of 13. Door County Advocate, May 2, 1919. Door County Advocate, July 23, November 5, 1920. Door County Advocate, August 10, 17, 1922. List of Merchant Vessels of the U.S., 1914, p. 317.

373) *G.M.A. Herrmann*, #86171, Fish Tug, Dynamited September 1922.

In July of 1919, the *Herrmann* was purchased by James Larson of Minneconne and was to be removed from the shipyard. Apparently she never made it. In September of 1922, the *Herrmann* was lying just outside the dock on the south side of the Sturgeon Bay Dry Dock Company's yard. She was half submerged and had to be blown up to make way for the launching of a new ship.

The *Herrmann* was built at Milwaukee in 1891 and registered 34 gross tons. She measured 61.6 feet in length, 14.6 feet at the beam and 6.5 feet in depth. DOOR COUNTY ADVOCATE, July 25, 1919. DOOR COUNTY ADVOCATE, September 28, 1922. List of Merchant Vessels of the U.S., 1911, p. 189.

374) *Bonita*, #3554, Yacht, Abandoned prior to 1924.

The *Bonita* had been owned by Senator Isaac "Ike" Watson Stephenson. In an April 15, 1924 issue, the GREEN BAY PRESS-GAZETTE described the yacht as one of many vessels laying in the marine graveyard in the Fox River between the two railroad bridges in Green Bay. The story reflectively asks,

"Where floats there now anywhere on the Great Lakes, a yacht with such proud connections as the old Bonita's? *For when the* Bonita, *handsome property of the famous "Ike" Stephenson, put to sea, people on the wharves knew that ere she returned, a new chapter would be written in the political history of Wisconsin. It was aboard the* Bonita *that the early campaigns of the present Senator La Follette were planned; and as the yacht cruised lazily about the blue waters of Lake Michigan, Stephenson and his cohorts planned one by one, the various moves which eventually brought 'Fighting Bob' into power. The establishment of the* MILWAUKEE FREE PRESS-*the great battle against the railroad barons and hundreds of lesser moves: these are tales that the stripped cabin of the boat could tell were it given tongue. And now her rakish bow thrust over the low shore line, her stern deep in the Fox, there is nothing ahead for her but the axe and the fire."*

In 1961 bottom surveys for the Army Corps of Engineers

The Bonita, private yacht of Isaac Watson Stephenson.
Photo courtesy of the Great Lakes Marine Collection of the Milwaukee Public Library/Wisconsin Marine Historical Society

271

found an "old wooden hulk about 100 feet long" between the railroad bridges—the approximate area where the Bonita was abandoned. The wreck was described in the 1963 Great Lakes Pilot as "headed into the bank and about 50 feet off shore and its stern about 150 feet into the channel." Soundings indicated 13 feet of water over the stern.

The *Bonita* was built at Detroit in 1892 and registered 73 gross tons. She measured 110.2 feet in length, 16.6 feet across the beam and 6.6 feet in depth. GREEN BAY PRESS-GAZETTE, April 15, 1924. DOOR COUNTY ADVOCATE, April 25, 1924. List of Merchant Vessels of the U.S. U.S. Army Corps of Engineers, Great Lakes Pilot, 1963, Detroit, Michigan, p. 130.

375) *Nerita*, #206344, Sea-Going Yacht Abandoned prior to 1924.

The *Nerita*, like the *Bonita*, found a resting place in the boneyard of Green Bay in the Fox River between the two railroad bridges. She had once been owned on the Atlantic coast. Later she became the property of a Wisconsin excursion line that used her to carry sightseers around Green Bay and Lake Michigan. At the time of her abandonment, she was owned by Captain Pickney S. Roulett of Green Bay. GREEN BAY PRESS-GAZETTE, April 15, 1924. DOOR COUNTY ADVOCATE, April 25, 1924. List of Merchant Vessels of the U.S., 1914, p. 254.

376) *Lakeland*, #126420, Steel Steamer, Foundered December 3, 1924.

The *Lakeland* was bound from Kenosha to Detroit with a cargo of automobiles and was ten miles off the Sturgeon Bay canal when she developed a bad leak. Captain John T. McNeely ordered her brought about for the canal and the steamer was just nine miles short of there when the engines had to be shut down to divert steam to the pumps. When the fight seemed hopeless, McNeely ordered all but a skeleton crew into the lifeboats. An SOS had been sent out and the steamer *Ann Arbor No. 6* as well as the Sturgeon Bay Coast Guard arrived on the scene. By that time the vessel was listing 45 degrees to port and Coast Guard Captain Robert Anderson ordered the boat abandoned and took the remaining crewmembers and Captain McNeely aboard their cutter. Shortly thereafter, the *Lakeland* slipped below the waves stern first with her lights still flickering until the last spar disappeared. As she started downward, the force of air bursting through the chambers, blew her cabins and hatches forty feet into the air. The vessel settled to the bottom seven miles east of the canal in 220 feet of water. The *Lakeland* was valued at $500,000

The following summer, 22 insurance companies owing $450,000 on the sunken ship started an investigation on the loss. Local vessels dragged for the ship for days and the project was about to be given up when H.C. Hansen, representing the insurance companies, hired Albert Kalmbach and two of his fish tugs. Kalmbach made a drag and had it towed around behind the fishtugs, *Albert C.* and the *Four Brothers*. They were finishing their second pass when they snagged the *Lakeland*.

Five weeks later, in early August of 1925, the salvage barge *Chittendon*, towed all the way from New York City for the project, was anchored over the wreck. A special team of divers assembled for the job, started exploring the *Lakeland*. Three divers were from Overseas Salvors, Inc. One of them, S.J. Drillishak, had set the world record, 306 feet, when, as a Navy diver, he was helping to rescue the crew of a sunken submarine. The crew also included two Navy divers. The team used a new breathing medium, helium and oxygen—never used before in a working situation—to prevent narcosis of the depth. Divers made numerous dives over four weeks time and finished Labor Day weekend.

That fall, sixteen insurance companies took the Thomson

The steamer Lakeland entering Milwaukee Harbor.

Photo courtesy of the Wisconsin Maritime Museum, Manitowoc, Wisconsin

Transportation Company to court in Cleveland in an effort to prove that Captain McNeely had conspired with the ship's owners to scuttle his vessel and help the financially weak company. Despite testimony by three divers that the seacocks were open, the jury deadlocked and the case was dismissed.

In February of 1926 the case went to trial a second time. This time the jury decided that claims of collusion between the captain and the owner were unfounded. The Thomson Transportation Company was awarded full indemnity and interest. A third case was attempted but never came to trial.

Over and above what they spent for legal fees, the insurance companies spent $60,000 just for the diving expedition. While the court case was a failure, the diving expedition was a wild success. It is interesting to note that this technology of using "mixed gas" for diving has been greatly developed. It has effectively increased the acceptable depth of diving from 200 to 2,000 feet. The U.S. Navy used it to salvage the submarine, *Squalus*, in 1939. E.A. Link used it for his Man-In-The-Sea project and Jacques Cousteau used it for his Conshelf project. It is now used extensively for oil field diving and is even being used for advanced sport diving. But before it was used anywhere else in the world, it was used at Sturgeon Bay, Wisconsin.

The *Lakeland* was a steel steamer built at Cleveland in 1887 as the *Cambria*. She registered 2,425 gross tons and measured 280 feet in length, 40 feet across the beam and 20 feet in depth. Green Bay Press-Gazette, December 3, 1924. Milwaukee Journal, December 3, December 4, 1924. Door County Advocate, December 5, 1924. Door County Advocate, June 26, August 14, 21, September 11, October 30, 1925. Door County Advocate, February 12, 26, 1926. Door County Advocate, August 19, 1927. List of Merchant Vessels of the U.S., 1924, p. 66.

377) *Fox*, Side-Wheel Steamer, Abandoned 1927.

The *Fox* was a sidewheel tug boat built in Oshkosh in 1900 for the Army Corps of Engineers. She was used on the Fox River system for many years. In 1927 she was pushed into the shallows at the mouth of the river and abandoned. A few years later, the Green Bay Yacht Club adopted the old vessel for their club house. The *Fox* served in that capacity for thirty years, until a new club house was built in 1963. The old sidewheeler was bulldozed and covered with a parking lot.

The side-wheel steamer Fox.

Photo courtesy of the Wisconsin Maritime Museum, Manitowoc, Wisconsin

The *Fox* measured 139 displacement tons with a length of 107.5 feet, a beam of 18.8 feet and a depth of 5 feet. GREEN BAY PRESS-GAZETTE, "Sunday Magazine" section, May 17, 1964. Herman G. Runge Collection of the Milwaukee Public Library/Wisconsin Marine Historical Society.

378) *I.N. Foster*, #100031, Barge, Abandoned 1927.

The *I.N. Foster* was built in 1872 as a schooner, converted to a steamer in 1893 before finally being reduced to a barge. She is often reported a having been lost on Rock Island. The *Foster*, still rigged as a schooner, ran aground on the island on August 8, 1887 and was released 53 weeks later. She served on the lakes for another forty years before being abandoned in Sturgeon Bay in 1927. The *Foster* registered 319 gross tons with a length of 134.9 feet, 26.2 feet, and a depth of 11.5 feet. DOOR COUNTY ADVOCATE, August 18, 1888.

Herman G. Runge Collection of the Milwaukee Public Library/Wisconsin Marine Historical Society. List of Merchant Vessels of the U.S., 1895, p. 257.

379) *Frances IV*, Canadian Motor Yacht, Exploded August 6, 1927.

The *Frances IV* was one of several yachts from the Chicago Yacht Club that were bound from Sturgeon Bay to Georgian Bay, Ontario. She was four miles out from Horseshoe Bay on a line with the west end of Chambers Island when witnesses saw a plume of blue smoke rise from the yacht. She blew a distress signal and moments later an explosion in her engine room blew seventy feet into the air. C.W. Johnson, owner of the vessel, and his daughter, Frances, age nine, jumped into the water and were picked up by one of the yachts from their club. Mrs. Johnson was killed by the explosion. Her body was later recovered and taken to Sturgeon Bay. Captain of the yacht, Walter Banks, and steward, Yasu "Pete" Kamatami, also jumped into the water. Both were thrown life preservers by a passing boat as it was on its way to rescue Johnson and his daughter. When rescuers returned, both Banks and Kamatami were missing. The body of Walter Banks was later recovered. Yasu Kamatami, a Japanese student, working his way through Oberlin College with summer employment on the yacht, was never found.

The *Frances IV* burned for two hours before she sank. She was described as an express cruiser and measured 65 feet in length. DOOR COUNTY ADVOCATE, August 12, 19, 26, September 2, 1927.

380) *Cynthie*, #208967, Gas Fish Tug, Burned September 19, 1928.

The *Cynthie* burned and sank with the loss of two men "about five miles off Sherwood Point on the Sturgeon Bay -Marinette course." The tug's engine backfired setting fire to kerosene kept on board to preserve fish nets. The whole interior of the cabin was soon in flames. Three men were on board: her owner, Dan Henry of Marinette; Arthur Frohmeier, a relative of Henry's from Chicago; and Tom Anderson of Marinette, the boat's engineer. When the boat caught fire, Henry and Frohmeier immediately jumped overboard. Anderson ran forward and grabbed three life preservers before jumping over the side. By that time Henry had gone down. Frohmeier was satisfied that he was safe resting on a floating box and declined a life jacket. He later tired and dropped from sight. The tug, *Florence*, later arrived on the scene and rescued Anderson, the sole survivor. In spite of a Coast Guard search, Henry and Frohmeier were never found.

The *Cynthie* was built in Sturgeon Bay in 1907. She featured an eight horse gas engine—the engine that caused her demise, and registered eight gross tons. She measured 27.5 feet in length, 8.8 feet across the beam and 3.3 feet in depth. Door County Advocate, September 21, 1928. List of Merchant Vessels of the U.S., 1924, p. 159. List of Merchant Vessels of the U.S., 1929, p. 911.

381) *Leila C.*, Fish Tug, Foundered October 3, 1928.

The *Leila C.* was sunk in a collision with the ore freighter, *S.B. Coolidge*. Her owner, Leslie Cornell, and Alfred Johnson were on their way out to set the 4,000 hooks they had on board. Cruising through a slight haze, "but not enough to interfere with vision," they collided at right angles with the *Coolidge* which was bound for Escanaba. The collision occurred two miles southeast of Pilot Island. The *Leila C.* sank inside of fifteen minutes in 150 feet of water. Cornell and Johnson grabbed life preservers and jumped overboard. They were rescued by the *Coolidge's* crew and placed aboard the ferry, *Wisconsin*. Ironically, the *Coolidge's* captain, "Mac" Johnson, was also a Washington Island native and may have been related to Alfred Johnson of the sunken *Leila C.* The Plum Island Coast Guard attempted to drag for the boat but were unsuccessful due to the rock ledges that made up the bottom contour in that area.

The *Leila C.* had just recently been built and this may explain why she was not listed in the government list. Just a few days prior, as she was leaving her slip, one of the cylinders in her "new type Kahlenberg engine" went through itself, almost wrecking the machinery. She was brought to the Sturgeon Bay Boat Works for repairs.

Two days after the *Leila C.* was lost, two Coast Guard boats, the fishtugs, *J.W. Cornell, Clara C., Velox Iona Estella, Fred,* and the small freighter *Diana* searched for almost twelve hours but failed to find the tug. An airplane from Escanaba assisted for an hour, but no trace of the tug was found.

The *Leila C.* measured forty feet in length and was valued at $8,000. There was no insurance. DOOR COUNTY ADVOCATE, October 5, 12, 26, 1928.

382) *Michael J. Bartelme,* #116723, Steel Steamer, Stranded October 4, 1928.

The *Bartelme* was steaming north through a thick fog when she ran aground on the shoals of Cana Island. She had been making a regular circuit of carrying coal from Ashtabula, Ohio, to Milwaukee and returning with iron ore from Escanaba. This was her thirteenth trip.

The steamer attempted to release herself but only pulled herself broadside to the island. The ship pounded in south winds and large boulders were hammered up through the the steel plating of her bottom. The big wrecking tug, *Favorite,* arrived on the scene but no serious effort to pull the steamer into deep water could be made until pumps could be put aboard. The *Favorite* could not deliver the equipment due to the shallow depth of the water and by the time the tug *Arctic* arrived from Manitowoc with a lighter, winds had picked up and both tugs had to run for cover. As the lake began to roll, the *Bartelme* pounded on the bottom again and the Coast Guard decided it was time to remove the 26 crewmen on board.

Marine architect John Smith was brought in from Detroit to survey the hull and based on his report the insurance companies concluded that they were not going to pay the estimated $150,000 to repair the *Bartelme* valued a $200,000.

A crew of salvors was put aboard the ship and the task of stripping the hull was begun. The *Bartelme* was sitting with her bow in four to five feet of water and her stern was in fourteen feet. On November 5th, one month after she grounded, the ship broke in two. The stern section settled in deeper water, flooding the engine room. In spite of this, part of the crew remained on board and continued pulling out anything moveable. Fifteen carloads of equipment, valued at over $20,000, were taken off the *Bartelme*. By June of 1930, the engines and boilers were also removed.

The vacant hull of the *M.J. Bartelme* sat on Cana Island for five years. The wreck became such a popular tourist attraction that the road to the island had to be rebuilt. At one point, lighthouse keeper William Sanderson, reported nearly 200 cars were parked near the island and the road leading to it. The road was so narrow that cars leaving the area could not get around cars arriving.

In August of 1933, workmen started cutting up the hull of the *Bartelme*. The steam barge *M.H. Stuart* was chartered to transport the iron from the wreck to Sturgeon Bay on scows with a derrick scow being used to load the scows.

The *Michael J. Bartelme* registered 3,400 tons with an overall length of 352 feet, a beam of 44 feet and a depth of 22 feet. For all of this bulk, only a few plates, some cable

The steamer Michael J. Bartelme

Photo courtesy of the Great Lakes Marine Collection of the Milwaukee Public Library/Wisconsin Marine Historical Society

and a few fixtures mark the spot where the steamer ended her career. She was built as the *Central West* and had her name changed the year before she was lost. She was built at Cleveland in 1896. Door County Advocate, October 5, 12, November 2, 9, 1928. Door County Advocate, June 6, 1930. Door County Advocate, August 11, September 15, 1933. List of Merchant Vessels of the U.S., 1933, p. 75.

383) *Pathfinder*, #202225, Gas Screw, Stranded March 10, 1929.

The List of Merchant Vessels of the U.S. for 1930 describes the *Pathfinder* as having gone ashore at Baileys Harbor and dropped from the registry. She was built as the *Minnie R.* and under that name collided with the *Pere Marquette 17* at Kewaunee in 1914 and dropped from the registry. Four people were aboard—all were saved. The *Pathfinder* was built in Manitowoc in 1905 and registered ten tons. She was designed for miscellaneous service and measured 32.2 feet in length, with a beam of 9 feet and a depth of 3.0 feet. List of Merchant Vessels of the U.S., 1911, p. 249. List of Merchant Vessels of the U.S., 1914, p. 429. List of Merchant Vessels of the U.S., 1930, p. 918.

384) *Coila*, #207117, Gas Screw, Stranded March 10, 1929.

The *Coila* was listed in the List of Merchant Vessels of the U.S. as having stranded at Jacksonport. No other information was given on the circumstances. The *Coila* registered 6 gross tons with a length of 29 feet, a beam of 8 feet, and a depth of 3.6 feet. She was built in Manitowoc in 1902. List of Merchant Vessels of the U.S., 1928, p. 276. List of Merchant Vessels of the U.S., 1929, p. 911.

385) "Mystery Plane," Crashed October 30, 1929.

A plane of unstated size and description was seen dropping into the bay according to a number of witnesses. A storm was blowing at the time. Four men near the Menominee county airport had seen her fly into the storm swept bay on a line with the harbor piers and Green Island. A woman at Gosling's, in Menominee, also saw a plane go into the Bay of Green Bay about a mile and a quarter from the Michigan shore at the same time. Shortly before, workers on Chambers Island saw the craft southwest of the island flying in a westerly direction. The Plum Island Coast Guard, with the assistance of an airplane and a number of fishtugs, searched the area for 24 hours. No trace of the plane was found. DOOR COUNTY ADVOCATE, November 1, 1929.

386) Franc Minor, #120615, Schooner, Burned December 8, 1929.

The *Minor* was towed from Cedar River to Marinette in September of 1919. She was shoved on the banks of Meriman Island and her owner, Orin Angwall, intended to have her overhauled. The craft was left laying in the mud for years. In December of 1929, a group of boys, skating on the river, were apparently using the vessel as a wind break for a bonfire. The fire spread to the old schooner. The blaze was only discovered after it had a good start. By the time the fire department arrived, flames were leaping from every corner of the craft. The loss was not covered by insurance. As late as the 1960s, the remains of the vessel could be seen at low water.

The *Franc Minor* was a small trading schooner that was used for freighting along the peninsula years before. She registered 45 gross tons with a length of 68 feet, a beam of 17.3 feet and a depth of 5 feet. She was built at Fort Howard in 1885. DOOR COUNTY ADVOCATE, September 12, 1919. DOOR COUNTY ADVOCATE, December 13, 1929. List of Merchant Vessels of the U.S., 1914, p. 31.

387) *Adriatic*, #106676, Schooner, Abandoned in 1930.

Adriatic, it might be remembered, was the fellow consort of the *City of Glasgow* when that vessel met its fate in Lily Bay. Unlike the *Glasgow*, the *Adriatic* was pulled off and repaired at Sturgeon Bay. The schooner was purchased in early 1913 by Thomas Smith and rebuilt to haul stone for the Leathem & Smith quarry. The quarry had just been equipped with a new rock crushing machine and was given an all new cement wharf. In preparation for her part in the increasing stone trade the *Adriatic* was altered, given a new coat of red and green paint and a hoisting rig. (Construction was held up when the rig's four ton drum broke through the ice and could not be retrieved until the ice went out.) The barge took her first load in early June of 1913. Still not satisfied, the *Adriatic's* owners had her equipped with a new self-unloading boom. News accounts reported, "The conveyors are on the same principle as those on the *Wyandotte* and other boats of this type, the stone being carried from hoppers in the hold on belts to a receptacle that dumps the material onto a belt on a 60 foot crane that carries it over the side onto the dock. The equipment will cost in the neighborhood of $5,000 without the installation. The capacity will be 200 yards an hour." The equipment arrived in Sturgeon Bay in early December and by mid-summer the barge was ready to rejoin the stone trade. The unloading boom proved too heavy for the design and an A frame was added to help bear the weight. With her new hoppers and boom the barge was equipped to carry 1,000 yards of stone and it was estimated that she could unload herself in about four hours.

By 1928, the *Adriatic* was downgraded to an unrigged barge and, two years later, was abandoned and dropped from the government list. In October of 1947, the 36 foot fishtug, *Lady Marie*, was sunk when she ran on an obstruction off the Smith Coal Company dock. The obstruction was reported to be the wreck of the *Adriatic*.

The *Adriatic* was built as a schooner in 1889 at West Bay City, Michigan, and originally registered 915 gross tons. She measured 202 feet in length, 34.7 feet at the beam, and 16.6 feet in depth. Door County Advocate, January 23, February 27, March 20, April 13, 1913. June 12, October 30, December 11, 1913. Door County Advocate, May 28, July 16, 1914. Door County Advocate, May 2, 1919. Door County Advocate, October 10, 1947. List of Merchant Vessels of the U.S., 1895, p. 64. List of Merchant Vessels of the U.S., 1930, p. 627.

388) *Cabot Brothers*, #213459, Gas Screw, Burned October 25, 1930.

The *Cabot Brothers* was a gas screw of eleven tons that burned at Sawyer, Wisconsin, according to the List of Merchant Vessels of the U.S. No other details of the story are given. An old fish boat laying just off the drop off from Potawatomi Park may be the *Cabot Brothers*. It is appropriately due south of a spot called Cabot's Point. The sunken hulk is burned down to the waterline and little is left except for the keel, parts of the bottom, part of the engine, the propeller, shaft and shoe.

The *Cabot Brothers* was built at Sturgeon Bay as the *Johanna W.* in 1915. She measured 30.2 feet in length, 9.2 feet across the beam, and 3.6 feet in depth. List of Merchant Vessels of the U.S., 1929, p. 258. List of Merchant Vessels of the U.S., 1931, p. 939.

389) Leathem D. Smith, #218159, Tug, Abandoned about 1930.

The *Smith* was built in 1893 as the *Light Ship No. 59* and for many years saw service at Bar Point and elsewhere before being sold for the humiliating figure of $340. The old light ship was given an engine, new super structure and a name, *Leathem D. Smith*, and put in service in 1919. She served the Leathem & Smith Company or one of its off

The Leathem D. Smith (on the right) after she was abandoned into the Sturgeon Bay bone-yard.

Photo courtesy of the Wisconsin Maritime Museum, Manitowoc, Wisconsin

shoots until the early 1930s when she was taken to the Leathem Smith yard and left. She went largely unused but was left on the government list until 1943. She was one of the vessels that escaped damage at the Sturgeon Bay ship yard in the 1935 fire. The *Leathem D. Smith* was wood hulled, and registered 122 gross tons with a length of 89.2 feet, a beam of 21 feet and a draft of 9.5 feet. Herman G. Runge Collection of the Milwaukee Public Library/Wisconsin Marine Historical Society.

390) *Empire State*, #7229, Steam Barge
391) *Ida Corning*, #44283, Barge
392) *Oakleaf*, # 19106, Schooner, All Burned June 21, 1931.

These three vessels burned at the Sturgeon Bay Stone Company where they had been scuttled for use as a pier. A cigarette dropped by a careless fisherman is thought to have started the the fire on the *Ida Corning*. Flames quickly spread to the *Oakleaf* and *Empire State*. The fire was left unchecked and burned for four days. Charred ribs still lay in the shallows off the old dock and the remnants of the hulls are still filled with burned embers.

The *Empire State* caught fire at an earlier date, July 28, 1929, once again, due to a careless smoker. The local fire department was able to extinguish the blaze but the fire re-ignited that night. Returning firefighters allowed it to burn, standing by only to prevent the spread of sparks. Whatever the fire of 1929 left, the fire of 1931 destroyed.

The *Empire State* was built in Buffalo in 1862 as a steam propeller and was, at one time, considered one of the finest passenger and freight steamers on the lakes. The steamer was later purchased by the Sturgeon Bay Stone company and in 1908 was cut down for use in the stone trade. She was the sister ship of the steamer, *Fountain City*, which at the time of the fire, was sitting in the "boneyard" for ships

The steamer Empire State.

Photo courtesy of the Great Lakes Marine Collection of the Milwaukee Public Library/Wisconsin Marine Historical Society

on the east side of the bay. The *Fountain City* had also been burned.

In 1868, the *Empire State* accidentally ran into and sank the schooner *Dunderberg* resulting in the death of Mrs. O. Wilcox. The steamer was libeled for $60,000 and authorities arrested second mate John Longley for "manslaughter on the high seas." Longley had been in control at the time of the accident. The second mate was later released on a legal technicality. According to maritime law, a ship's officer could not be held responsible for the death of a person on another ship. The Steamboat Inspectors' Board of Inquiry found Longley negligent in his duties, however, and his pilot license was revoked

In 1870, the *Empire State* again claimed notoriety when she rammed and sank the steamer, *Wabash* in sixty feet of water. In her heyday, the *Empire State* registered 1,116.53 gross tons and boasted a length of 212 feet, a beam of 32.7

The schooner Ida Corning.
Photo courtesy of the Great Lakes Marine Collection
of the Milwaukee Public Library/Wisconsin Marine Historical Society

feet and a depth of 12.2 feet. CHICAGO TRIBUNE, August 19, 1868. CHICAGO TRIBUNE, August 20, 28, September 1, 10, 1868. CHICAGO TIMES, June 9, 1870. DOOR COUNTY ADVOCATE, January 30, 1908. DOOR COUNTY ADVOCATE, August 2, 1929. DOOR COUNTY ADVOCATE, June 26, 1931. List of Merchant Vessels of the U.S., 1895, p. 242.

The *Ida Corning* was built in 1881 for use as a tow barge to freight lumber from Marinette and Menominee to Chicago. In later years, she was purchased by the Sturgeon Bay Stone Company for the stone trade. When that trade slumped and her services were no longer needed, she was scuttled in her present position. She was built at East Saginaw, Michigan, and registered 444.71 gross tons and had a length of 168 feet, a beam of 31 feet, and a depth of 10.9 feet. DOOR COUNTY ADVOCATE, June 26, 1931. List of Merchant Vessels of the U.S., 1895, p. 92.

The *Oakleaf* was built as a lumber ship and was used for that purpose for many years until she was taken over by the Sturgeon Bay Stone Company for hauling stone. About 1910, that trade slumped and the vessel was scuttled in her present position. The *Oakleaf* was built in Cleveland and measured 160 feet in length, a beam of 31 feet, and a depth of 10.7 feet. DOOR COUNTY ADVOCATE, June 26, 1931. List of Merchant Vessels of the U.S., 1895, p. 156.

393) *Georgia*, #125873, Steamer, Abandoned Mid-June of 1932

On June 13, 1932, the old steamer, *Georgia*, was released from the boneyard in Sturgeon Bay, where she had been sitting since 1926. She was taken in tow of the stone carrier, *Fred W. Green*, and the *Marquis Roen* and brought to Summer Island where she was to be sunk for use as a breakwater for the Northwest Sand and Gravel Company's new quarry. Everything of value was taken off the steamer. Her wooden life boats were sold and many were remodeled into pleasure craft in Door County. Gunder Gunderson of

The steamer Georgia

Photo courtesy of the Wisconsin Maritime Museum, Manitowoc, Wisconsin

Nasewaupee removed the cabins for use as a store and soft drink parlor on the "Little Sturgeon Road."

The *Georgia* was built as the *City of Ludington* in 1880 for the Goodrich Company. She was constructed in Manitowoc and spent half a century running between Chicago and Mackinac Island. The steamer registered 842.33 gross tons and was powered by a 325 horsepower steam engine. She measured 195.7 feet in length, 34.4 feet at the beam and 12 feet in depth. DOOR COUNTY ADVOCATE, June 17, 1932. List of Merchant Vessels of the U.S., 1895, p. 229.

394) *Captain Lawrence*, #107569, Schooner, Stranded September 19, 1933.

The *Captain Lawrence* was taken up to Poverty Island to seek what had been described, at the time, as "King Strang's gold." (See Legendary Treasure of Poverty Island). She was anchored off the island when she was overwhelmed by a southwest storm. When her anchor cable broke, she drifted ashore and broke up on the rocks of Poverty Island. The vessel had been acquired by Wilfred Behrens, who with Alfred Graham, his son, Immanuel, and Walter Hartman comprised a dive team intending to find the treasure reported to be somewhere between the island and Middle Gull Island. All four reached the safety of Poverty Island with the help of lighthouse keeper Nels P. Jensen and his assistants, Ben Johnson and Abe Jessen. The light keepers gave the four salvors temporary shelter and aid in recovering any part of the wreck that could be removed.

The *Captain Lawrence* was built as the schooner *Alice* in 1898 at Green Bay by Horace Conley. She had several different owners, including the Sea Scouts, a nautical arm of the Boy Scouts, before she was laid up in the Menominee River for two years. She was purchased by Behrens who sailed her in the area for two seasons prior to her demise.

The loss of the schooner was covered in numerous news-papers. Some stories conflict on where she was going—the MANITOWOC HERALD reported she was sailing for Beaver Island to look for King Strang's treasure there—but all agree she was lost on Poverty Island in search of gold.

As the *Alice*, she was outfitted with a 40 horsepower gas engine in 1919. The Sea Scouts took her over in 1924 and gave her the name, *"Captain Lawrence."* She is occasional-ly listed as the *"Gay Captain Lawrence."* This may be from some confusion around her new description of "gas yacht" being abbreviated to "ga. y."

The *Lawrence* had been docked in Sturgeon Bay during part of the sailing season of 1932. The craft was rigged like a New Foundland fishing schooner and drew much atten-tion because of her appearance. The DOOR COUNTY ADVOCATE, in describing the loss of the schooner, stated that she had been built for Marshall Field of Chicago for use in the Spanish-American War.

The *Captain Lawrence* registered 43 gross tons, and measured 60.8 feet in length, 16.2 feet across the beam and 9 feet in depth. ESCANABA DAILY PRESS, September 15, 1933. GREEN BAY PRESS-GAZETTE, September 19, 1933. DOOR COUNTY ADVOCATE, September 29, 1933. Edward Carus, "Great Lakes Marine Notes", MANITOWOC HERALD-TIMES, March 31, 1934. List of Merchant Vessels of the U.S., 1931, p.782.

395) *Mueller*, #135954, Steamer, Burned September, 1933.

The *Mueller* was moored at the Leathem D. Smith Dock Company's yard when she caught fire. She was pushed in the mud until her future could be determined. She was finally dropped from the government list in 1936.

The *Mueller* was built as the *Edwin S. Tice* at Manitowoc in 1887. In her heyday, the steamer boasted 699 gross tons with a 500 horsepower steam engine and a crew of eleven. She measured 172 feet in length, 18.7 feet across the beam and 8.7 feet in depth. DOOR COUNTY ADVOCATE, September 29, 1933.

396) *Mary Ellen Cook*, #90763, Schooner, Burned February 27, 1934.

The *Cook* was burned at the shore by the Door County Country Club where she had been laying for the last twelve years. Her deck was rotted away and her mizzen mast fell over. In the fall of 1933, her main mast was taken out before it fell. About February of 1934, the foremast with the yard arm and remaining rigging fell over. Only her hull remained and it was decided that it should be burned.

The Mary Ellen Cook.
Photo courtesy of the Great Lakes Marine Collection
of the Milwaukee Public Library/Wisconsin Marine Historical Society

The *Cook* was built at Grand Haven in 1875, and had been the pride of the sailing fleet on Lake Michigan. She made maritime history when, while under command of Captain J.M. Valentine, she rode a large wave over the Chicago breakwater while entering that harbor in a storm. By 1922 she had outlived her usefulness as a working schooner and was taken to the Door County Country Club where she was painted white and sunk for use as a novelty pier. Even as a pier she was admired by thousands of

The steamer Mueller.

Photo courtesy of the Great Lakes Marine Collection of the Milwaukee Public Library/Wisconsin Marine Historical Society

tourists and was used as a mooring place for yachts. The *Mary Ellen Cook* had carried a crew of 4 and registered 132 gross tons. She measured 118 feet in length, 25 feet at the beam and 7 feet in depth. DOOR COUNTY ADVOCATE, June 16, 1922. DOOR COUNTY ADVOCATE, March 2, 1934. List of Merchant Vessels of the U.S., 1911, p. 78.

The Wisconsin was the subject of a number of post-cards including this picture of her preparing to leave Washington Island.

Photo courtesy of the Great Lakes Marine Collection
of the Milwaukee Public Library/Wisconsin Marine Historical Society

397) *Wisconsin*, #120499, Steamer, Scuttled in 1935.

The *Wisconsin* was built in 1882 as the *F. and P.M. No. 1* for the Flint and Pere Marquette Transportation Co. By 1935 she had changed owners, changed appearances and changed names and, by this time, as a scow, had outlived her usefulness. She was taken out in the bay to a point north of Green Island and sent to the bottom. In her prime, as the *F. and P.M.*, she measured 769 gross tons with a length of 181 feet, a beam of 30.2 feet and a depth of 12.1 feet. She was built in Detroit. List of Merchant Vessels of the U.S., 1900, p. 236. List of Merchant Vessels of the U.S., 1935, p. 604.

398) *Beaver*,#155225, Tug,
399) *Lucia A. Simpson*, #140097, Schooner
400) *Petosky*, #150425, Steamer
401) *Swift*, #81432, Steamer
402) *E.G. Crosby*, #127731, Steamer, All burned December 3, 1935

These five vessels were destroyed in a fire that swept over the Sturgeon Bay Shipbuilding and Drydock Company. Also burned were the steamers, *Waukegan*, and *Kenosha* which were repaired and restored to some form of service. Fire started from a welding torch used in the *Crosby*, a steel steamer being cut down for use as a barge. From there, the flames spread to the other vessels. None of the ships were insured.

The *Beaver* was a steam tug that had actually been abandoned the year before and had been left in the yard awaiting her destiny. Partially rotten, the tug had been pulled up almost onto the beach. The *Beaver* was built in 1892 at Grand Haven, as the *Oval Agitator* for service as a passenger vessel. The tug had been equipped with a 350 horsepower steam engine and originally carried a crew of eleven. The vessel registered 121 gross tons with a length of 98.4 feet, a beam of 19.6 feet and a depth of 8.6 feet. Door County Advocate, December 6, 1935. List of Merchant Vessels of the U.S., 1911, p. 137.

The *Lucia A. Simpson* was the last three-masted schooner on the Great Lakes. Some years before she was purchased by a West Allis diver who had planned to take her to Lake Superior for a wreck salvage operation. After a bad encounter with a squall off the canal, the schooner was taken to the ship yard and left. Later, she was to be towed to Chicago for use as headquarters for a new yacht club being built there, but the plans fell through. The *Simpson* was the sister ship of the schooner, *Our Son,* the last sailing schooner to work on the Great Lakes. The *Our Son* foundered on Lake Michigan several years before.

The *Lucia Simpson* had been considered valueless at the time of the fire and little effort was made to save her. Nonetheless, only the bow of the old schooner was destroyed. The stern section was left with two of her masts still standing. What was not burned was scrapped.

The *Lucia A. Simpson* was built in Manitowoc in 1875 and registered 227 gross tons. She measured 127 feet in length, 28 feet across the beam and 8.7 feet in depth. DOOR COUNTY ADVOCATE, March 11, 1932. DOOR COUNTY ADVOCATE, December 6, 1935. List of Merchant Vessels of the U.S., 1931, p. 586. List of Merchant Vessels of the U.S., 1936, p. 1035.

The *Petosky* was a wooden hulled steamer built in 1888 at Manitowoc. She registered 770 gross tons and measured 171.3 feet in length, 30.4 feet at the beam and 12.2 feet in depth. DOOR COUNTY ADVOCATE, December 6, 1935. List of Merchant Vessels of the U.S., 1931, p. 141. List of Merchant Vessels of the U.S., 1935, p. 1032.

The steamer *Swift* was built as the *Wotan* at Marine City, Michigan, in 1893 and had been used by the Nessen Transportation Company of Chicago to haul lumber. She was a wooden vessel of 886 gross tons and measured 191. 5 feet in length, 36.5 feet across the beam and 13.6 feet in depth. DOOR COUNTY ADVOCATE, December 6, 1935. List of Merchant Vessels of the U.S., 1931, p. 174. List of Merchant Vessels of the U.S., 1936, p. 1032.

The *E.G. Crosby*, the original source of the fire, was an

298

oil burning, steam driven propeller built in 1903. Fire gutted the vessel of her wooden trim work, interior and anything else burnable, leaving a steel frame and hull. Nothing was stated about her ultimate disposition, however, later issues of the government's List of Merchant Vessels declare the *Crosby* destroyed on December 3, 1935. She was probably cut up for scrap metal.

The *E.G. Crosby* had an interesting career that began under the name *City of South Haven* as a luxury passenger steamer running between Chicago and South Haven. Her original owners had her built to rival the ill-fated steamer *Eastland* which later capsized in Chicago. The *South Haven* was later renamed *E.G. Crosby* in memory of Great Lakes ship captain Edward G. Crosby, who as a passenger, was lost with the luxury liner *Titanic* in 1912. During the prohibition era, the *Crosby* was renamed *City of Miami* and taken to the east coast where she ran between Miami and Havana, Cuba as a floating tavern. Later, she was returned to service on Lake Michigan under her former name of *E.G. Crosby*. She had most recently been purchased by Roen and Wolter of Sturgeon Bay for conversion to a barge.

The *Crosby* measured 247.7 feet in length, 40.3 feet across the beam, and 21.7 feet in depth. She registered 1,879 gross tons and rated a propulsion capability of 2,000 horsepower. DOOR COUNTY ADVOCATE, December 6, 13, 1935. List of Merchant Vessels of the U.S., 1936, p. 52, 53. List of Merchant Vessels of the U.S., 1965, p. 270. Walter Lord, A Night To Remember, New York: Holt Rinehart & Winston, 1955, p. 113.

403) *Sidney O. Neff*, #116377, Steamer, Abandoned in May of 1939.

The *Sidney O. Neff* had served on the Great Lakes for forty years. In 1931 federal steamboat inspectors condemned the vessel and her owner, the Marinette

The steamer Sydney O. Neff shortly before she was taken out and abandoned in the Bay.

Photo courtesy of the Wisconsin Maritime Museum, Manitowoc, Wisconsin

Transportation Company decided to abandon her. She was left to rot but in 1934, the old steamer was seized and put up for sale by Federal Marshals in Milwaukee for claims against her. The highest bid was $500 from Captain Orin Angwall of Marinette. Her stack and worn out machinery were taken by the crew of the steamer *Mindemoya* which then took everything out into the lake and dumped it. Deprived of her equipment, the *Neff* was to be taken over by the Marinette Fuel and Dock company where it was to be filled and sunk for a pier. She was later towed outside the harbor by the fishtug, *Four Brothers*, awaiting removal of other salvageable items before she was to be pushed ashore on Green Island. However, nothing further was ever done with her and she was left to break up in eight to ten feet of water 1,700 feet south of the pierhead at Menominee harbor. As of a year later, three to four feet of the starboard side of the hull still showed above the water.

The *Sidney O. Neff* was built in 1890 in Manitowoc for the Marinette Transportation Company. She was used primarily in the lumber trade and was later used to haul pulpwood. The craft was powered by a 350 horsepower steam engine and carried a crew of 24. She registered 435 gross tons and measured 149 feet in length, 30.2 feet at the beam and 10.4 feet in depth. DOOR COUNTY ADVOCATE, December 21, 1934. MENOMINEE HERALD-LEADER, May 16, October 28, 31, 1939. GREEN BAY PRESS-GAZETTE, June 1, 1940. List of Merchant Vessels of the U.S., 1938, p. 71.

404) Unknown Steamer, Abandoned Circa 1905.

This unidentified shipwreck near Claflin Point in Little Sturgeon Bay is thought to be a steamer or lake tug of at least 150 feet in length and, based on artifacts found on site, abandoned sometime after the turn of the century. The state sponsored underwater investigation, led by Dr. Bradley Rodgers, was unable to positively name the vessel.

They finally measured the wreckage and compared the dimensions of the wreck with those of every steamer of appropriate size and design. The steamer *Puritan*, 172 feet in length, 23 feet across the beam, built of wood in 1887, was the only candidate that matched. That particular vessel burned at her dock in Manistee, Michigan in 1895. The survey speculated that the burned hull of the *Puritan* was brought to the Sturgeon Bay area for conversion to a stone barge.However, a 1979 survey of the Manistee wreck confirmed the identity of that vessel as the *Puritan*.

The *Puritan* was built at Benton Harbor, Michigan, for the Graham & Morton Transportation Line and registered 289.67 gross tons. Bradley A. Rodgers, Phd., 1995 Predisturbance Wreck Site Investigation at Claflin Point Little Sturgeon Bay, Wisconsin. Maritime Studies Program East Carolina University, p. 28. List of Merchant Vessels of the U.S., 1895, page 290. Herman G. Runge Collection of the Milwaukee Public Library/Wisconsin Marine Historical Society.

405) *Reliance*, #223255, Fish Tug, Foundered December 11, 1943.

The *Reliance* sank with all hands in an unknown location somewhere in Lake Michigan. Despite warnings from other fishermen that they were overloading their vessel, brothers Albert and Ronald Tallman together with Perry Pardee, had taken on three tons of nets and 1,500 pounds of coal as well as other equipment at their slip in Fairport, Michigan. The Tallmans' father, Rudolph, an experienced fisherman himself, pleaded with his sons not to leave. Despite this, the *Reliance* pulled out of her slip and set out to join other Fairport fishing vessels at Boulder Reef near Fox Island for an annual expedition for whitefish. They passed Point Detour and were never seen again. A heavy wind was blowing at the time and developed into a gale with twenty to thirty foot waves. Local fishermen said it was worse than the Armistice Day Storm of 1940. Max

Kreshefisk of Van's Harbor, left after the Tallman boat did but never saw their fishtug and described the storm as a "howling terror" adding, "I lost all of my nets, everything, even boxes lashed to the cabin top with one-inch rope, but I got back." Fred Ranguette, a fellow fisherman from Fairport, used the Tallman's slip to load his nets. Ranguette speculated that the Tallman's vessel had been stove in at the stern by a wave and sunk. The *Reliance* was not known to be missing until several days later when the other fishtugs returned and asked why the Tallmans and Pardee never joined them. A region wide search was started by fishermen assisted by the Coast Guard and local airplane pilots. The Fox Island lighthouse crew, familiar with the *Reliance*, stated that she never appeared in their area. The Fox Islands and the northern shore of Lake Michigan were checked for the *Reliance* or some trace of it. Nothing was found. Rudolph Tallman spent the rest of his life trying to find some vestige of the fishermen.

The *Reliance* was built in Naubinway, Michigan in 1923 and measured 31.2 feet in length, 9.5 feet at the beam and 4 feet in depth. ESCANABA DAILY PRESS, December 16, 17, 18, 1943. Fred and Vida Ranguette, personal interview, August 8, 1987. Robert Tatrow, personal interview, August 8, 1987. Garden Peninsula Historical Society, Our Heritage, Garden Peninsula Delta County, Michigan 1840 - 1980, Garden, Michigan. p. 240. List of Merchant Vessels of the U.S., 1931, p. 478.

406) *Nauti-Girl*, Motor Yacht, Foundered August 26, 1945.

The *Nauti-Girl*, a fifty foot diesel powered cruiser, had been on her way from St. Ignace to Sturgeon Bay when she was overtaken by a southerly gale. She came to anchor two miles south of Cana Island about a mile off shore and was weathering the storm until the vessel sprung a leak. One of the eight passengers, Thomas Leech, set out to get help in a life raft, drifting straight towards the Cana Island light. He was washed ashore into the small bay immediately south of the island where he was helped by keeper, Michael Drezdzon, who had already contacted the Coast Guard. Leech had left behind his wife, as well as owner, Frank B. Whiting and his wife, their daughter and son-in-law, Mr. and Mrs. Robert Schroeder, and Frank Hichrodt. As Leech was helped ashore, "the yacht which had been pitching and tossing wildly in the mounting waves, disappeared from sight." Those left on board donned life jackets and launched the remaining life raft. They hung onto their little craft for an hour and finally they washed ashore near the lighthouse. The yacht sank in what was thought to be 40 feet of water.

Several days after the vessel sank, George Meredith of the Cherryland Airport and Francis Moore of the Roen Steamship company flew over the sight to locate the *Nauti-Girl* for the insurance company. They located the cruiser in 25 feet of water. Moore, Captain John Roen and diver Joe Beatty later went out to the wreck to see if it was worth salvaging. The yacht was deemed salvageable and the Roen barge, *Industry*, was sent out two weeks later. However, in the interim, the *Nauti-Girl* washed ashore and broke up. Only the vessel's diesel engines were salvageable and those were recovered by a Baileys Harbor fisherman, Cliff Winninger. Door County Advocate, August 31, September 7, 28, 1945.

407) Navy Rescue Boat, Scuttled 1946.

This 45 foot cabin cruiser was built by the Sturgeon Bay Boatworks (now Palmer Johnson Yachts) as a rescue boat for the U.S. Navy. Before the craft could be delivered to the War Department, World War II ended. The boat was paid for and technically belonged to the government who had no use for it. The War Department required that it be destroyed. Yard employees took off anything useful and the boat was taken out into Lake Michigan and scuttled.

Top: The Navy rescue boat during her water test at the Sturgeon Bay Boatworks, now Palmer Johnson.
Bottom: As she appeared ready for delivery to the War Department.

Photos from the author's collection

William Eckert, personal interview, May 18 and July 20, 1996.

408) *Satisfaction*, #116628, Tug, Abandoned in 1946.

The *Satisfaction*, like her cohort, the *Bob Teed*, was owned by the Waterways Engineering Corporation. She was built as a fishtug for Edward Groch at Sheboygan in 1894. She served the fishing trade for almost twenty-five years before being purchased by the Greiling Brothers of Green Bay, who converted her for towing. She was taken over by the Waterways Engineering Company in 1930. The *Satisfaction* was ultimately stripped of her equipment and left to sink near her slip at the Waterways Engineering dock. She was later joined by the *Bob Teed*. The *Satisfaction* registered 47 gross tons with a length of 64 feet, a beam of 16 feet and a depth of 8 feet. Herman G. Runge Collection of the Milwaukee Public Library/Wisconsin Marine Historical Society. List of Merchant Vessels of the U.S., 1895, p. 297.

409) *Pup*, Fish Tug, Foundered November 25, 1946.

The *Pup's* owner, Fred Ranguette had taken two hunters to Big Summer Island. When a southeast wind arrived with a snow storm Ranguette was forced to leave the tug at anchor and return to the island where he sought shelter with the hunters. The next day when he went down to the shore the break in the rocks was evident where the anchor had pried loose. The vessel sank in forty to fifty feet of water off the northeast corner of Big Summer Island. Ranguette was rescued from the island by Norm Casey, a commercial fisherman from Fairport (and his father-in-law). The remains of the *Pup* were thought to have been found in later years by divers from the Michigan State University's science camp on the island. The *Pup* was valued at $1,000 and measured eight net tons. Fred and Vida Ranguette, personal interview, August 8, 1987.

410) *Seabird II*, #244446, Fish Tug, Foundered April 10, 1947.

The *Seabird* was crushed by ice and sunk in thirty feet of water off Marinette. An S.O.S. was sent out and picked up by the Coast Guard lighthouse tender, *Sun Dew*, but poor visibility prevented the ship from making the rescue. Crewmen Michael Brodzinski, Floyd Jarman and Clinton Gamlin were able to escape the sinking tug and walked across the ice to shore. The *Seabird* was owned by Tom Coffey and was a wooden craft, of 20 gross tons and was powered with a 60 horsepower engine. She was built in Marinette in 1941 and measured 43 feet in length, 11.4 feet across the beam and 4.2 feet in depth. DOOR COUNTY ADVOCATE, April 18, 1947. List of Merchant Vessels of the U.S., 1944, p. 293.

411) *Bob Teed*, #3262, Tug, Abandoned October of 1947.

The *Bob Teed* was built in 1883 at Saugatuck, Michigan, for Thomas Teed, Sr. of Chicago. She was used for general towing up and down Lake Michigan before being purchased in 1941 by Waterways Engineering Corporation of Green Bay. The *Teed* was registered as having a wood hull, but was actually a composite hull—iron framing with wood planking. By 1947, she was sixty-four years old and her steam engine was ancient and surrounded by a world of war surplus diesel engines. The old tug was stripped of her engine and boiler and abandoned in her slip at the Waterways Engineering dock where she settled to the bottom of the Fox River. Sometime later the vessel caught fire, possibly at the hands of youngsters using the wreck as a fort or as a wind break for skating.

The tug's wooden planking and missing cabin belied her original design and the 1963 Great Lakes Pilot described her as a simple "wooden dump scow." Soundings obtained for the Great Lakes Survey in 1958, found 13 feet over the deepest part of the wreck, however, the river bottom has since filled in around the wreck.

The *Bob Teed* registered 45 gross tons and measured 64.2 feet in length, 18.7 feet across the beam and 8.7 feet in depth. Herman G. Runge Collection of the Milwaukee Public Library/Wisconsin Marine Historical Society. U.S. Army Corps of Engineers, Great Lakes Pilot, 1963, Detroit, Michigan, p. 130. List of Merchant Vessels of the U.S., 1895, p. 223.

412) *Bridgebuilder X*, #208790, Tug, Foundered December 15, 1959.

The *Bridgebuilder X* had been brought to Sturgeon Bay where the Sturgeon Bay Shipbuilding and Dry Dock Company had given her a dry dock check and rudder repair. With her repairs done, the tug pulled out of the yard at 8:30 that morning, cruised out to Lake Michigan and disappeared with both of her crewmen. She had been bound for South Fox Island. The Coast Guard crews from Plum Island and Traverse City searched for the missing tug for five days assisted by helicopter and airplane patrols. No sign of the tug was found. Lost with the vessel was Sterling Nickerson, Jr. and Glenn Roop. The tug was owned by Sterling Nickerson & Sons and had been one of the vessels used in the construction of the Mackinac bridge. Most recently, she had been used for towing logs between Northport and South Fox Island.

The *Bridgebuilder X* was a steel hulled, diesel powered tug, built in Lorraine, Ohio, in 1911. She had, in her earlier days, been used as a tour boat at the Soo Locks. She registered 53 gross tons and measured 61 feet in length, 16 feet across the beam and 7.2 feet in depth. GREEN BAY PRESS-GAZETTE, December 19, December 21, 1959. DOOR COUNTY ADVOCATE, December 22, 1959. List of Merchant Vessels of the U.S., 1960, p. 76.

413) *Roen Salvage Derrick Barge No. 93*, Foundered October 20, 1969.

The tug Bob Teed at her mooring in Green Bay at Waterways Engineering dock. Immediately next to her is the tug Satisfaction.

Photo courtesy of the Great Lakes Marine Collection of the Milwaukee Public Library/Wisconsin Marine Historical Society

The Bridge Builder X as the Bide A Wee, a tour boat operating on the Soo Canal.

Photo courtesy of the Great Lakes Marine Collection of the Milwaukee Public Library/Wisconsin Marine Historical Society

The scow was loaded with sixty tons of assorted construction equipment including a work boat and was in tow of the tug *John Purves*. The entourage under the command of Captain Nick Wagener, departed Sturgeon Bay on the late evening of a blustery, rainy day bound for Rogers City, Michigan. They were off Rock Island passage early the next morning when the *Purves* was forced to slow down because the barge was sitting low in the water and was taking water over her prow. Forty-five minutes later, the barge sank to the bottom in 110 feet of water near Little Gull Island. The tow line was cut and the *Purves* continued on to her way.

The barge was owned by Roen Salvage company, but was in tow of a vessel owned by the Roen Steamship company. The craft and equipment were insured for $80,000 which was paid by Roen Salvage's insurance company. The insurance company, in turn, sued Roen Steamship for the loss. The case was settled out of court six years later for the sum of $20,000. John H. Purves, <u>Roen Steamship Company: The Way It Was, 1909 - 1976</u>, 1983, p. 89, 90.

414) *Peter W.*, Fish Tug, Scuttled 1979.

Little information is available on the *Peter W* and the small amount that is, remains conflicting. The *Peter W* is a small fish tug of about thirty feet laying off the drop off in Wisconsin Bay. According to Wisconsin Department of Resources officials, she was illegally scuttled. She sits in sixty feet of water devoid of any engine or cargo. Joel McOlash, telephone interview, September 27, 1995.

415) *Buccaneer*, Catamaran Houseboat, Foundered July 1, 1981.

The *Buccaneer* was on her way from Egg Harbor to Menominee for repairs when the rubber gasket around the lower unit of her starboard engine began to leak. At 7:05

a.m., owner, Nick Zivalich radioed the Sturgeon Bay Coast Guard. A 41 foot rescue boat arrived on the scene 30 minutes later by which time only 10 feet of the boat was still above water. Coast Guardsmen removed Zivalich and his partner, Helen Standard. Ten minutes later, the *Buccaneer* settled to the bottom in 100 feet of water four miles off Egg Harbor. A buoy was tied to the sinking vessel before she went down, but the line was too short and the Buccaneer dragged her marker down with her. As the catamaran sank, air pressure, building up inside the cabin, blew the roof off. Her owners intended to raise the craft and have her repaired, but the exact location was lost.

Zivalich and Standard left Egg Harbor about 6:15 that morning hoping to cross the Bay under calm conditions. When the yacht sank, 2 to 5 foot waves were prevailing. The two owners were landed safely at Egg Harbor. They had jointly purchased the boat only a month before. Only a few pieces of furniture were recovered.

The *Buccaneer* was built of steel oil drums by the Bergen Tank Company and measured 54 feet in length. She was valued at $10,000. DOOR COUNTY ADVOCATE, July 2, 1981. Nick Zivalich, telephone interview, March 2, 1997.

416) *Eagle*, Gas Yacht, Stranded September 3, 1984.

The *Eagle* was a dive boat belonging to Frank Hoffman of Mystery Ship fame. Hoffman, despondent over the dilapidated state of his museum ship, the *Alvin Clark*, took his father and set out for a cruise along the bay. Concerned friends came after him and took him home in their tug, the *Southern Marine*, leaving his *Eagle* moored at the old life saving station pier on St. Martin Island. When a heavy gale came up, she sprung her mooring lines and went ashore just west of the pier. That fall Hoffman, with the aid of local fishermen, was able to plug the holes in her bottom and tow her off the beach. Once again she was moored at the Coast Guard pier in preparation for a long journey to the repair yard. Once again a gale blew her on the beach. Before Hoffman and his friends could retrieve her a second time, the *Eagle* broke up. Friends of the family that visited the site said they never realized that the elements could so effectively flatten a steel hull. The dive boat was a steel 32 foot twin engine Roemer. She had been used in a number of Hoffman's efforts, most recently, the attempt to raise the *Erie L. Hackley*. Dick Ranguette, personal interview, September 23, 1995. Dave Olsen, telephone interview, November 1, 1995. Ed Hoffman, telephone interview, December 14, 1995.

Part 5:
Vessels of note that were salvaged

There are a number of vessels that were sunk and later salvaged, or in some way have made maritime history.

The *Annie Marie* had the ill-fortune to sail into the "Big Blow of 1880." She capsized off Two Rivers 'and in her overturned condition was blown down the lake. One sailor, Tom Benson, was lost. Captain O'Brien, his wife, and five sailors strapped themselves to the bottom of the vessel where frequently they were buried under tons of water by the huge waves. The seven survivors rode out the storm like this for 36 hours before they were rescued by the schooner *Reindeer* and put ashore at the lake entrance to the canal. The schooner was thought to have broken up somewhere along the lakeshore, but she was later found near Baileys Harbor. She was righted and towed to Baileys Harbor where it was thought that she only needed new spars. DOOR COUNTY ADVOCATE, October 21, 28, 1880. DOOR COUNTY ADVOCATE, April 28, 1881.

The schooner *Apprentice Boy* was reported ashore in September of 1869 at the "Schuller Place" a mile south of the "portage" where the Sturgeon Bay canal was dug years later. She was scuttled to prevent her from pounding on the bottom. Her owners planned to tow her off with a tug boat when they could find one. Within a month the schooner was declared a total loss. The *Apprentice Boy* was likewise reported ashore or sunk in several different places, but in 1910, the Door County Advocate reported that the old vessel was used to fill in "the old Wabash slip" in Chicago. DOOR COUNTY ADVOCATE, September 30, October 28, 1869. DOOR COUNTY ADVOCATE, September 29, 1910.

The schooner *Blue Belle* found her way onto the north reef at Baileys Harbor where she had the company of the schooners, *Magic* and *Fairfield*. The *Blue Belle* was libeled by the owners of the tugs that tried to pull her off. She was ultimately towed off by the tug *David Smoke*. Her creditors were in Milwaukee and she may have been taken to that port. DOOR COUNTY ADVOCATE, December 9, 16, 23, 1869. Reprinted from the MANITOWOC PILOT by the GREEN BAY ADVOCATE, December 30, 1869. Reprinted from the MANITOWOC PILOT by the GREEN BAY ADVOCATE, June 6, 1870.

While trying to find her way through a dense fog, the steamer, *Bulgaria*, ran aground on Fisherman's shoal June 6, 1906. She was deemed unsalvageable, declared a total loss and abandoned to the underwriters. Her death knoll, not withstanding, the *Bulgaria* was loaded with 2,000 tons of coal. Her owners and her insurers considered the vessel doomed, but her valuable cargo guaranteed that someone would try. The steamer was purchased by Green Bay merchant B. Abramson who brought in wrecking master Thomas Isabel. The hull was jacketed in canvas where needed, pumped free of water and finally pulled clear of the shoal. She was taken to West Harbor on Washington Island where additional repairs were made in preparation for the journey to Sturgeon Bay. On her way to that port she ran aground again, this time in Strawberry passage. In spite of setbacks, the *Bulgaria* arrived in Sturgeon Bay, August 15, 1906, to the greetings of steam whistles and cheers of several hundred people. She was repaired at Manitowoc and returned to service. DOOR COUNTY ADVOCATE, June 15, July 5, 12, August 16, 1906.

The steamer *Comet*, bound from Buffalo to Green Bay, ran on the rocks at Washington Harbor, in a storm June 26, 1865. To prevent her from breaking up, her captain ordered

The steamer Bulgaria

Photo courtesy of the Great Lakes Marine Collection of the Milwaukee Public Library/Wisconsin Marine Historical Society

her scuttled in thirteen feet of water. On board were fifty passengers and $10,000 of merchandise mostly consigned to Green Bay merchants. The U.S. steamer *Survey* was asked to proceed to Green Bay to seek the assistance of the steamer *George L. Dunlap*. Ten minutes after receiving word, the *Dunlap* was bound for Washington Island. Within a week she returned with the *Comet's* passengers and the soaked cargo of teas, coffee and dried fruit. The cargo was considered worthless but was insured.

The disabled steamer was taken in tow for Milwaukee where she was drydocked and repaired. Weeks later she was reported traveling her usual route. Ironically, her captain, Captain Gaylord, stranded several miles to the south, ten months earlier, while piloting the *Comet's* sister ship, the *Rocket*. It is just as ironic that both vessels sank in 1875, the *Comet* near Detroit, Michigan and the *Rocket* near Whitefish Point, Michigan. KEWAUNEE ENTERPRISE, July 5, 12, August 30, 1865. GREEN BAY ADVOCATE, July 6, 1865. CHICAGO TRIBUNE, May 10, 1878.

The *Corona* was a sidewheel steamer that plied the trade on the Bay of Green Bay. In June of 1888 she ran aground on a shoal south of Squaw Point. The tug *Lucille* was sent to pull her off and also went aground. The tug *Lotus* finally released the first two vessels from the spot now called Corona Shoal. From the ESCANABA IRON PORT by way of the DOOR COUNTY ADVOCATE, June 30, 1888.

The scow-schooner *David Stewart* was bound for Escanaba to pick up a cargo of iron ore when she went ashore on Pilot Island October 10, 1868. The ship was without cargo at the time and Captain William Crowl and his crew were able to escape in safety. The tug *G.W. Wood* was immediately dispatched to her rescue and was later joined by the steamers, *Magnet*, *Saginaw* and the wrecking tug, *Escanaba*. The combined effort of four ships could not

The side-wheel steamer Comet.

Photo courtesy of the Great Lakes Marine Collection of the Milwaukee Public Library/Wisconsin Marine Historical Society

release the stranded schooner and her underwriters decided to leave her till spring.

The decision was reconsidered and Captains Charles Roach and John Prindivile went to Pilot Island to see the *Stewart's* status for themselves. The captains were advised by the Pottawotami Lighthouse keeper that the *Stewart* had grounded and pounded vigorously on the rocks and her bottom "must be badly used up." The salvors concluded for themselves that the schooner was "shook" but worth the effort to retrieve her. The tug, *Union* and steambarge, *H. Warrington* were sent north and later assisted by the steamer, *George Dunbar*. Passing ship captains reporting upon arrival at Chicago stated the the schooner could not be released until the weather quieted, however she had been lifted with six derricks in readiness. She was moved twelve feet but the expedition continued to wait for total release until good weather could facilitate the long tow to a safe port. The expedition suffered a minor setback when a steamer, pulling on the *Stewart*, snapped its towing hawser breaking Captain Prindiville's leg. Up to this point, news reports continued to celebrate the small successes and voice continued hopes of releasing the ship. After the accident, nothing more was reported on the rescue of the *Daniel Stewart* and she was listed with the shipping losses for the season at the end of the year. The following July, the schooner was successfully pulled off and towed to Detroit by the steamer *Magnet*. She was rebuilt and returned to service the next year. The *Stewart* was owned at Milan, Ohio by Kelley & Co. registered 545.41 gross tons. Loss from the vessel was estimated at $38,000 of which $19,850 was covered by insurance. CHICAGO TRIBUNE, October 13, 20, 22, 29, 30, November 4, 6, 7, 20, 23, 27, December 14, 1868. DOOR COUNTY ADVOCATE, December 31, 1868. CHICAGO TRIBUNE, July 8, 1869. MARINE CASUALTIES ON THE GREAT LAKES, 1868. List of Merchant Vessels of the U.S., 1867, p. 45.

The schooner *Duncan City* blew ashore on the east side of Summer Island in the spring of 1889. She was described as laying in a comfortable position and *"has but little water below the hatches, it is questionable whether any attempt will be made to get her off this season at least, in view of the unfavorable outlook for vessel property. Should business improve and that class of bottoms appreciate in value, there is no question but what the* Duncan City *will be rescued in good time."*

The *Duncan City* was left to sit in the shallows of Summer Island throughout that year and into the following spring. In June of 1890, the DOOR COUNTY ADVOCATE, reported, "The schooner *Duncan City*, which has been on Summer Island since last fall, was released by the tug Monarch last Friday. She was not much injured." In spite of her reported rescue, the Duncan City was removed from the Federal Register. Her ultimate disposition is unknown. DOOR COUNTY ADVOCATE, August 17, 1889. DOOR COUNTY ADVOCATE, June 28, 1890. List of Merchant Vessels of the U.S., 1889.

A Ford coach carrying John W. Cornell, Jr., Norman Nelson, Raymond Richter, Leroy Elnarson, Roy Stover and Ralph Wade broke through thin ice March 10, 1935 as the six men were on their way back to Washington Island from a basketball game in Ellison Bay. The group had spent the night in Sturgeon Bay and was supposed to rendezvous back at Ellison Bay with other cars before driving across the ice to the island. The coach arrived first and the six men decided to set out across the ice taking a short cut. When the other cars arrived at Washington Island and no sign of the men was found, a search was started. Someone in Ellison Bay had seen the coach head north and a trail was followed to a hole in the ice two miles north of Gills Rock. Coast Guardsmen and local fishermen were able to recover the bodies of the six men as well as the Ford coach. (Author's note: while this is not a shipwreck per se, we've covered sunken airplanes, railroad cars, etc. This story does figure prominently in the local history and is therefore included here.) DOOR COUNTY ADVOCATE, March 15, 1935.

The steamer Corona

Photo courtesy of the Great Lakes Marine Collection of the Milwaukee Public Library/Wisconsin Marine Historical Society

The 38 foot sloop *Half Moon* was returning to Sturgeon Bay from a race to Menominee, June 30, 1946, when it was overcome by a squall five miles off the mouth of Sturgeon Bay. As the cockpit of the yacht quickly flooded, the life jackets were swept away. The vessel's owner, Leathem D. Smith, president and general manager of the Smith Ship Building Co., was able to retrieve one jacket and strapped his daughter, Patsy and her college roommate, Mary Loomis, into it before being lost with the *Half Moon*. Also lost were Elton Washburn and Howard Hunt, employees of the shipyard. Mary and Patsy swam for shore and had a mile to go when Mary tired out and gave up. After swimming for six hours, Patsy, the sole survivor, reached shore near Little Harbor. Bodies of the four victims were recovered within a week. The death of Leathem Smith received nation-wide coverage, appearing in everything from newsreels to church sermons. TIME MAGAZINE'S obituary for Smith described him as the "the Henry Kaiser of Great Lakes ship building."

The *Half Moon* had originally been owned by James Roosevelt, son of President Franklin Roosevelt. Young Roosevelt had altered the design of the cabin, removing a bulkhead, so his disabled father, FDR, could make his way around the furnishings more comfortably. Maritime experts reasoned that this contributed to the sinking of the yacht. Initial efforts to raise her proved unsuccessful, but in November the sloop was finally lifted to the surface and taken to the shipyard for repairs. She was purchased for $525 from the insurance company by Emmett Platten, a Green Bay liquor dealer. Platten intended to take the yacht to the Gulf coast. DOOR COUNTY ADVOCATE, June 28, July 5, 19, October 4, November 15, 22, 1946.

The steamer *Michigan* was coming into Green Bay harbor in November of 1863 when she was cut through by ice and sunk. She was raised, stripped of her machinery and converted to a lumber barge. She was lost in Lake Erie in 1868. MARINE CASUALTIES ON THE GREAT LAKES, 1863. CHICAGO TRIBUNE, August 25, 1869.

The steamer *Minneapolis* ran aground on an uncharted reef on the north end of the Bay of Green Bay on June 3, 1898. The chart showed a depth of 82 feet in the vicinity. The steamer was pulled off and required drydocking for repairs, leaving behind only her name. Four weeks later Minneapolis shoal was buoyed. DOOR COUNTY ADVOCATE, July 2, 9, 1898.

The steamer *Ogemaw*, laden with iron ore, foundered in sixty feet of water near Burnt Bluff in early December of 1891. She had two consorts in tow and, before she sank, these were moored along side the stricken vessel in hopes of keeping her afloat. The pressure was so great that their decks burst open and the consorts had all they could do to get away. The *Ogemaw's* crew was rescued by the barges.

The following October it was reported that a salvage expedition had succeeded in raising the hull to the surface so that the outline of the steamer was plainly evident. Everything seemed to be in place for pumping the *Ogemaw* free of water. Nothing is certain of her ultimate disposition, however, a vessel of the same name was lost in Lake Erie in the early 1920s. This may be the same steamer. DOOR COUNTY ADVOCATE, December 12, 1891. DOOR COUNTY ADVOCATE, October 8, 1892.

The schooner *Riverside* is considered a popular diving site. In fact, the schooner ran aground on Pilot Island October 15, 1887 and was considered a total loss. She was bound for Chicago with a load of coal at the time. Several early efforts were made to float the hull off the reef but none were successful. The vessel sat on the reef for months but was ultimately released in mid October of 1888, almost exactly one year after she ran aground. The *Riverside* was brought to Green Bay where the damage was declared "comparatively trifling". She was repaired, returned to service and sold to Detroit interests. On October 14, 1893, almost exactly six years after she was supposedly wrecked on Pilot Island, the *Riverside* sank with all hands in Lake Erie. DOOR COUNTY ADVOCATE, October 22, 29, 1887. DOOR COUNTY ADVOCATE, June 16, July 14, October 20, December 8, 1888. DOOR COUNTY ADVOCATE, October 28, 1893. Herman G. Runge Collection of the Milwaukee Public Library/Wisconsin Marine Historical Society.

According to the U.S. government's "Marine Casualties-1864" the steamer *Rocket* was sunk at Washington Harbor. The GREEN BAY ADVOCATE ran a small story that year explaining that the *Rocket*, on its way from Buffalo to Green Bay, ran on the Rock Island reef August 22, 1864. The steamer was able to release herself but only after jettisoning most of the cargo including general groceries, hardware, pianos and miscellaneous freight. Passengers and officers joined together in throwing luggage and cargo, in some cases their own goods, overboard. The value of the lost cargo was valued at $30,000. Passengers aboard the *Rocket* were so concerned about the professional reputation of the steamer's Captain Gaylord that they ran a public notice in the Green Bay paper absolving him of any indiscretions. Gaylord was transferred to the *Rocket's* sister ship, the *Comet*. The following June, that vessel ran aground in a storm near Washington Harbor, while under his command. Both vessels sank in 1875, the *Comet* near Detroit, Michigan and the *Rocket* near Whitefish Point, Michigan. GREEN BAY ADVOCATE, August 25, 1864. CHICAGO TRIBUNE, May 10, 1878.

The steamer Ogemaw.

Photo courtesy of the Great Lakes Marine Collection of the Milwaukee Public Library/Wisconsin Marine Historical Society

The schooner *S.B. Pomeroy* had a couple of encounters with fate. In September of 1871, she capsized off Menominee. Crewmen James Merehie, John Davidson, Archibald Dickey and William Steele were all drowned attempting to reach shore. The vessel was salvaged and returned to service. The following September, the *Pomeroy* ran aground on Whale Back shoal while on her way to Chicago with a cargo of lumber. The cargo was thrown overboard and the schooner was thought ready to go to pieces. The following week tugs from Escanaba and Cedar River pulled her free with no serious damage. MARINETTE EAGLE reprinted by the DOOR COUNTY ADVOCATE, September 21, 1871. GREEN BAY ADVOCATE, October 3, 1872. MENOMINEE HERALD reprinted by the DOOR COUNTY ADVOCATE, October 17, 1872.

The sandsucker, *Sinola*, was dredging along the north end of the bay when she was overwhelmed by what would later be dubbed "The Armistice Day Storm of 1940." The steamer anchored in the lee of Washington Island, but seventy-mile-per-hour winds from the south tossed her up the bay. When the steam line broke and the generator was damaged, the crew of 23 was left cold and helpless in the darkened fury of the storm. Hatches froze shut and the men waded through flooded compartments hoping the ship would run aground before she foundered. The *Sinola* finally grounded near Sac Bay, Michigan. There the crew was able to float a line to shore with a buoy as over three hundred people gathered on the shore ready to offer assistance. Pulling a skiff back and forth the crew was rescued by area fishermen. The bow of the *Sinola* was farther out and continuously washed by waves. Crewmen in the forward cabin had to be rescued by the Coast Guard with a Lyle gun and a breeches buoy.

The vessel was later salvaged by the Roen Salvage Company. On December 21, 1940, the *Sinola* was finally

The schooner S.B. Pomeroy.

Photo courtesy of the Great Lakes Marine Collection of the Milwaukee Public Library/Wisconsin Marine Historical Society

towed into Sturgeon Bay to the greetings of steam whistles and horns. She was later taken to Manitowoc for repairs. DOOR COUNTY ADVOCATE, November 15, November 22, December 6, 1940. GREEN BAY PRESS-GAZETTE, November 13, 1940. Fred Ranguette, personal interview, September 16, 1995.

The schooner *Vermont* was driven on the beach at Garden Bay, Michigan where she had been taking on a cargo of Christmas trees. Her captain, Hans Hanson, ordered her scuttled to prevent her from being pounded to pieces on the bottom. Nonetheless she was declared a total loss anyway. Within a week, however vessel and cargo were raised and taken back to Milwaukee. KEWAUNEE ENTERPRISE, November 30, December 7, 1900. DOOR COUNTY ADVOCATE, December 1, 1900.

The steamer *Waverly* was bound from Chicago for Buffalo, July 28, 1896, when she ran aground near Death's Door. The DOOR COUNTY ADVOCATE reported "...it was found necessary to throw about three thousand barrels of flour and other freight overboard before she could be released. The flour was picked up by the people residing in that region and it is estimated that there is enough of the staff of life there to maintain the inhabitants for a year or more to come." The loss of cargo was estimated at $30,000. The vessel was released but is remembered for having named Waverly shoal. The *Waverly* sank July 22, 1903 in Lake Huron after colliding with the steamer *Turret Court*.

Some other shoals and bays that were named for the vessels running aground are Europe Bay for the the steamer *Europe*, and Dunlap Reef for the steamer *George L. Dunlap* and Hanover Shoal for the schooner *Hanover*. Driscoll Shoal was named for Captain George H. Drisko, who had written to the ESCANABA IRON PORT about the presence of an unmarked reef in the north end of the Bay

The steamer Waverly.

Photo courtesy of the Great Lakes Marine Collection of the Milwaukee Public Library/Wisconsin Marine Historical Society

of Green Bay. The shoal was buoyed in June of 1880. Door County Advocate, December 3, 1887. Escanaba Iron Port, August, 23, 1879. Escanaba Iron Port, June 26, 1880.

Appendix A:
Great Storms and Squalls

Northern Lake Michigan has been swept by a number of storms of note. A big gale hit the area in 1847, but few people were here to experience it. Other storms like the Armistice Day Storm of 1940, and the great storms of 1905, 1913 and 1929 are also remembered for their ferocity. By far, the most fearsome storm that has ever hit this region was the "Big Blow of 1880."

The shipping season of 1880 had been blessed with few storms and many warm sultry days. Ship captains made best use of a season that lasted late into the year.

The Weather Bureau, founded by Door County pioneer Increase Claflin, was a mere youth of eleven years. It can not be said that vessel captains mistrusted the Bureau, trusted their own instincts more, or simply liked to take chances, but when storm warnings were displayed on Thursday morning, area ships went on with business as usual. Warnings of an approaching gale went unheeded for almost two days until the evening of Friday, October 15, 1880. That night winds began to blow out of the southeast. As the night went on the wind increased and ships started looking for shelter. Few found it. By the next day 70 to 90 mile per hour winds blew down the length of Lake Michigan. North Bay offered little protection from the wind, but with nowhere else to go, over fifty ships sought an anchorage there. Ships riding out the storm off Cana Island, in thirty feet of water, were pounding on the bottom of the lake. And for the first time that any resident could remember, waves were sweeping into the woods. When the Canadian schooner *Two Friends* went ashore at North Bay, a local fisherman rowed through the surf to the stranded ship. Reaching the wreck eight times, he returned to shore with one man until all of the crewmen were rescued. At Baileys Harbor, local towns people and ships' crews banded together to rescue the crew of the schooner *Peoria*, stranded on the outer reef.

At Cana Island, waves swept over the island crashing down the door to the lighthouse and splashing ten feet up the tower. Lighthouse keeper William Sanderson reported that the sidewalks and his flock of chickens were washed away. Sanderson had to remove his family to the safety of the boathouse in back. A visitor who stayed with the light-keeper reported, "We had a terrible time of it here on the night of the storm, the sea at times making almost a clean break over the house. The lantern at a height of one hundred feet was continually enveloped in spray throughout the night, but notwithstanding a good light was maintained."

The scow, *N.M. Dunham*, ashore at Whitefish Bay, was so overwhelmed by the waves that the crewmembers had to climb the rigging to keep from being swept away. When the waves subsided, onlookers could walk around the vessel without getting their feet wet.

Over twenty ships were blown ashore between Kewaunee and Washington Island. Although salvage took almost a year in some cases, all but three vessels, stranded that night, were saved. Farther down the lake, the steamer, *Alpena* and the schooner, *David A. Wells* both sank with all passengers and crew.

News dispatches placed losses on Lake Superior at $35,000, and $61,000 on Lake Ontario. Lake Erie interests were thought to have suffered $74,000. On Lake Michigan, where the storm rolled down the length of the lake, damage was figured at $311,000, at least four times what it was elsewhere.

As the years went by, the region experienced other great

storms. Some like the Armistice Day Storm of 1940 have gone down in history...remembered as a benchmark by which other storms are compared. However, no storm has ever compared with the "Big Blow of 1880." Door County Advocate, October 21, 28, 1880, November 4, 11, 18, 1880. Door County Advocate, May 5, 26, 1881.

Squalls

In his song, "White Squall." Canadian folk musician Stan Rogers sings of a storm...

> *"There's a thing that us old timers know*
> *...in a sultry summer calm,*
> *there comes a blow from nowhere*
> *and it goes off like a bomb."*

The lyrics aptly describe summer squalls that occasionally roam the Great Lakes. These storms are of short duration, ten to twenty minutes usually, but as the song explains, happen in relative calm and pounce with wind of 40 to 100 miles per hour. One source defines a white squall as a waterspout in development.

Telling of his life and times one old lake captain told of the "squally" season of 1898... "I was caught out in one of those squalls this summer, and it came so suddenly and with such violent force as to blow the head sails out of the bolt ropes. The vessel was loaded with bark and when the squall struck her the wind picked up part of the deckload and hurled it into the air as high as the cross-trees*." A schooner with 2,000 square feet of sail set would have little protection and sometimes no warning from such a storm. This may explain the loss of some ships such as the schooner *Thomas Hume*. The *Hume* disappeared mysteriously on Lake Michigan in May of 1891. No trace of her,

her cargo or her crew of seven was ever found. *The height of the cross-tree could vary from ship to ship, but 80 feet seems to be a reasonable figure. Door County Advocate, June 6, 1891. Door County Advocate, October 8, 1898. W.A. McEwen and A.H. Lewis, Encyclopedia of Nautical Knowledge, Cambridge, Maryland: Cornell Maritime Press, 1953, p. 526.

Appendix B:
Early Salvage Techniques

The northwest quadrant of Lake Michigan has been the scene of thousands of shipwrecks—far more than the hundreds of vessels listed here might suggest. The demand for vessel property and creative uses for even old ships lead to creative measures for salvaging ships.

Some of these techniques were simply the tried and true procedures used in shipyards, carried to the scene of a wreck. When the *Iver Lawson* went ashore, salvors, using jack screws, raised the hull high enough to build a launch ramp beneath her. Plan called for pulling her down the ways with a tugboat. The *Lawson* didn't budge and eventually fell apart on her expensive cradle.

When the *City of Ludington* went ashore at Eagle Harbor, salvage crews raised her with three hydraulic jacks on each side of the hull. Dispensing with the ramp, the crew pulled on her with tugs. Figuring that if they could lift her high enough, when offshore tug boats pulled on her, she would jump ten feet. They estimated that with three lifts and pulls each day, they could get the Ludington to deep water in a week. For as strenuous as it must have been on the hull, dropping it a couple feet over twenty times, the scheme must have worked. The *City of Ludington* was successfully refloated within three weeks.

Ships lost in deep water were a different matter. Hand-operated diving compressors of the time could accommodate two divers to thirty feet or one diver to sixty feet. Only the hardiest of divers could descend deeper. When a ship was lost in deep water all salvage captains could hope to do was grapple for the hull and try to drag it to a shallower, more manageable depth. Usually this only resulted in pulling the hull apart.

One unique salvage effort in shallow water involved the sinking of the tugboat, *Wright*. The *Wright* had been punching a path through ice in the Sturgeon Bay area. Backing down her "track," she would build steam and repeatedly ram a hole through the ice. On one pass, as she hit the ice, the oakum in the seams of her bow froze to the ice shelf. When she backed up for another pass, she pulled the caulking out and sank in eighteen feet of water.

The tug settled on her side. To "right" her so she would rise through the hole she had made, a timber, with cable attached, was sunk in the ice next to the tug. The cables were made fast to the mast of the tug and hoisted until the vessel was sitting upright. Diver Captain Thomas Isabell was then sent down to jacket the gangways and most of the upper works with boards and canvas. The scuppers were plugged and the pockets, below decks on each side of the boiler and engine hatch, were given water tight bulkheads. A large quantity of horse manure was then thrown around the outside of the hull and a suction hose put into the ship. As the suction pump drew water out of the hull, manure was drawn into the seams temporarily caulking them. Five times, suction was either lost or stopped to set up a second pump and each time the *Wright* settled to the bottom again. Finally, four and a half days after she sank, the tug was raised to the surface and steam raised in her boiler. They then went about cleaning her up and shortly thereafter, she went back to breaking ice.

Ships that were raised or old and leaking but unable to find help in a shipyard were often given a temporary berth on a nearby mud bank. The soft mud provided a custom formed cradle and also had the effect of filling in opened seams. Local mud flats usually became ship graveyards, congested with old vessels that ultimately became forgotten and abandoned. Sturgeon Bay had such a problem with abandoned hulls that in 1915 the city council obtained information from the Navy department showing the location of the wrecks in the area and naming their last known owners. Preparations were being made to have the wrecks removed. KEWAUNEE ENTERPRISE, April 25, May 16, 1890. DOOR COUNTY ADVOCATE, April 8, 1899. DOOR COUNTY ADVOCATE, March 21, 1903. DOOR COUNTY ADVOCATE, March 4, 1915.

Appendix C:
Some Notes on Rigging

Wire rigging had been popular in England from its inception in the 1850s and made its way to the eastern seaboard. After the Civil War, the use of wire cable found its way to the Great Lakes

Though they were more expensive, wire shroud lines were popular for their low maintenance and were considered the mark of a first class vessel. Hemp shrouds and lanyards required regular maintenance which included a constant coating of tar to protect it from the elements. Hemp also stretched and while this relieved the strain on the mast during a storm, it required a vessel to pull into a quiet bay and tighten her lines a dozen or more times a season. A ship with slack in her standing rigging was said to be "loose in stays" which impaired her ability to sail close to the wind.

A compromise was found by rigging the wire shrouds with deadeyes and hemp lanyards as opposed to the usual turnbuckles. This gave a slight stretch relieving the strain on the mast in foul weather.

Though wire rigging required less maintenance and fewer adjustments, it did not stretch. This was popular with vessel owners, though it was disliked by sailors who had to endure the dismasting of a sailing vessel in a storm and more than one vessel captain had his wire rigging sold and replaced with hemp. DOOR COUNTY ADVOCATE, November 3, 10, 1894.

Appendix D:
The Legendary Treasure
of Poverty Island

A book about sunken ships would not be complete without a story about pirates and gold treasure. We are fortunate in having the "Legendary Treasure of Poverty Island".

There are differing versions of this legend of missing gold, however the most widely recognized account states five chests of gold, a loan of $4,500,000 from a European nation, was on its way to the Confederate States through the Union's back door. This gold shipment had come in through the Great Lakes and was being transported by ship when it was waylaid near Poverty Island, Michigan. The ship's captain, fearing that his vessel might be searched, chained the chests together and threw them overboard with hopes that they could be snagged at a later time. The chests were supposedly lost until years later when a ship, attempting to pull itself off the island reefs, pulled up a chest on a chain.

The first recognition of a "treasure" came in September of 1933 when a group of salvors sailing a converted yacht, the *Captain Lawrence*, began searching near Poverty Island for what was described as "King Strang's Gold."[1] ("King" James Strang was a self-styled leader of a Mormon sect living on Beaver Island, on the other side of Lake Michigan. Strang was murdered and his followers were forcibly removed by area vigilantes in the 1850s.) The *Captain Lawrence* was lost September 14, 1933, when she dragged her anchor and went ashore on Poverty Island. The four crewmen were rescued by the lighthouse keeper and his assistants and returned to the mainland.

The gold was given further recognition in 1940 when a Works Project Administration book, "Michigan: A Guide to the Wolverine State" announced, "The largest prize in Michigan waters is said to be in the safe of a vessel lying near Poverty Island off Big Bay de Noc, not far from Escanaba. The identity of the vessel has not been made known, but there is no secret regarding the four and a half million dollars' worth of gold bullion in her safe."

The treasure was given almost thirty years of obscurity until 1969 when SKIN DIVER magazine published an article about the treasure. The article used as its primary resource a Washington Island tavern owner, Karle Jessen. Jessen maintained that as a boy in the 1930s, while visiting his lighthouse keeper-father on Poverty Island, he had seen a group of salvors searching for the treasure. One day when their diving bell was pulled up, the crew members went in "ecstatic dances all over the deck" ostensibly celebrating the finding of the gold. According to Jessen, the expedition came to an abrupt halt the next day, when the salvage vessel, the *St. Lawrence*, was wrecked off shore from the island.

If the story of the gold has its roots in fact, the $4.5 million dollars in gold has to be the flower of fancy. The simple circumstance of that amount of gold, in a single block would be the size of a refrigerator and would weigh over twelve thousand pounds. Packed into five chests, it would take some hefty seamen to lift it over a railing.

Speculating that the legend may be concocted from bits and pieces of other stories, the different parts of it may be explainable. Karle Jessen's story of the salvage vessel, *St. Lawrence*, is incredibly close to the story of the salvage vessel, *Captain Lawrence*, in spite of Jessen's insistence that it was a different ship. The account of the ship dredging up the chain with the chest attached bears a remarkable likeness to a story originally published in the GLADSTONE DELTA and later reprinted in the DOOR COUNTY ADVOCATE. So that the reader might not wonder what parts have been left out, the article is reprinted here in its entirety.

"The steamer Etruria *came in Monday with 7,000 tons of coal, and cleared Friday. Capt. Green reports a singular occurrence which took place Monday. He came by Poverty Island at 12:05 that morning and let go anchor at 12:55 on account of thick weather, in about ten fathoms of water. At 1:30 he heaved anchor, and found that it had caught the cable chain of a vessel, as well as some wreckage and a chest, which sank as soon as it appeared on the surface. Attached to the chain was an old fashioned "Swedish" anchor with rotted stock. The anchor by some means broke loose, but the chain was saved. It is a hand made chain of seven-eighths inch iron and links about five inches long. There was about thirty-two fathoms in the piece. The captain estimated from the size anchor and chain that it had belonged to a vessel of four or five hundred tons burden. From the spot where the anchor was found, Peninsula point light bore N. W. and Rock Island due south. This brings the place about seven miles E. S. E. of the Eleven Foot Shoal. Captain Green is of the opinion, from the surrounding circumstances, that he dropped his anchor on the hulk of a vessel that had been sunk years ago, from some cause or other. Captain Green would like to know what vessel of this description was sunk inside Poverty Passage."*

While no marauding pirates of the SKIN DIVER magazine account have been documented anywhere, the north end of the bay of Green Bay is not without its pirate tales. In the early 1850s, a group of "desperadoes" roamed the north end of Lake Michigan. A Green Bay resident received a letter from Summer Island describing a group of thieves in a boat "clinker built, square stern, with two sails, one colored and the other white." These robbers came ashore on the island and stole "nearly everything belonging to the inhabitants." Several weeks before, desperadoes were seen passing counterfeit money in the Grand Traverse, Michigan area. Residents followed them to a cove. Only three of the thieves were seen making sail. As the residents closed in they saw that the bottom of the boat was filled with armed men who rose up and aimed their carbines at their pursuers. The pirates were generally believed to be from Beaver Island and at one point made an appearance in Mackinac harbor where, by presenting themselves as customs officials, they boarded, then seized the schooner, *Seaman*. According to the Beaver Island, ISLANDER the gang boarded the vessel about midnight in "great force," beat up the captain and "commenced cutting the stays and destroying sail and rigging." They suddenly became quiet and "as anxious to get rid of their prize and prisoners as they had been to take them." Other stories in the ISLANDER were quick to point out that while these "pirates" might have been from Beaver Island, they were not part of the Mormon sect living there.

Research for this book has not uncovered any stories of five chests crossing Union territory bound for the Confederacy. However, a story has been found of five chests bound from the Confederacy for Canada. The story of the five chests of gold bound for the South, sounds, in a fractured fashion, like the details of the State Department records of the Confederate States.

In early April of 1865, as Union troops were closing on Richmond, Virginia, a train left that city with the Confederate treasure and archives. The treasure found its way to Washington—not Washington D.C. — but Washington, Georgia, where a Confederate Captain, M.H.

Clark was given the task of overtaking the duties of Treasurer of the Confederacy and paying what debts could be paid with the remaining funds of the Confederate States of America. Clark maintained that the treasury contained several hundred thousand dollars, all of which was paid out by him with receipts to corroborate. Following on Clark's trail were numerous Union investigators, convinced that the treasury was somewhere to be found and amounted to more than $5,000,000.

Also removed on April 2, 1865, were the records of the State Department of the Confederate States of America stored in five chests. These records were hidden away from Union troops until they could be secreted away to Canada. All orders concerning the papers were intentionally verbal, so as to leave no paper trail. Years after the war, Colonel John T. Pickett negotiated with the Federal government for these archives and they were ultimately sold to the United States and are now on file at the Library of Congress. These chests contained, among other things, information concerning the £5,000,000 loan from the Emile Erlanger & Co., a French banking trust, to the Confederacy—the loan around which the legend seems to have been woven. Oddly enough, if you want to research the foreign loans, to the Confederacy, that supposedly lead to "Legendary Treasure of Poverty Island" you will find yourself paging through the "Pickett Papers."

It is wildly ironic that the story of a missing treasure should be so closely associated with an island named "Poverty." In fact, the island's name has nothing to do with this legend. The islands to the north and south of Poverty Island have all been utilized by pioneers for fishing, lumbering and quarrying. Poverty Island, on the other hand, was not endowed with any kind of natural harbor conducive to fishing or quarrying. What few trees it has are too gnarly for timbering. Early settlers quickly concluded that if you were going to live on this island you had better be prepared for a life of poverty. Though the island does not offer any major commerce, it does brandish the intrigue of a limitless legend and a supposedly haunted lighthouse.[2]

The story of the steamer *Etruria* locating a chain and chest is interesting. Why was a chest attached to an anchor chain? Sailors occasionally suspended a weight or "sentinel" on an anchor cable to give it greater effect, however, in this case, the weight applied would be a mere fraction of what was appropriate. This leads us to believe that this ship's captain was hiding something...something waterproof and bulky. And he was hiding it from someone who could out run his vessel or from someone he could not be certain he could trust.

Almost three decades have passed since SKIN DIVER magazine ran the article on the Poverty Island Treasure. In that time, hundreds of treasure seekers have scoured the area with equipment ranging from the highly technical to the laughable. Stories abound of divers using magnetometers, side-scan sonar, fortune-tellers and we cannot forget the two doctors who went out with divining rods. Likewise, there are numerous stories of people who claim to have found treasure. One man maintained that he found one chest and took the proceeds out west where he started a construction company. Another story relates how one diver located part of the gold and hid it in an engine block.

This chapter should end with this caveat. Even if the 1904 story of the chest is accurate and, moreover, the chest did indeed contain gold...even if this gold still lays on the bottom of the bay, unfound...it is covered by a lot of water. Should any readers decide to search for the treasure they should invest only as much money, time and effort as they can afford to lose with a smile. Because, if you spend a lot, as the pioneers said of the island, you had better be prepared to live in poverty.

¹Author Carl Norberg, in his article, "The Lost Treasure of the Beaver Island Mormon Colony," tells the story of a brass box, belonging to James Strang, and containing the tithings of the Beaver Island Mormons. This box, according to the story, was smuggled off the island, after Strang was shot, and taken to nearby High Island where it was buried.

²In the 1980s two different acquaintances contacted the author to say that each was going to the island with the other fellow and did I know him. These two divers stayed on the island, in the lighthouse, for about a week, accompanied by several other divers. My acquaintances quickly concluded **a**: they had an intense dislike for each other. and **b**: the lighthouse was haunted. Within weeks of their returning home both divers called to tell me what a 'jerk' the other guy was, and both gave me remarkably similar stories of a lantern toting apparition walking the lighthouse catwalk and a bunkbed that shook off its rather startled occupant.

GREEN BAY ADVOCATE, May 15, 29, 1851. GREEN BAY ADVOCATE, July 22, 12, 1852. GREEN BAY ADVOCATE, May 19, 1853. M.H. Clark, Account of the Evacuation of the Confederate Treasury, Southern Historical Society Papers, December 1881. GLADSTONE DELTA, July 9, 1904. DOOR COUNTY ADVOCATE, July 16, 1904. Edwin Denby, Secretary of the Navy, Official Records of the Union and Confederate Navies in the War of the Rebellion, Washington: Government Printing Office, 1922, Series II, Vol., p. 16. DOOR COUNTY ADVOCATE, September 15, 29, 1933. GREEN BAY PRESS-GAZETTE, September 19, 1933. MANITOWOC HERALD-TIMES, March 31, 1934. Works Project Administration, Michigan: A Guide to the Wolverine State - 1940. Ivan H. Walton, "Marine Lore" p. 122. Margaret Coppess, Island Story: The History of Michigan's St. Martin Island, Iron Mountain, Michigan: Mid-Peninsula Library Co-operative, 1981, p. 52. SKIN DIVER, March 1969, p. 22. SKIN DIVER, March 1986, p. 28. Doyle Fitzpatrick, The King Strang Story by National Heritage, Lansing Michigan: 1970, p. 191-196. Carl Norberg, "The Lost Treasure of the Beaver Island Mormon Colony" Inland Seas, Quarterly Journal of the Great Lakes Historical Society, Vol. 43, Fall 1987, No. 3, p. 188-193. Barada, William, telephone interview, 25 January 1984. Jessen, Karle, telephone interview, 12 October 1986. Reetz, Aurthur, telephone interview, 12 April 1984. "Treasure," Unsolved Mysteries, narrated by Robert Stack, NBC, WLUK, Green Bay, 11 November 1994.

Comparison of Vessels
by Length and Tonnage

Erastus Corning▼
Schooner, 832.43 gross
tons, 216 feet in length.

Granite State▼
Steamer, 428.82 gross tons,
approx. 160 feet in length.

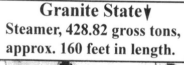

Spatula⌐
Yacht, Approx. 2
gross tons, 28 feet
in length.

Mueller↑
Steamer, 699 gross tons,
172 feet in length.

Le Griffon↓
Bark, 45-60 gross
tons, approx. 80 -
90 feet in length.

← Author
Homo Sapien,
.0775 gross tons,
5.6 feet in length.

345

Glossary of Terms

Able-Bodied Seaman: a sailor trained in' the ways of a ship such as line handling, steering a course and handling cargo. This rating usually followed a three year apprenticeship. Sailors not having attained this level were **Ordinary Seamen**. In the 1870s and 1880s and Able-bodied Seaman could expect to make $2.75 to $3.50 per day depending upon the time of year. Ordinary Seamen were usually 50 cents less than their more experienced counterparts.

Amidship: the center of a ship, half way between the bow and the stern.

Ballast: counter weight on a ship placed low on the vessel to help lower the center of gravity. Ballast can be lead or iron ingots, stones and in modern vessels, water.

Bark: a three-masted sailing vessel with the two forward masts rigged with square sails. Also spelled **barque**.

Beam: the width of a ship, measured at its widest part.

Beating: sailing against the wind in a zigzag fashion.

Breeches Buoy: life saving harness used to rescue shipwreck sailors by pulling them along a cable.

Brig: a two masted sailing vessel with squared sails.

Bucket: a propeller blade.

Centerboard: a removable board lowered when a ship is sailing close to the wind. The centerboard was housed in a water tight chamber, the centerboard box, from which it could be lowered directly through the bottom of the ship.

Chainplates: metal strap fastened to the side of the ship to which the shroud lines are attached for steadying the masts.

Clamshell: hinged shovel for scooping sand, gravel or coal, etc. A wire cable pinches the clamshell shut as it lifts it up.

Cross-trees: brackets for holding the shroud lines away

from the mast for better support. Now commonly called spreaders.

Deadeyes: round blocks of hardwood drilled and laced with lanyards and used for tightening shroud lines or other rigging. Deadeyes have been replace with turnbuckles on modern sailing craft.

Dredge: a crane usually set on a barge for digging underwater channels.

Forecastle: cabin or living quarters in the bow of a ship. The forecastle usually housed the sailors and could be a structure on deck or set up below deck.

Fore and aft rigged: used to describe sailing vessels with sails usually cut in a triangular or trapezoidal pattern, laced to the fore, main, or mizzen masts, and rigged in a fashion parallel to the ship's hull. Fore and aft rigged sails can be set perpendicular to the hull for, say, sailing with the wind. A fore and aft rigged ship was easier to adjust for variable winds and for tacking.

Gale: strictly speaking, a gale is a storm with winds of 40 to 65 miles per hour. Many times the term was used loosely.

Galley: ship's kitchen.

"Grub Up": just as today we gas up a car, a ship's crew would take on fuel or **"coal up"** and **"grub up"** when they were taking on food and provisions.

Hawser: a heavy rope of wire or hemp used for towing or mooring. Hawsers made of hemp were usually coated with sheep tallow to preserve them.

Head: ship's bathroom. Can also refer to that part of a ship forward of the foremast.

Head Sails: jib or other sails rigged between the foremast and the bowsprit on the bow of a ship.

Hogged: common description for a ship's hull that has been bent out of alignment.

Hooker: small sailing craft with one mast usually, used for fishing.

Ironed Off: refers to the protective steel sheeting on the bow of a wooden vessel. This sheeting was designed to protect vessels, usually tugs or steamers, from damage by ice or other hazards. A vessel so equipped was said to be "ironed off."

Master: captain of ship. Sometimes as opposed to a ship's captain who has control over the ship and its crew, a ship's master is a representative of the owner in business.

Making Water: leaking in the hold of a ship especially at a fast rate.

Missed Stays: as a sailing vessel would "tack" or zigzag against the wind she would have to reset the sails and come about. The ship at some point has lost the power of the wind and has to rely on its forward momentum to glide into a new position and regain the wind. If the procedure is not done fast enough the forward momentum is lost and the ship has "missed stays."

Mizzen Mast: rear mast of a sailing ship.

Oakum: caulking used between the wooden planks of a ship's hull.

Ordinary Seaman: See **Able-bodied Seaman**.

Reef: reducing the area of a sail. Sails are equipped with reef points at different levels allowing several degrees of sail adjustment in compensation to increasing wind. If the first level of sail is taken in, a vessel is reefed, if the second level of sail is take in, the vessel is double reefed, etc. **Reef**, in reference to water level, means a shallow area.

Rudder: a blade or board hinged and rigged to the stern of a ship for purposes of steering.

Scow: a flat nosed vessel usually of shallow draft.

Scuttle: an access hole in a ship's hull such as a coal scuttle or lumber scuttle. **Scuttle** can also refer to the intentional sinking of a ship.

Shoe: extension of the keel to accommodate the ship's propeller and rudder.

Shroud Lines: Standing Rigging rigged to help support the mast.

Spars: loosely speaking, any mast or boom on a ship whether it's rigged horizontally or vertically.

Standing Rigging: any rigging set to support or steady masts, etc. as opposed to **running rigging** which is used to raise or lower sails.

Square rigged: describes a vessel, usually a large one, using square or rectangular sails rigged from horizontal masts set across the beam of the ship. This as opposed to a **Fore and aft rig.** A square rigged vessel's sails could be pulled around almost parallel with the ship's hull. A square rigged ship could make best use of a steady wind but the sails required a lengthy time to set.

Tacking: the process of zig-zagging into the wind. Sailing with the wind blowing on the starboard side of the vessel was the **starboard tack** and vice versa for the **port tack**. For sailing vessels approaching each other during **tacking**, the vessel on the **starboard tack** had the right of way.

Topsail Schooner: a schooner with a square sail rigged at the top of the foremast.

Yawl: among discriminating yachtsmen, a yawl is a two masted yacht with a large foremast or main mast and a small aftermast or mizzen mast set in back of the rudder. A yawl can also be a ship's rowboat.

Index of Ships

M

Z

Index of Individuals

A

B

Buset, Peter, p. 229
Butler, D., p. 4

C

Caffery, John, p. 13
Cardwell, Captain William, p. 32
Carroll, Captain John, p. 55
Carroll, Thomas, p. 28
Carlson, A., p. 40
Carus, Captain Edward, p. 240
Casey, Norm, p. 305
Casey, Captain Pat, p. 234, 243
Cauwenberg, Jules, p. 232
Cavalier, Robert Rene, Sieur de La Salle, p. 1
Ceaser, p. 156
Chamberlain, Philo, p. 82
Christenson, Captain Thomas, p. 173
Christiansen, Captain Sam, p. 258
Christianson, Captain, p. 79
Christianson, Andrew, p. 267
Christianson, Jacob, p. 79
Christianson, Captain Ole, p. 133, 225
Claflin, Increase, p. 331
Clark, Alvin S., p. 20
Clark, John Pearson, p. 20
Clark, Captain M.H., p. 342
Clark, Maggie, p. 109
Cleveland, Dell, p. 205
Clow, Captain David, p. 85, 138, 142
Clow, Captain James, p. 170
Cochems, M. p. 86
Coffey, James, p. 188
Coffey, Tom, p. 307
Cofrin, Ashley, p. 152
Cointe, A.J., p. 100

D

Devine, Captain John, p. 194
Dickinson, Robert, p. 14
Dickey, Archibald, p. 326
Dier, Superintendent Adam, p. 186
Dingman, Captain William, p. 84
Doak, Alexander, p. 14
Doak, Captain John R., p. 42, 52
Dohl, Ole D., p. 197
Donley, Charles, p. 119
Dorner, John, p. 25
Downey, J., p. 46
Doyle, p. 38
Dreutzer, Yngve, p. 52
Drew, Frank, p. 199
Drezdzon, Michael, p. 304
Drillishak, S.J., p. 273
Drisko, Captain George H., p. 328
Duchaine, Clifford, p. 247
Dumann, Henry, p. 168
Dunlap, James, p. 93
Durbin, Captain, p. 30
Dwyer, Frank, p. 104

E

Elliot, Captain A.M., p. 123
Elnarson, Leroy, p. 320
Emmet, Robert, p. 33
Emms, C.T., p. 116
Erskine, Lincoln, p. 81, 191
Evans, Captain Robert, p. 223

F

Faith, Captain Henry, p. 38
Fellows, Captain C.L., p. 63, 107, 145
Ferguson, Captain, p. 39

Field, Marshall, p. 293
Flynn, Owen, p. 82
Foss, Matthew, p. 151, 193
Foss, Henry, p. 151
Fowler, p. 216
Fredrickson, Lynn, p. 267
Frohmeier, Arthur, p. 278
Frontenac, Count, p. 2

G

Gamlin, Clinton, p. 307
Garbosky, Louis, p. 116
Garbowski, Dick, p. 19
Gardener, F.B., p. 100
Gardes, Louis, p. 62
Gaylord, Captain, p. 317, 324
Genneisse, August, p. 100
Gilbert, Francis, p. 4
Gillilland, T.F., p. 25
Glockner, Captain William, p. 196
Glantz, Deputy Marshall E.H., p. 185
Goble, George, p. 64
Goodell, Nathan, p. 4, 5
Goodenow, S., p. 182
Goodman, Captain James, p. 126
Gorham, Captain Alex, p. 109
Graham, Captain Alfred, p. 214, 291
Graham, Captain E.B., p. 63, 90
Graham, Immanuel, p. 291
Graham, Captain Robert, p. 22
Griffin, Captain William, p. 101
Grimm, Jacob, p. 29, 40
Green, Captain, p. 340
Green, Adolph, p. 254
Green, Otto, p. 254

Groch, Edward, p. 305
Gross, Charles, p. 7, 8, 9, 15
Gumm, J.H. p. 97
Gunderson, Gunder, p. 290
Gunderson, Captain S., 41
Gunderson, Captain C., 99

H

Hackett, Captain Fletcher, p. 29
Hackett, Captain Francis, p. 243
Hagedon, Luther, p. 4
Halgren, Captain Emanuel, p. 218
Halley, John, p. 48
Hammer, Captain N.A., p. 95
Hampton, Joseph, p. 116
Hansen, G.M., p. 131
Hansen, Captain Gunder, p. 222
Hansen, Jacob, p. 11
Hansen, H.C., p. 273
Hanson, Andrew, p. 237
Hanson, Captain Hans, p. 328
Hanson, Captain Peter, p. 177
Harlow, Richard, p. 81
Harrington, Joseph, p. 161
Harris, Joseph, p. 11
Hart, Captain, p. 25
Hart, Asabel, p. 75
Hartman, Walter, p. 291
Hatchell, p. 43, 44, 45
Hauser, Captain, p. 30
Hayes, Captain John, p. 219
Hayes, Captain William, p. 264
Heald, Charles, p. 267
Heins, Captain George, p. 220
Helmholtz, William, p. 168

Hennesey, Peter, p. 81
Hennepin, Father Louis, p. 1
Henry, Dan., p. 278
Herdmanc, Joseph, p. 16
Herter, Henry, p. 29
Hichrodt, Frank, p. 304
Higgie, p. 19
Hill, Frank, p. 61, 63
Hill, John, p. 180
Hines, Captain, N.P., p. 61
Hoffman, Frank, p. 19, 79, 104, 199, 312
Hogenson, Captain Fordel, p. 172, 202
Hogg, Frank, p. 27
Holland, Captain M.M., p. 64
Horton, Captain J.W., p. 77
Hunt, Howard, p. 322

I

Icke, Captain Albert, p. 146
Ingraham, W.P., p. 57
Innis, Charles, p. 265
Isabell, Captain Thomas, p. 150, 160, 168, 185, 197, 203,
    205, 213, 217, 229, 231, 315, 335
Isabell, Frank, 213

J

Jackson, George, p. 37
Jackson, Captain William, p. 11, 41
Jacobs, William, p. 116
Jacobsen, p. 218
Jacobson, Captain, p. 79
Jameson, William, p. 13
Jarman, Floyd, p. 307
Jensen, Nels P., p. 291
Jepsen, Nels, p. 106

L

M

R

S

Bibliography
Books

Beasly, Norman. Freighters of Fortune, The Story of the Great Lakes. New York: Harper & Brothers, 1930. p.23

Beeson, Harvey C. Beeson's Inland Marine Directory, Chicago, Illinois, 1896, p. 47

Clark, M.H. Account of the Evacuation of the Confederate Treasury: Southern Historical Society Papers, December 1881

Coppess, Margaret. Island Story: The History of Michigan's St. Martin Island. Iron Mountain, Michigan: Mid-Peninsula Library Co-operative. 1981, p. 52

Denby, Edwin. Secretary of the Navy, director, Government Printing Office. Official Records of the Union and Confederate Navies in the War of the Rebellion, Washington, D.C. 1922, Series II, Vol., p. 16

Fitzpatrick, Doyle. The King Strang Story. Lansing Michigan: National Heritage. 1970, p. 191-196

Garden Peninsula Historical Society. Our Heritage, Garden Peninsula Delta County, Michigan 1840 - 1980. Garden, Michigan, p. 173

Hennepin, Fr. Louis, A New Discovery of a Vast Country in America, 1681, reprinted from the second London issue of 1698 by Reuben Gold Thwaites, A.C. McClurg & Co., Chicago, 1903, p. 82 - 144

Hennepin, Fr. Louis, A Description of Louisiana, translated from the edition of 1683 by John Gilmary Shea, New York, 1880

DOOR COUNTY ADVOCATE, August 23, 29, September 5, October 3, 1930

History of the Great Lakes, Illustrated. Chicago: J.H. Beers & Co. 1899. Vol. 2, p. 66 - 67

Knudsen, Arthur and Evelyn. A Gleam Across the Wave: The Biography of Martin Nicolai Knudsen, Lighthouse Keeper on Lake Michigan, p. 61

Knudsen, Martin, Light Keeper. Journal of the Lighthouse Station at Porte Des Morte, on Pilot Island, entries for October 28, 29, 1891, November 5, 14, 15, 26, 1891, April 20, 1893, December 14, 1894, July 21, 1898.

Lord, Walter. A Night To Remember. New York: Holt, Rinehart & Winston, p. 113

The Mystery Ship from 19 Fathoms Au Train, Michigan: Avery Color Studios, 1974, p. 35 - 42

Purves, John H. Roen Steamship Company: The Way It Was, 1909 - 1976. 1983, p. 89-90

Directory of Marine Interests of the Great Lakes, Detroit Michigan, R.L. Polk & Company, 1884, p. 56

Rodgers, Bradley A., Phd. 1995 Predisturbance Wreck Site Investigation at Claflin Point Little Sturgeon Bay, Wisconsin. Maritime Studies Program East Carolina University, p. 28.33

U.S. Army Corps of Engineers. Great Lakes Pilot, 1963,

Detroit, Michigan, p. 130

U.S. Government. MARINE CASUALTIES ON THE GREAT LAKES,
  1863 - 1873

U.S. Government Printing Office. Medal of Honor
  Recipients 1863 - 1978. Washington, 1979, p. 7-10

U. S. Government Printing Office. The List of Merchant Vessels of
  the U.S. Washington, D.C.: 1867 - 1935

W.A. McEwen, W.A. and A.H. Lewis, A.H. Encyclopedia
  of Nautical Knowledge. Cambridge, Maryland: Cornell
  Maritime Press, 1953. p. 526

Walton, Ivan H. "Marine Lore" p. 122

Works Project Administration. Michigan: A Guide to the
  Wolverine State, 1940. Compiled by the Works Project
  Administration - 1940,

Collections

EDWARD CARUS MARINE NOTES, Wisconsin Maritime Museum,
  Manitowoc, Wisconsin
Herman G. Runge Collection of the Milwaukee Public
  Library/Wisconsin Marine Historical Society

Interviews

Barada, William, telephone interview, 25 January 1984
Cornell, James, personal interview, 18 August 1996
Eckert, William, personal interview, 18 May, 20 July 1996
Harold, Steve, Manistee Historical Museum, telephone
  interview, 9 January 1997
Hoffman, Ed, telephone interview, 14 December 1995

Jessen, Karle, telephone interview, 12 October 1986
McOlash, Joel, telephone interview, 27 September 1995
Murphy, Edward F., Secretary of the Medal of Honor
   Historical Society, Mesa Arizona, telephone interview,
   October 13, 1996
Olsen, Dave, telephone interview, 1 November 1995
Ranguette, Fred and Vida, personal interview, 8 August
   1987
Ranguette, Richard, personal interview, 23 September
   1995
Reetz, Aurthur, telephone interview, 12 April 1984
Tatrow, Robert, personal interview, 8 August 8 1987
Zivalich, Nick, telephone interview, 2 March 1997

Periodicals

Newspapers read in complete series:
AHNAPEE RECORD-HERALD 1873 - 1900
CHICAGO TIMES 1870 - 1872
CHICAGO TRIBUNE 1865 - 1880
DOOR COUNTY ADVOCATE 1862 - 1955
GREEN BAY ADVOCATE 1846 - 1906
GREEN BAY GAZETTE 1871 - 1915
GREEN BAY INTELLIGENCER 1833 - 1836
GREEN BAY REPUBLICAN 1841 - 1844
KEWAUNEE ENTERPRISE 1859 - 1955

Newspapers and periodical cited for specific stories:
AHNAPEE RECORD-HERALD 6 June 1895
BUFFALO COURIER 6 October 1875
Carus, Edward. "Great Lakes Marine Notes", MANITOWOC
   HERALD-TIMES 31 March 1934
CHICAGO TIMES 22 September 1865
DAILY STATE GAZETTE [Green Bay, Wisconsin] 17
September 1891

ESCANABA DAILY PRESS 16, 17, 18, December 1943
ESCANABA IRON PORT 23 August 1879
ESCANABA IRON PORT 26 June 1880
ESCANABA IRON PORT 11 November 11 1886
ESCANABA IRON PORT 17 November 1888
ESCANABA IRON PORT 22 June 22 1889
ESCANABA MORNING PRESS 8 October 1913
ESCANABA MORNING PRESS 2 June 1915
ESCANABA TRIBUNE 9, 16, December 1869
ESCANABA TRIBUNE 31 May, 7 June 1873.
ESCANABA TRIBUNE 16, 23, October 1875
ESCANABA TRIBUNE 31 March 1877
ESCANABA TRIBUNE 25 August 1877
GLADSTONE DELTA 9 July 1904
GREEN BAY ADVOCATE 18 September 1851
GREEN BAY GAZETTE 25 October 1899
GREEN BAY PRESS-GAZETTE 15 April 1924
GREEN BAY PRESS-GAZETTE 3 December 1924
GREEN BAY PRESS-GAZETTE 19 September 1933
GREEN BAY PRESS-GAZETTE 1 June 1940
GREEN BAY PRESS-GAZETTE, "Sunday Magazine" section,
    17 May 1964
GREEN BAY PRESS-GAZETTE 14 December 1969
GREEN BAY REPUBLICAN 5 December 1843
MANISTIQUE PIONEER-TRIBUNE 21 December 1906
MANITOWOC HERALD-TIMES 31 March 1934
MARINETTE STAR 31 1899
MENOMINEE HERALD 12, 17 November 1913
MENOMINEE HERALD-LEADER 16 May, 28, 31
    October 1939.
MILWAUKEE JOURNAL 3, 4 December 1924
Norberg, Carl. "The Lost Treasure of the Beaver Island
    Mormon Colony", Inland Seas, Quarterly Journal of the
    Great Lakes Historical Society, Vol. 43, Fall 1987, No. 3,
    p. 188-193

PORT LIGHT [Sturgeon Bay] 19 September 1944
SKIN DIVER, March 1969, p. 22
SKIN DIVER, March 1986, p. 28

Television Productions

"Treasure," <u>Unsolved Mysteries</u>, NBC, WLUK, Green Bay, Wisconsin, narrated by Robert Stack, 11 November 1994